Ideal Surroundings
Gender and Domestic Life in a Working-Class Suburb in the 1920s

The 1920s are seen by historians as a crucial period in the formation of the Canadian working class. In *Ideal Surroundings*, Suzanne Morton looks at a single working-class community as it responded to national and regional changes. Grounded in labour and feminist history, with a strong emphasis on domestic life, this analysis focuses on the relationship between gender ideals and the actual experience of different family members.

The setting is Richmond Heights, a working-class suburb of Halifax that was constructed following the 1917 explosion that devastated a large section of the city. The Halifax Relief Commission, specially formed to respond to this incident, generated a unique set of historical records that provides an unusually intimate glimpse of domestic life. Drawing on these and other archives, Morton uncovers many critical challenges to working-class ideals. The male world-view in particular was seriously destabilized as economic transformation and unemployment left many men without the means to support their families, and as the daughters of Richmond Heights increasingly left their class-defined jobs for service and clerical positions.

Drawing on recent theoretical and empirical work, Morton expertly combines interpretive and narrative material, creating a vivid portrayal of class dynamics in this critical postwar era. Her focus on the home and domesticity marks an innovative move towards the integration of gender in the study of Canadian history.

(Studies in Gender and History)

SUZANNE MORTON is an assistant professor in the Department of History, McGill University.

STUDIES IN GENDER AND HISTORY

General editors: Franca Iacovetta and Craig Heron

Ideal Surroundings:

*Domestic Life in
a Working-Class Suburb
in the 1920s*

SUZANNE MORTON

UNIVERSITY OF TORONTO PRESS
Toronto Buffalo London

© University of Toronto Press Incorporated 1995
Toronto Buffalo London

Printed in Canada

ISBN 0-8020-0474-1 (cloth)
ISBN 0-8020-7575-4 (paper)

Printed on acid-free paper

Canadian Cataloguing in Publication Data

Morton, Suzanne
  Ideal surroundings : domestic life in a working-class
  suburb in the 1920s

  (Studies in gender and history series)
  Includes index.
  ISBN 0-8020-0474-1 (bound) ISBN 0-8020-7575-4 (pbk.)

  1. Richmond Heights (Halifax, N.S.) – Social life
  and customs. I. Title. II. Series

  FC2346.52.M67 1995   971.6'225   C94-932217-2
  F1039.5.H17M67 1995

Illustration credits: The photographs in the book are both from the Halifax
Relief Commission photographic collection at the Public Archives of Nova
Scotia. P. xi: Harry Thompson in his Kane Place garden, 1923, N-7064; p. xii:
Merkel Place, Hydrostone development, 1921, N-7016.

University of Toronto Press acknowledges the financial assistance to its
publishing program of the Canada Council and the Ontario Arts Council.

This book has been published with the help of a grant from the Social Science
Federation of Canada, using funds provided by the Social Sciences and
Humanities Research Council of Canada.

Contents

Tables and Illustrations

Acknowledgments

'Mother was a very private person,' the ninety-four-year-old woman began; 'she never wanted anyone to know her troubles.' With these words, a prospective informant gently let me down. She had reconsidered her original assent to an interview about her early family life in Richmond Heights and, upon the advice of her extended family, decided not to talk with me. This woman's decision not to be interviewed undoubtedly reflected her deceased mother's wishes. In claiming a place in Canadian history for the group of people studied in this book, I am aware that in including them I am destroying the privacy that many people cherished. For this trespass I sincerely beg their pardon and hope that my alteration of individual surnames offers some protection. In light of the importance of privacy, I am especially grateful to those informants who willingly spoke about the past.

I complete this project with an extensive list of debts for intellectual challenges and support. At Dalhousie University, I was fortunate to benefit from the wisdom of Michael Cross and Ruth Bleasdale, who challenged my conceptions and encouraged my exploratory detours. Judith Fingard and David Sutherland offered additional support and expanded my inquiry by their questions. I am in particular debt to David Sutherland, who originally suggested I might find the Halifax Relief Commission correspondence interesting. Janet Guildford provided friendship and humour and never tired of explaining Halifax to a 'come from away.' Fellow Halifax travellers Michael Earle, Jim Frost, Bonnie Huskins, Joey Power, Jane Arscott, and Lesley Barnes shaped my thinking in innumerable ways. Janet Kitz graciously shared her extensive knowledge about the Halifax explosion and its survivors. The Dalhousie University Faculty of Graduate Studies provided financial assistance in the form of fellowship and research grants. It would not have been possible to contemplate the original research involved in this project without this support.

From the very beginning of this project Ian McKay has been characteristically generous with his enthusiasm and his files. Bettina Bradbury offered extensive comments on the dissertation on which this was based. The rethinking of that dissertation was assisted by Lykke de la Cour, Sandra den Otter, Karen Dubinsky, Nancy Forestell, Margaret Little, Lynne Marks, Kate McPherson, Cecilia Morgan, George Rawlyk, and Shirley Tillotson. I am also grateful to Gerry Hallowell, Rob Ferguson, Franca Iacovetta, and Margaret Allen of University of Toronto Press. Friends of Anglo-Celtic descent unwittingly provided fictitious surnames that did not overlap with actual names (and those excluded have instant insight into the correct surnames). Sarah Bradshaw and David Docherty, Diana Hilton and Toby Lennox opened their homes and offered generous hospitality. In my debts, my largest is to my family. My sister Janet visited an archives on my behalf and found it a very strange place, while my parents, Anne and Garry Morton, provided emotional, grammatical, and financial support.

An earlier version of chapter 5 appeared as 'Women on Their Own: Single Mothers in Working-Class Halifax in the 1920s,' in *Acadiensis*, 12, no. 2 (Spring 1992): 90–107, and some material in chapters 4 and 7 appeared as 'The June Bride as the Working-Class Bride: Getting Married in a Halifax Working-Class Neighbourhood in the 1920s,' in Bettina Bradbury, ed., *Canadian Family History: Selected Readings* (Toronto: Copp Clark Pitman 1992).

Harry Thompson stands proudly in his Kane Place garden after receiving first prize in the Halifax Relief Commission 1923 Garden Contest.

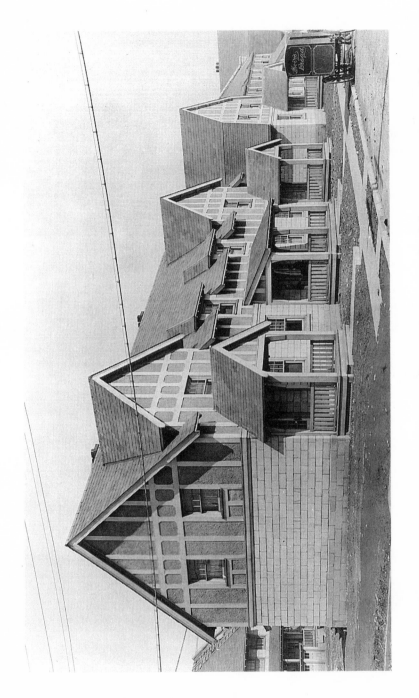

Merkel Place, Hydrostone development, 1921. The cement-like building material and the attempt to create a varied streetscape are evident in this photo.

IDEAL SURROUNDINGS

Introduction

A man stands by the front porch of his Kane Place home in September 1923 stiffly facing the camera. He wears a straw boater, dark suit coat, white shirt, and straight tie. Harry Thompson, a carpenter at the military hospital, has just won first prize in Richmond Heights' annual garden contest. The narrow and short yard, bordered by a low, wooden latticed fence, testifies to his after-hours labour. Except for a footpath and a flagpole where the Red Ensign limply hangs in the still air, the house's frontage is completely filled with flowers. In fact, the abundance of the garden overflows into flower boxes on the window, a hanging basket, and vines clinging to the porch supports.[1]

In another photograph, taken five years later, an elderly woman stands by the porch of her Livingstone Place residence. Her hands folded across her stomach, she wears a dark, unfashionable, button-down dress with a touch of modern style, a fox-fur collar. Mrs Fleck, who lives with a widowed daughter and her family, is the recent winner of a local newspaper's Mother's Day contest. She is understandably proud of her achievement of being the forebear of 105 grandchildren.[2]

The images of a proud gardener or grandmother are at first difficult to integrate with other visual representations of the Canadian working class during the 1920s. A number of other images come to mind: an assembly-line worker in one of the new car factories in Oshawa or Windsor, a foreign-born radical in isolated western lumber or mining camps, a pretty young shop-girl strutting along Sunnyside boardwalk in Toronto, or a couple driving their black Model T home from a dance or silent picture. Harry Thompson and Mrs Fleck, on the other hand, appear in neither a workplace nor a commercial leisure setting. The domestic orientation suggested by the images of the well-dressed home-improver or the extraordinary grandmother redirects the attention of the historian away from the workplace and the union hall into the world of the family and the home.

This book will examine class, age, and gender in the specific context of one Canadian working-class suburb in the 1920s. Richmond Heights, a working-class suburb of Halifax, Nova Scotia, is of special interest for at least three reasons. First, its construction played a pioneering role in the history of Canadian urban planning and working-class housing. In addition, the dramatic events surrounding the 1917 explosion in Halifax Harbour and the reconstruction of the city are stories in themselves worth telling. The reconstruction of the city also generated a unique set of historical records that offers a rare glimpse into the domestic life of early-twentieth-century working-class Canadians. Finally, as a neighbourhood in Halifax, Richmond Heights witnessed at first hand the dramatic restructuring of the city and the regional economy during the 1920s, with the shift from manufacturing and transportation to service and trade. This economic reorientation was relevant to other Canadian communities, for, in fact, the rapid transformation of the local Halifax economy foreshadowed a much slower national transition. Change occurred throughout the country but at different rates and at different times according to local circumstances. As I have argued elsewhere with Janet Guildford, Atlantic Canadian history and women's history share certain parallels, since they are often discounted as atypical or somehow outside the mainstream of what 'really happened' in the Canadian past. In suggesting the broader implications of an Atlantic Canadian study, I hope to promote a broader definition of Canadian history as truly including the East, in the same way that women's history has fostered important reconceptualizations of the past to include both men and women.[3]

While an Atlantic Canada case study can inform and offer insights into other places, context is important. Even today, in what we recognize as a more homogeneous North American culture, there remain distinct ideals of masculinity and femininity that correspond to class, race, age, sexual orientation, and region. We easily identify different manifestations of masculinity in the Anglo-Celtic fisherman from Trinity Bay, Newfoundland, the sophisticated purse-carrying Montreal businessman, the young African-Canadian student in Toronto, the Albertan cowboy of Ukrainian descent, the elderly gay activist from Vancouver, and the second-generation Italian-Canadian who works the line at General Motors in Oshawa. These representative images and their differences do not negate the many aspects of men's lives that may be the same, but rather emphasize important variances in experience. The variety of masculinities reflect differing degrees of power and autonomy, fused by class, age, region, sexual orientation, and race. There is not one single way to act like a man in Canada in the 1990s, and therefore discussions of gender ideals must be specific in their circumstances. The gender ideals for men and women in Richmond Heights in the 1920s, although they shared many similarities with those for other Canadians, were specific to that particular time and place and the particular conditions of the neighbourhood.

The use of a community study permits historical generalizations to be tested in a precise time and place. It is an approach that, while pioneered in Canada by sociology, has also been influenced by anthropology and geography and, in history, the Annales school. Community studies have been adopted most frequently by those interested in social and economic history, such as historians of immigration, the family, and the working class.[4] The study of a community as a microcosm of a larger society allows the historian to conduct the intensive research necessary to reconstruct the daily lives of ordinary people and to explore questions about living conditions, identity, and culture. Though community studies offer the exciting prospect of examining a number of themes at the same time and also satisfy the historian's desire for specificity, we must always be cautious about the extent to which conclusions can be applied elsewhere. In this book, an attempt is made to situate Richmond Heights in a comparative framework by referring to other studies. This effort is important, for it is through such critical evaluation that community studies contribute to the development of theory and an overall synthesis in historical understanding by alerting us to differences and similarities. It is therefore not surprising that this study offers some insights that are specific to Halifax and others that might be applied across Canada or North America.

Class, gender, and age are real and interconnected relationships, but they are rarely experienced in any consistent, hierarchical manner. Haligonians simultaneously shared many different identities that came into focus at different times or over different issues. Class identity was evident during the 1920 Halifax Shipyards strike; gender determined how one was likely to feel about prohibition, and old age united people with similar memories of the past. Furthermore, a regional identity was apparent in the widespread practice of eating baked beans and brown bread on Saturday or supporting the Maritime Rights movement.

When discussing men and women, I have used the word 'gender' rather than 'sex' in order to emphasize the historical and social construction rather than biological differences between men and women. Gender ideals were quite distinct from reality, since they concerned how men and women were expected to behave. The fluctuation in the distance between expectations and reality meant that gender ideals were by definition always shifting and relative.[5] Gender ideals are not exclusionary, and a society can have several ideals at the same time for the same gender. For example, young women were not expected to behave in the same manner as their grandmothers. Furthermore, gender ideals are class or community specific. As stated previously, they must be examined in a particular context. For the purposes of this study, gender ideals of Richmond Heights were shaped by the widespread heterosexual capitalist assumptions about a 'family wage' with a male breadwinner and a dependent wife. While this model remained impractical for many individual households, the ideal of the breadwinner-housewife dichotomy was embodied not only in trade-union and state policy, but also in popular perception.[6]

We know surprisingly little about how working-class Canadians experienced the 1920s, but American studies and preliminary Canadian explorations have underscored how different members of the working class had become from their mothers and fathers of a generation earlier. This 'new' working class, which took form after 1920, has usually been explained in terms of a combination of factors. Emphasis has been placed on the homogenizing power of mass culture and consumption, the fragmentation of the working class by ethnic and racial divisions, and the impact of monopoly capitalism, particularly new management techniques supported by the state.[7] In the most famous community study of the twenties, *Middletown: A Study of Contemporary American Culture*, Robert and Helen Lynd investigated Muncie, Indiana, and settled upon the importance of consumption and mass culture in changing people's lives.[8] More recently, labour historians have responded to Susan Porter Benson, who noted in a 1987 review article that the 1920s were a watershed with regard to women's waged employment, so that gender must be central to the way in which historians of the working class approach the decade.[9] Gender analysis has been effectively mixed into interpretations of the rise of mass culture and the entrenchment of monopoly capitalism by Joy Parr in her innovative study of industrial workers in two Ontario small towns and by Elizabeth Faue in an examination of gender and the labour movement in Minneapolis, Minnesota, in the interwar period.[10] The present study differs from the works of both Parr and Faue because it shifts the focus towards what was happening at home and how domestic life shaped the entire class experience rather than concentrating primarily on the workplace or formal working-class institutions such as labour unions.

Historians of the Canadian working class have understandably been attracted to moments of action and crisis when men and women developed a critique of society and participated in movements that sought to bring about change. Men and women were also important actors in the making of their history inside the household, but the focus on the household reveals the degree to which they were always vulnerable to forces beyond any possible control. Birth, death, disease, or a cold winter that exhausted limited resources of coal could and did disrupt the delicate balance of their lives. Investigation of domestic life exposes the important role luck could play in the equilibrium between survival and disaster.

An independent working-class culture did not disappear or die in the 1920s, but it certainly changed. Labour historians have portrayed working-class culture as something that was created by and partially defined labouring men. It could reinforce and possibly foster class consciousness through developing male bonds beyond the workplace in public areas such as those historian Bryan Palmer referred to as 'the street, field and hall.' Indeed, in examining working-class culture in an earlier period, historians have often found it difficult to see women. For to do so, it is necessary to look closely at the composition of the crowds attending a parade or a baseball game, to ask who trade unionists were waltzing with at their many dances, to surmise who had prepared the picnic lunches eaten on summer excursions, and to see the working-class wife as primary consumer and critical linchpin in the success of any organized consumer boycott. By the early twentieth century such conjecture is no longer necessary, since women were simply more obvious and visible in their public daily activities. Furthermore, with the gradual decline of domestic service and as the site of waged labour moved into more public occupations, women became more conspicuous participants in the workforce. Although the experience of class and that of gender were never distinct, in an earlier period this connection had been easier to ignore. By the 1920s, any conception of class and class culture had to include women – the young women engaged in retail and clerical work, the widow struggling without a male breadwinner, and the married homemaker at the forefront of working-class

RICHMOND HEIGHTS

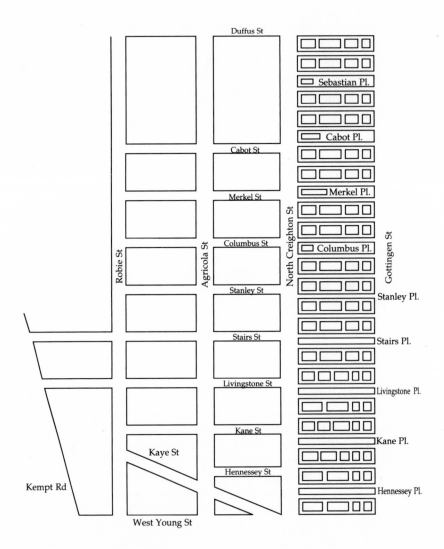

Street plan of Richmond Heights. The Hydrostone development stretched between Gottingen Street and North Creighton Street.

domestic consumption. Women did not undermine class or an independent class-based culture; rather their acknowledged presence makes understanding the ways in which class worked much more complex. Working-class culture looked very different when women were visible participants.

RICHMOND HEIGHTS

Richmond Heights was situated at the far North End of the Halifax peninsula, west of the harbour, beyond the steep incline of Fort Needham and Gottingen Street. The name Richmond Heights was selected by its residents in the 1920s in an unsuccessful attempt to include its neighbouring streets and replace the more restrictive and in the end permanent label of 'the Hydrostone District.' Richmond Heights is therefore a historical community that no longer exists in the psyche of the local geography. On its western border was Kempt Road, which separated the built-up area from undeveloped land, much of it employed for agricultural production. To its north, above Duffus Street were prison lands around Rockhead, Africville, and the Bedford Basin. South of Young Street lay the city centre, the city's more prosperous neighbourhoods, and finally the open Atlantic.[11] Nestled between Fort Needham, the prison lands, Kempt Road, and Young Street, and bisected by North Creighton Street, Richmond Heights was composed of a planned residential development to the east and a haphazard assortment of houses on the west. The perimeter of this subdivision measured just under two kilometres and could easily be walked in twenty minutes.

The weather in Halifax has always been the stuff of daily conversation. Although the city sits in a temperate zone, vestiges of winter can last into May. The North Atlantic winds moderate most extremes in temperature, but the average annual temperature between 1870 and 1947 remained at a cool forty-four degrees Fahrenheit. Halifax annually received an average of nearly fifty-six inches of rain and seventy-one inches of snow. Some form of precipitation fell almost every other day in the year, regardless of the season. The number of hours of bright sunshine in Halifax was not measured until 1940 and then ranged between 88 hours in November and 239 hours in July.[12]

While the residents of Richmond Heights may have measured time by the scarcity of rain in a season or the severity of one winter compared to another, this study imposes the arbitrary period of a decade on the life of the community. The use of a decade such as the 1920s for investigation can at times be unsatisfactory, since it imposes an artificial marking of time on the lives of individuals. In this particular case it proves useful, however, as the beginning of the decade corresponded with the construction of the housing development: the first tenants moved into their new homes in the fall of 1919. Furthermore, the twenties also coincided with an economic cycle in Halifax, since the decade was bracketed at either end by a sudden shift from prosperity to depression. By ending before 1930, the study avoids the circumstances surrounding the Great Depression. Finally, the 1920s were a critical period for the Canadian working class. The dramatic rise and collapse of the labour movement after the First World War created the impression of a sharp break with the past. The study of a working-class suburb in the 1920s furthers our understanding of what happened after the 1919 labour revolt.

Richmond Heights was primarily composed of a section of the working class considered 'respectable,' since most men were employed in skilled or semi-skilled positions and attempted to support their families (see appendix table A). The definition of class to be used here is determined by the broader historical questions raised by this study. For this purpose, the label 'working class' corresponds in the most general way to occupation and the decision to live in what was recognized as a working-class suburb, and encompasses all members of these households. Very few households were not supported by waged labour, and in the case of exceptions such as pensioners, petty shopkeepers, and small contractors, their standard of living gave them much in common with their neighbours. The suburb's residents experienced de facto segregation, since only the well paid or households with a number of wage-earners could afford the rents, which were slightly higher than those in other working-class Halifax neighbourhoods. The community can also be considered to have been self-selected. Richmond Heights tenants chose to commit a significant portion of their income in exchange for above-average housing, a decision that in part reflected the importance they placed on their home life and domesticity.

Although Halifax was situated on the periphery of the North American continent, it was almost entirely integrated into the continental culture. For example, in September 1923, the *Evening Mail* claimed that more than a thousand copies of records or sheet music of the song 'Yes, We Have No Bananas' had been sold in the city, the equivalent of one copy to every ten homes.[13] Haligonians watched Hollywood movies, tuned into radio signals from the American Northeast, and had front-row seats for viewing the exciting attempts to cross the Atlantic by air. Commercialized sports, such as American major-league baseball and boxing, were complemented by a revived commercialized version of local schooner races that featured the *Bluenose*.[14] New forms and choices in entertainment and interests were available but often required a surplus income beyond the consumer capabilities of some Richmond Heights residents. A North End Halifax teacher noted that several girls in her grade-eight class had never been to a movie theatre.[15]

In 1931, the population of Halifax was nearly stagnant at 59,273. The city boasted 122 miles of streets, 28 of which were paved, and had 54 miles of sewers.[16] Symbols of progress could be deceptive, because the 1920s were hard on the Maritimes as a result of lower prices for resources, increased freight rates that made local goods uncompetitive in large central-Canadian markets, and the resulting capture of local retail and manufacturing markets by successful central-Canadian firms.[17] As the city experienced what was coyly described as 'economic readjustment,' the decade cemented the fact that Halifax was to be not a place where products were made but rather a city where products and services were consumed.[18]

Halifax is a particularly interesting city in which to examine the private world of the working class in the 1920s, since it did not experience the prosperity of new industrial manufacturing centres; nor did it have an immigrant population that needed to be 'Americanized.' In 1921, nearly 80 per cent of the total population had been born in Nova Scotia, and some of the city's residents were proud of its homogeneity and the fact that there was 'no large mass to be Canadianized, no "Ghetto" nor "Little Italy."'[19] Although Halifax had a largely homogeneous population, not all residents of Richmond Heights were born in Nova Scotia; nor were all Anglo-Celtic. Thirty-six residents were identified by newspaper comments or obituaries as not being born in the province. Most of the immigrants identified were men who came from England or Ireland with the army or navy. Three men and four women were identified as being born in Newfoundland, two brothers were born in Italy, and one man living on Stairs Street was born in France.[20] A number of households with Acadian names took up residence, but these few exceptions, like the occasional immigrant, could be assimilated into the community. More important, although the city of Halifax had a large African–Nova Scotian population and a number of Asian families, they did not live in Richmond Heights, which was a uniformly white subdivision.[21]

Immigration and racial tensions were important in explaining class fragmentation in the North American context but do little to explain the working-class experience in this relatively homogeneous Halifax community. This is not to ignore the fact that the largely homogeneous Anglo-Celtic community had a very strong sense of its own racial superiority. A neighbourhood woman felt that no further explanation was necessary when she defended her respectability with the cry, 'I am an Englishwoman!' Racial attitudes held by Richmond Heights residents in fact could also contain strange twists. While minstrel shows complete with blackface were the favourite form of entertainment performed by all the nearby churches, the girls of St Joseph's Church followed their 1928 minstrel show by a production of *Uncle Tom's Cabin*.[22]

The same uniformity in the community's racial composition was also seen in its household structure. Households in Richmond Heights were primarily composed of immediate family, but the term 'household' is preferable to 'family' for a variety of reasons. Firstly, it is the way residents were perceived by the primary record group used in this study. At the heart of this investigation are the records of the Halifax Relief Commission (HRC) regarding its tenants and, more important, the responses and requests of the tenants to the commission. Usually written by a woman in her role as domestic manager, sometimes literate and legible and at other times barely decipherable, the scraps of paper – pieces of envelopes, pages of children's school scribblers, and in one case a history textbook – permit members of a usually silenced group of the past to speak in their own words. These pencil scrawls were written on behalf of households and should be regarded in this context.[23] Other sources such as church, voluntary association, charity, legal, and municipal records were useful in flushing out individuals who composed the household's membership. The Canadian manuscript censuses for 1921 and 1931 and school records may not be released to the public for another twenty or thirty years, and city directories must be approached with great caution. Examination of leases, municipal voters' lists, telephone listings, and city directories has permitted identification of a total of 3,443 individuals living in the suburb between 1920 and 1929. Although many of these people appeared in a variety of record groups, the total base underestimates the population, as it excluded all children, nearly all married women before 1926, many young adults, and most of the aged living within the household. Some information on these less conspicuous groups could be gleaned from local newspapers.[24] Since the afternoon newspaper contained the most local news, the *Evening Mail*, Halifax's largest evening daily, was read for the entire decade. These or similar sources would be available for most communities; unique to this study, however, are the valuable sources created by the HRC. The material generated by the HRC in its dual role as landlord and pension arbitrator must be read critically, for the commission was in a perpetual state of judging the residents of Richmond Heights according to a 'respectable' ideal. In response, some tenants doubtless provided the commission with what they thought it wanted to read, perhaps suppressing their own thoughts and feelings in the hope of a sympathetic response when the rent was late or not to be forthcoming. But this is not true in all cases. The contrite appeasement practised by some tenants contrasts with the defiance and pride of their neighbours. This occurred notwithstanding what appears to have been their equally vulnerable households. Examining the community at the household level allows the variety of responses to become apparent.

Looking at the household also allows us to see people in relation to the economic unit in which they lived. Combined wages and/or income from boarders and lodgers were often necessary to maintain a tenancy. Therefore, the use of household reminds us not to assume the presence of a two-generation nuclear family. Households could include a variety of people, kin or otherwise. Finally, the word 'family' is loaded with emotional overtones and, as Linda Gordon has reminded us, can falsely suggest a homogeneous unit by masking intrafamily conflict, particularly conflict over the concerns of women and children.[25] Households generally placed value upon privacy, and as a result much of domestic life remains invisible. Important questions about internal power division, relations with neighbours, and individual aspirations remain unanswered.

The organization of this book reflects the importance of age and marital status in gender analysis. Gender was experienced differently at different ages. A focus on distinct subgroups within the household and suburb draws attention to the fact that class was experienced differently by individuals throughout the community, even within the same household. With the importance of generation in mind, I have organized the study loosely along a reversed life cycle – one that begins with the elderly and ends with young single women.[26] While this is counter to the usual life-course approach, it is hoped that this organization will emphasize the element of change. In chapter 1 the social geography of

Richmond Heights is explored with particular emphasis on the built environment. The second chapter concentrates on the values of the people inside the houses, notably respectability and consumerism. With the background complete, the third chapter addresses the elderly, especially their relationship to the labour market and their efforts to maintain independence. Chapter 4 investigates the difficulty that married adults experienced in attempting to live up to the demanding gender ideals of mother, father, wife, and husband. Not all households in Richmond Heights were fortunate in having a male breadwinner or access to his wage, and these female-headed households are the subject of chapter 5. Men and young single women are the subject of the last two chapters, since the interactions of class and gender are examined in a time of shifting occupations. Although the study stresses the importance of generational differences, it does not consider children. Children were not active participants in the creation of gender ideology, but were more often the intended subjects of socialization. As well, the inclusion of children would introduce questions about long-term mobility that are beyond the book's parameters.

This is a feminist study, and although I appear to hold young women responsible for much of the transition, it is worth keeping in mind that there was nothing idyllic about the industrial working-class culture that these women challenged. Pre-explosion Richmond was no 'Camelot' for the male worker, and family members would certainly not have claimed that it was. At the same time, the emerging dominant domesticity was also not the answer. The new working-class suburb was indeed partly marked by overstretched consumption and by a depersonalized mass culture. Change did not begin or end in the 1920s; but through an examination of the ways in which class, gender, and age interacted in a specific time and location, it is possible to approach an understanding of the reciprocal links between the political and the domestic life.

1

Richmond Heights

On the morning of 6 December 1917, in the narrows at the base of the Richmond slope, a munitions ship bound for Europe and packed with 2,600 tons of explosives collided with a relief ship. The resulting explosion killed nearly 2,000 people, injured 9,000, and totally devastated a large section of the North End of Halifax. In literally an instant, trees and telephone poles snapped into pieces as the wooden houses collapsed onto their hot coal stoves and caught fire. In the place of what had been the working-class suburb of Richmond lay 325 acres of charred ruins, the result of one of the largest pre-atomic man-made explosions.[1]

An observer of the December 1917 events remarked that the explosion blew Halifax into the twentieth century.[2] The image of the city being blown across time is powerful: the explosion changed both the physical environment of much of Halifax and the context in which daily life occurred. In the wake of the explosion, Halifax was besieged by experts on almost every aspect of domestic life, ranging from public health and social work to town planning and architecture. The experts brought with them the most modern and scientific methods and theories and, in the vacuum created by the destruction of a working-class community, proceeded to implement their knowledge and fill the empty space.

In fact, however, Richmond was not a clean slate; for although the houses, churches, schools, and factories were gone, many of the survivors returned to rebuild their homes and former lives. These men and women, boys and girls, provided a measure of continuity with the past. They had been there before the catastrophe, and now, with newcomers, the mix of old and new came together to build the neighbourhood of Richmond Heights.

The intervention of outside experts was complemented by the intrusion of the state, for post-explosion Halifax was beleaguered by many forms of government intervention. The now-vacant land along the waterfront was expropriated by the minister of marine, who, concerned about the shortage of Canadian ocean tonnage during the war, entered into an agreement with Roy Wolvin, president of the Montreal Transportation Company. In exchange for the establishment of the Halifax Shipyards Limited, the government offered the old naval graving dock, sufficient space for a plant, and four government contracts for ships. In June 1918, Roy Wolvin and J.W. Norcross, president of Canada Steamship Lines, organized Halifax Shipyards Limited, the first building block in what would become the British Empire Steel Corporation.[3]

The most important intervention by a government body was the creation of the Halifax Relief Commission (HRC). The voluntary organization of local citizens that responded to the emergency was replaced in late January 1918 by a federally appointed, state-supported, three-man agency.[4] The HRC was given further legal jurisdiction by the Nova Scotia legislature under the provincial HRC Act. The commission was responsible for investigating losses, damages, and injuries and for awarding compensation, and, most important for the purpose of this study, was empowered within a defined area of 325 acres to expropriate land, create zoning regulations, rebuild, and carry out a town-planning scheme.[5] The HRC's responsibilities for compensation and reconstruction were integrated through a plan that proposed to have the rent of the rebuilt homes finance future pension payments. Hence, the HRC was inadvertently given a public mandate to create the first public housing project in Canada. This quasi-governmental agency served as the primary landlord in Richmond Heights from the fall of 1919 until well into the 1950s.

The explosion and its devastation made possible a form of urban planning that had been discussed in theoretical terms for a number of years.[6] The explosion then functioned as something of a catalyst – albeit a fortuitous one – for a grand urban experiment in a real Canadian situation in which the need for some measure of urban planning was unquestioned. The residential planning focused on the most prosperous portion of the urban working class, since the HRC stated from the beginning that it desired to make Richmond Heights 'one of the best residential portions of the city for persons of moderate means.' Single-family detached dwellings on the harbour slope would form the 'most desirable residential area,' while west of North Creighton Street frame wooden houses of 'a somewhat cheap type' were to be erected 'for the poorer classes.'[7] Between the two developments there would be a 'screen' or 'buffer' to separate the desirable homes on the slope and the 'inferior district of the west.'[8] The screen took the form of a group development built for families of skilled workmen and offered the most enduring reminder of the explosion, a housing project known as the Hydrostone District.[9]

The Hydrostone District was built on ten short parallel east-west streets. In the centre of eight of the streets was a large boulevard of communal green space, a grassy island that was supposed to serve as a play area for children. These islands were surrounded by narrow streets designed to restrict traffic by permitting only single directional flow. The eighty-six buildings contained three offices and thirteen stores on Young Street and 324 homes arranged in sections of two, four, and six dwelling units. The terraced houses faced the boulevards, with parallel service lanes in the rear. Their appearance, some with false timbering, stuccoed second storey, and hipped roof, reflected a transatlantic attraction to the Tudor style that supposedly created the ambience of cosy workers' cottages. Concern for privacy in the Hydrostone District was apparent in the architects' attempt to separate entrances. Indeed, the development reflected a moment in time; had it been built even five years later, it might have looked completely different. Within the design there was no provision for private automobiles, and the back service lanes for tradesmen and delivery reflected a pre–'cash-and-carry' way of shopping. The design and appearance of the Hydrostone District also reflected early-twentieth-century concern about Canadian working-class housing and the emergence of the garden suburbs in England.

Before the explosion, Halifax working-class housing was generally poor. Hugh MacLennan in his famous novel about the Halifax explosion, *Barometer Rising*, described the city's North End houses as 'chocolate-brown,' 'cracker boxes standing in rows on a shelf.'[10] Most of the housing consisted of two-storey flats and single-family dwellings, sometimes shared among several families. Although there were few tenement blocks in Halifax, the narrow frontage and single room depth still resulted in limited light and ventilation.

Public concern around working-class housing drew connections between poor housing and the general health and morality of the population. The demand for progressive urban reform swept the country.[11] While progressives addressed problems of the urban core such as slums, overcrowding, poverty, crime, and high mortality, other residential op-

tions emerged with the advent and decline in the cost of public transportation. In many cities across North America, working-class suburbs
germinated on the periphery where land values were lower and household members could supplement wages with home-based production
such as gardening and small-scale animal husbandry. Suburbs are often
associated with the post-Second World War middle-class Canadian experience, but they have a much older and less homogeneous tradition.
These peripheral communities did not result in marked improvements
in public health among their working-class residents, since municipal
by-laws or sanitary facilities did not extend to the environs. Suburbs
merely shifted the location of the problem.[12] The pre-explosion suburb
of Richmond was one such outlying community, where factories, landlords, and home owners had been attracted north on the Halifax peninsula by the lower cost of land.

The dual problems of working-class housing in the urban core and
unplanned development on the periphery were experienced internationally. Urban reformers who blamed environmental factors for the
high incidence of disease, infant mortality, and a physically unfit labour
force believed that small, self-contained houses, gardens, and public
open spaces would help to produce a healthier and happier labour
force and, with it, perhaps an ideal society.[13] In England, an earlier
generation of housing reformers, including British industrialists George
Cadbury and William Lever, had initiated social experiments in the
planned rural company villages of Bournville near Birmingham in 1879
and Port Sunlight just outside Liverpool in 1888. The potential of
Bournville and Port Sunlight caught the progressive imagination, and
this excitement was reinforced by the 1898 publication of Ebenezer
Howard's *Tomorrow*. This book promoted garden cities that made use
of relatively cheap land on the outskirts of cities and provided the
residents with the best aspects of life in both town and country. The
success of pilot communities such as Bournville and Port Sunlight combined with the tremendous popularity of *Tomorrow* sparked a garden-
city movement that realized its ideal in 1903 with the establishment of
Letchworth Garden City, thirty miles north of London.[14] Garden cities
and the more practical garden suburbs involved the construction of
low-density housing, the creation of a trust or company that was responsible for regulating the use of public space, and carefully designed
layouts of roads so as to reduce the traffic flow. Letchworth provided a
concrete model of town planning in action and spawned the pre-war

Canadian derivative projects of Riverdale and Spruce Courts by the Toronto Housing Company.[15]

The link between the British garden-city movement and the post-explosion reconstruction of Halifax was Thomas Adams. Adams had been born in Edinburgh in 1871 and dabbled in a variety of areas including law school and dairy farming before trying his hand at journalism in London around 1900. Almost immediately, this thirty-year-old man with no background in housing became founding full-time secretary of the Garden City Association. With the development at Letchworth in 1903, Adams was appointed the first city manager. His pragmatic and less-than-Utopian views about town planning led him to resign in 1906 and enter a three-year period of private consulting and garden-city promotion. After the enactment of the first British town-planning act in 1909, Adams was appointed inspector, a position he held until 1914 when he was attracted to the Canadian Commission on Conservation to act as its town-planning expert. Garden suburbs such as the Lindenlea project in Ottawa and a settlement for returned soldiers in Lens, Saskatchewan, were constructed in Canada, but the First World War and the postwar recession generally interfered with Canadian projects. The reconstruction of Halifax therefore was a rare opportunity for Adams to supervise a garden suburb in this country.[16]

Before the explosion, Adams and the Halifax Civic Improvement League had envisaged a limited-dividend housing project, akin to the Toronto Housing Company, that would construct fifty double cottages on the harbour slope. These houses were to have the modern conveniences of water, electricity, indoor toilets, and annual rents of no more than $160 a year. Established contact with local urban reformers meant that Adams was familiar with the city's pre-explosion housing problems and topography and made him extremely well placed to advise on residential reconstruction. In this capacity, he responded with a detailed plan for the devastated district that included the group housing development, parks, and gradient diagonal roads crossing the slope. But Adams offered more than 'technical expertise.' His plans also expressed an ideological position that reflected the reformist ideas of architecture and design inherent in the British garden suburb movement, a supposedly 'more humane' perspective that contrasted with older theories of urban planning favouring social control and 'regulating the lives of the poor.'[17] But Adams also used an environmental determinist argument when it was convenient for him to do so. In a 1920 address to the Union of Nova Scotia Municipalities, Adams argued for a new domesticity founded upon improved working-class housing, stating that the worker living in decent housing was more likely to be 'the more reasonable human.' Furthermore, according to Adams, it was 'precisely the man who cares how his wife is housed, and it is precisely the man who cares for the environment in which his children are living that is most worth having in a factory.'[18] To be fair, it was perhaps impossible for urban reformers to separate the goals of improved working-class housing, domesticity, and the 'betterment' of the working class. Thus, it was with this triad in mind that the Hydrostone District was explicitly designed, the prospective tenants described alternatively as skilled workers, craftsmen, or just plain workmen – the presence of their families an unstated assumption.[19]

The Hydrostone District, with its low density of fewer than fourteen dwellings an acre, public green space, traffic management, and the grouping of houses with suitable variety, bore a strong physical likeness to its English antecedents. Moreover, the style and ideas of British architects Raymond Unwin and Barry Parker were apparent in the design; and it is evident that the much-praised Montreal architect of the Hydrostone District, George Ross, was largely influenced by earlier British plans.[20] Unwin and Parker may have been two of the most important contributors to working-class housing in the early twentieth century, having an important international influence on both the physical placement and the design of houses. The partners set an ideal density of between ten and twenty dwellings an acre, with dwellings positioned for maximum privacy and in such a manner that they were not an equal distance from the road. Homes had well-pitched roofs for maximum sunlight on the street, and the general shape of the dwelling changed from rectangle to square, with everything but porches under the same roof-line.[21]

All these tenets were introduced into the Hydrostone District development. There were six different plans for the thirty-five four-unit buildings, five versions of the nineteen six-unit buildings, and three different types of the twenty-nine two-unit flats and twelve apartments above the Young Street stores and offices. The houses were designed with small rooms that served specific functions. Within the group development, only 4 dwellings had four bedrooms, 190 had three bedrooms, and 130 had two bedrooms. Three-bedroom homes were probably regarded as optimal, since this design distributed separate rooms to the parents and to children of each sex. The buildings were made of nine-inch by twenty-four-inch blocks of hydraulically compressed concrete with the brand-name 'Hydrostone' that provided the development with its most enduring name.

The interior design incorporated many of the most modern conveniences yet did not contain elements that are now taken for granted. All dwellings had electricity, modern bathrooms, kitchen sinks, laundry trays in the basement, and closet space in most bedrooms. Water heaters may have been the most appreciated new feature, because they partially replaced the triple-purpose coal ranges. These ranges were for cooking and heated both water and the home, but they were dirty and their operation unnecessarily increased the temperature in the house in summer. Hot water and modern bathrooms must have been appreciated, but these homes were not completely equipped, as furnaces were not originally installed.[22] Other inconveniences were the small kitchens with neither cupboards nor counters and the necessity of going outside to get to the basement laundry sinks.

Yet among the designs were significant variations. The end units were larger than dwellings in the centre and boasted a living-room, dining-room, kitchen, and pantry on the first floor. Though the first floor of the smaller centre units lacked a separate dining-room, the kitchen allocated precious work space to a family eating area. The crucial area for food preparation that included the range, sink, and domestic water heater was partially screened to leave a large part of the kitchen free to be used as a dining room.[23]

In sharp contrast to the planned development of the 'Places' that composed the Hydrostone District, there was the less-organized and irregular housing on the extension streets. The area west of North Creighton had been farm land until a large portion was sold to the Halifax Land Company in 1891.[24] Development was slow and scattered in the area and by 1917 included approximately a hundred dwellings and the Fleming Brothers Foundry. The houses were owned by owner-occupants as well as by a 'small landlord class' who tended to live in the subdivision.[25]

The impact of the explosion on the pre-existing houses on the extension streets was uneven. Some houses were completely burned to the ground; others were damaged beyond repair, while their neighbours were able to replace glass and repair chimneys.[26] As a result, the area developed haphazardly to include a wide assortment of homes. The older, wooden, flat-roofed, two-storey dwellings typical of Halifax housing co-existed with shacks, flats, new HRC houses, and bungalows.

This diversity was also seen in the quality of the housing among the 128 houses assessed during the 1920s. On these streets, only one in four of the houses assessed for municipal taxes received a 'good' rating, and all had been built after the disaster.[27] Amenities also varied, since not all houses were connected to sewer, water, or electricity. Heating was provided almost universally by stove, 25 dwellings did not have toilets, and 64 did not have baths. Property assessments on the extension streets ranged from $5,000 for a new pair of flats at 7 Hennessey Street to $400 for what must have been little more than a shack at 26 Merkel Street. Some 88 of the 128 assessed properties fell between $1,000 and $2,500, with 13 below $1,000 and 27 above $2,500.[28] The great extremes in housing were further recognized by a 1932 report that condemned sections of Livingstone, Stairs, Stanley, and Kane streets for possessing some of the worst housing conditions in the city.[29]

Obviously, the explosion and the advice of experts did not alleviate all local housing problems. From the perspective of the tenants, the reaction to the new wooden and Hydrostone houses was generally positive. Some negative comments were made about the small size of the rooms, particularly the kitchens, which, as 'the poor man's principal room,' were without sufficient storage space for flour barrels or groceries.[30] Other critics referred to the design of the houses as 'pill boxes' or 'prison-like' in appearance.[31] At least as important as design to tenants was the fact that many units had wet cellars, because some of the development had been built on a swamp.[32]

The tenants also had mixed feelings about their landlord, the HRC. Feelings within Richmond Heights ranged from enmity to enthusiasm. One man felt particularly guilty about falling behind on his rent and wrote 'you will get your money as I know the rent is for poor people victims of the explosion and I would not do them out of a cent.'[33] In contrast, the housing officer, J.M. Hire, reported that upon issuing tenant Daniel Bolt with an eviction notice, 'He put forward the very much worn plea that the Relief Commission Houses were built for his kind and that the administration was indifferent and living on the "fat of the land."'[34]

The aspirations of Halifax's working-class citizens with regard to housing appear to have differed from those of workers in other Canadian cities. Richard Harris's study of 1931 home-ownership patterns in nine Canadian cities found that Halifax was the sole case where working-class home-ownership rates were lower than among the middle class.

Harris claimed that the low rates in Halifax could not be explained in terms of house affordability and that local factors must have been at work. While Harris suggested that the local housing market in 1931 might still have been feeling the long-term effects of the explosion, this explanation is difficult to accept since there was a high level of vacancy throughout the 1920s as a result of outmigration.[35] Rather, outmigration and the fragile local economy meant that many working-class Haligonians might not be around to reap the long-term gains of home ownership, so decent rental accommodation like that available in Richmond Heights provided an important option.

Richmond Heights was developed for people who had lost their housing in the explosion, and they formed a core population joined by many newcomers throughout the 1920s.[36] While ethnic divisions rather than class remained the primary residential determinant in cities such as Toronto and Winnipeg as late as 1930, in Halifax new class-based residential patterns appeared earlier. This trend was probably accelerated at least in part by the explosion. Janet Kitz noted that a number of the owners of old Richmond factories did not return to the area after the explosion except to maintain an affiliation with local churches. Similarly, L.D. McCann has stated that while white-collar clerks were often neighbours of blue-collar railway workers, the suburb of Richmond Heights was 'more solidly' working class in 1926 than its predecessor of Richmond had been in 1901 or 1912.[37] In terms of occupation and religion, both the railwaymen and the city's Roman Catholics claimed that their families had been the single most important group in the area affected by the explosion.[38] The 1891 and 1901 manuscript censuses for the district at the base of the slope around the old Richmond train station recorded many of the same families who resided in Richmond Heights during the 1920s. Railway families intermarried, and sons followed fathers and grandfathers onto the road or into the shops. By the 1920s, in Richmond Heights, there were railway families who could easily be traced back three generations.

Residents of Richmond Heights were not united only by the workplace or by the church. The suburb also housed the group of Haligonians most likely to support independent political action by labour and to adhere to the political tenets of labourism. No other polling district in Halifax was so consistent in its support of Labour party candidates in the provincial election of 1920, the federal election of 1921, and the federal by-election of 1922. In 1920, half the votes cast at the Richmond

Heights poll were in support of the Labour candidates, and even in 1922, when the wheels had fallen off the movement and levels of outmigration were high, the district was able to bring in a quarter of its votes for Labour. The names of neighbourhood residents, both male and female, appeared on the nomination papers of Labour alderman Robert Daw, and several men's names appeared on Labour's federal and provincial nomination papers in 1921 and 1925 respectively.[39]

Political action was a response to economic change, and nowhere in the city would the cycle of industrialization and deindustrialization have been experienced more sharply than in the North End working-class suburb of Richmond. As the terminal of the Nova Scotia and later the Intercolonial Railway since the 1850s, Richmond had attracted important industries such as the Nova Scotia Sugar Refinery located along the waterfront between the railway tracks and the deep harbour.[40] The advantages of rail and water transportation, reinforced by available land and a skilled labour force associated with the railway, attracted many industries to Richmond during the industrial expansion of the National Policy. At the Hillis and Sons foundry, skilled metal workers produced stoves, ranges, and furnaces. The Highland Spring Brewery, at the corner of Agricola and Sullivan, brewed and bottled ale and stout. Brandram-Henderson, a manufacturer of paint and varnish, opened its large site in 1880; and in 1891, the Halifax Graving Dockyard, precursor of the Halifax Shipyards Limited, began large ship repair. The community of Richmond was also dependent upon the Imperial Dockyard, which closed in 1907 and was reorganized in the early 1910s as Canada developed a naval policy.[41]

In the wake of the railway depot came the churches and the schools. Grove Presbyterian Church had its beginnings in 1861 as a Sunday school in the railway station until a building was completed in 1872. Kaye Street Methodist Church began in 1864 as a suburban mission, with a building opening in 1869. Grove Presbyterian and Kaye Street Methodist would join together to form United Memorial after the 1917 explosion, predating the formation of the United Church of Canada by seven years and offering a very concrete example of a community that could surmount sectarian difference.[42] An Anglican church, St Mark's, was erected in 1866. The Roman Catholic St Joseph's Church was opened in 1867, and the following year the Sisters of Charity opened a school, orphanage, and convent adjacent to the sanctuary. The vacant land to the north and west, between Richmond and the African–Nova Scotian community of Africville on the Bedford Basin, became the site of other less prestigious public institutions such as Rockhead prison and the infectious-diseases hospital in the 1860s. At the end of the nineteenth century, Richmond and the area encompassed by Ward Six comprised the fastest-growing area of Halifax, enhanced by industries, institutions, and transportation facilities and with land available for further growth.[43]

The decline of Richmond as an industrial suburb took much less time than its rise. By the mid-1890s, many Maritime capitalists found it increasingly difficult to compete successfully with central-Canadian enterprises, since they did not possess the local structures for the successful transition from industrial capitalism to financial capitalism. As a result, the region found itself in the middle of a three-stage process in which the Maritimes became a branch-plant economy, owned and operated by outside interests. The final stage of consolidation completed by the First World War brought about the rationalization of national industry, the closure of local factories and mines, and the region's development as a market for goods produced outside.[44]

What deindustrialization began, the 1917 explosion completed. It removed much physical evidence that industry had ever existed in Richmond. Although some of the railway wharves at Richmond were rebuilt, by the 1920s they had to compete with the railway, rerouted to the city's South End, and the newly completed Ocean Terminals near Point Pleasant Park. Important industries did not attempt to rebuild. The cotton-mill site on Robie Street, once an important employer of female labour, became a lumber-yard; and the demolished North End train station was now obsolete with the completion of the southern extension. The sugar refinery, which was already in the process of consolidating production, moved all operations across the harbour to its Woodside location.

The rise and fall of the North End industrial suburb embittered many workers who had lived through the cycle. In 1926, the *Citizen* published a piece of doggerel submitted by a worker and signed 'Old Timer' that, in the words of the paper, contained 'some poetry and a vast amount of truth.'

I remember in Halifax, not long ago,
When our boys leaving school had a chance;
They could learn a trade,
And in time, lead a maid
To a home, not a joy ride, or dance.

When the old shops at Richmond
Were going full swing,
With the cotton mill, dry dock and Moirs,
The Acadia refinery, the dockyard and Gunn's,
We had then lots of work for our boys.

Now, I'll tell you a tale that the older folks know,
It's enough to make anyone sob;
And we could have Halifax now on the map,
Only someone fell flat on the job.

Then something else happened, economy stuff,
With the works up in Richmond stripped bare;
There were hundreds of pay cheques just vanished like smoke,
When it gets far enough in the air.

Now the smiling-faced workmen are missed on our streets,
They are happy in some place, you bet;
They can smile at the building that's going on here,
That is, club resolution, and debt.

We can share all the glory, between Liberal and Tory,
For causing industry's fall;
They may call me a Mutt, but we're down in a rut.
It was brains, so-called brains, did it all.[45]

It was this grass-roots frustration, the feeling that Haligonians who had once experienced prosperity had now been betrayed, that proved rich soil for the Maritime Rights movement during the 1920s.[46] The memory of 'old timers' set a romanticized standard for what was possible and what had been lost. That this prosperity may have been largely an illusion mattered little by the 1920s. With the passage of time, images of the past grew clearer as non-essential details were stripped away and a streamlined version of past life in Richmond was offered.

During the 1920s, the economic rhythm of Richmond Heights was largely set by the level of activity in the shipyard. After the Canadian government reneged on its promise to build a merchant marine, the function of the shipyard became solely for repair. The shipyard still needed a large reserve of skilled labourers who could be called upon when a ship arrived for repair and then laid off at the completion of the project. Employment levels experienced sudden and dramatic swings. In the spring of 1920, before the shipyard strike, there were more than 2,000 men working on the *Canadian Mariner*. The number fell to less than 100 in January 1922.[47]

The railway also had its own rhythm, with the local peak between December and March when the St Lawrence River was frozen and use of the Port of Halifax was the heaviest.[48] Seasonal unemployment reflected the demand for different trades in the government-owned Canadian National Railways (CNR) and the Dominion Atlantic Railway. Those employed for track maintenance worked from April to October, those on the trains followed peak traffic, and shop workers were busy from January to July. The number of employees needed varied greatly and in 1928 national monthly employment totals for the CNR and the Canadian Pacific Railway (CPR) fluctuated by more than 33,000 workers.[49]

Another important employer of tenants in Richmond Heights was the military. Before the construction of the Hydrostone District, military tenants often had difficulty in obtaining rental accommodations, since they were unstable tenants subject to sudden transfers.[50] The HRC attracted military tenants and added clauses to their leases that allowed cancellation if the tenant was moved or ordered into barracks. Although the HRC willingly accepted military tenants, the decline of postwar operations in Halifax and the closure of the dockyard meant that, fewer soldiers and sailors were looking for local accommodation.

Unstable employment opportunities were reflected in the high level of vacancies and occupant turnover in the Hydrostone District. Names in the city directory indicate that slightly more than 1 per cent of all tenancies in the 1920s lasted nine or ten years, while nearly half lasted a year or less (see graph). During the winter of 1922–3, the commission estimated that 1,000 families passed through its hands and practically all were in arrears with its rent.[51] Of the 725 leases available, 128 extended beyond January 1930 and were thus artificially interrupted in this analysis. Nevertheless, more than half of these tenancies, or 426, were held for less than eighteen months, and only 34 lasted longer than five years. Although the turnover of leases was undoubtedly large, the number of short-term tenancies exaggerates the passage of people through the neighbourhood and the instability of the community, since many families held serial leases at different addresses. At least 150 people took out two leases in the same name; 23 were identified with three separate leases at different addresses, and 2 individuals had four

LENGTH OF TENANCIES

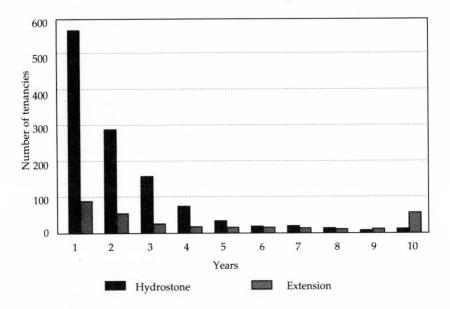

and five leases respectively. Recognition of multiple-lease tenants even underestimates the number of times the same people moved within the neighbourhood. Different individual members within the same household, such as wives, in-laws, and adult children, who undertook leases for the same household group cannot be traced except in rare situations. Although the leases suggest a high level of residential turnover, they also indicate that many moves were local, since households moved within the neighbourhood. One of the primary advantages of renting accommodation was the flexibility it permitted, and people took advantage of this option. Rental accommodation could meet the family's financial and spatial needs at very specific times. Residents of Richmond Heights used this flexibility to find suitable housing and so obtained the best housing possible within their means. The overall number of vacancies in the neighbourhood corresponded in a general manner to economic conditions. For example, in relatively good times, such as summer 1929, there were no vacancies in the development.[52]

The tenancy pattern of residents of the Hydrostone District compared to that on the extension streets was strikingly different. Residents on the extension streets were more likely to be owner-occupants who had held property before 1917 and tended to reside in the same homes throughout the 1920s. Only one-third of the tenancies were for a year or less, while 20 per cent lasted for nine or ten years. This may even underestimate the stability of the community, since construction on the extension streets continued throughout the decade and many houses were not available for longer residencies. The extension streets also differed from the Hydrostone in a relatively low level of vacancy, although empty houses on Livingstone Street were noted as a fire hazard.[53] The much lower level of vacancies on the extension streets might be explained by the poor condition of some of the rental housing and the correspondingly cheaper rent. On the other hand, those who owned their houses had a permanent commitment to the community and were less likely to leave Halifax, despite its limited economic opportunities.

Different forms of tenancies, ownership or renting, created different residential patterns. Moving around the neighbourhood or leaving the city were two ways of lessening pressure on the family economy. Life in the Hydrostone District could be similar to the description of Montreal in Gabrielle Roy's *The Tin Flute*, where each year households moved to suit their current financial position. May Day was the traditional moving day in Halifax, an urban adaptation of an older rural holiday.[54] The ambiguity around who was ultimately responsible for household decisions was reflected in the names in which leases were held. A number of leases were either solely in the wife's name or were jointly signed by husband and wife.[55] Despite the fact that the built environment was the result of modern theory and ideas, traditional tenancy patterns were unaffected. Residents continued to use mobility as an important survival strategy. The variance in lease-signing patterns also suggests the diverse decisions that could be made within every household. Perhaps some households were male or female dominated, while in other families housing decisions were undertaken jointly.

The dual impact of the explosion and reconstruction planted the community firmly within the context of the twentieth century, but it is important to note the large extent to which older ideas and ways of life co-existed with the new. Before the explosion, many of the lots in Richmond had been unusually large, allowing semi-rural domestic production. Many families kept animals and had extensive gardens for food production.[56] Although the households in the Hydrostone District had very little property, the subdivision remained close to the market gardens and farms on the perimeter of the city. Within Ward Six most of the area west of Kempt Road continued to be operated as farms. Those who lived in the wooden houses on the extension streets had more property and continued to meld an urban and rural lifestyle. In 1919 and 1921, new barns were built at 20 and 22 Kane Street, and in 1928 Fred Oliver of 24 Livingstone Street built a hen-house in his backyard.[57]

In an attempt to establish the same public-health standards as other Canadian cities, Halifax rather belatedly moved to restrict animals within its city limits. In 1922, Halifax forbade pig keeping in the city except by permit. It was noted in 1927, however, that there were several piggeries in the outlying areas of Ward Six and that there were 'more pigs in their Ward than in the other five wards put together.' Hens were kept by families in the wooden houses of Richmond Heights, and in one police case stolen hens were recovered on Kane Street. Poultry ran loose on the busy thoroughfares of North Creighton and Gottingen streets and throughout Richmond Heights, while wandering cows created a more serious menace on Robie Street. In 1926 a resident reported that two children had 'a narrow escape from being killed last Saturday by cows rushing pell mell down the street.' In the fall, complaints increased when cows entered people's yards, tipped garbage cans, and ate the contents.[58]

Municipal authorities had little success in eliminating what now appear as semi-rural aspects of life in the North End. They had even less success in regulating the use of public space. Street sellers were a particular source of tension, since they violated the general trend towards neutralized public space where areas were sharply defined for appropriate activities. Despite by-laws against door-to-door selling, strawberries and mackerel were sold in the streets by farmers and fishermen, who eliminated any middlemen. Each spring the weekly *Evening Mail* column 'North End Notes' complained about the presence of fresh-fish peddlers and warned of the impending nuisance of strawberry sellers, who walked the residential streets yelling late into the night. Similarly, in the autumn, residents were awakened at early hours in the morning by vegetable sellers.[59] Despite their noise and the complaints of newspapers, street hawkers must have found a worthwhile local market because they continued to visit the neighbourhood regularly. One suspects that the newspapers reflected the irritation of their advertisers, the local shopkeepers, rather than of female consumers, who could be virtually tied to their homes with small children and pleased to take advantage of producer prices.

The modern design of garden suburbia did nothing to alter the smells and noises of life on the outskirts of the city. Richmond Heights residents lived in new homes, but they continued to smell the pungent odours of the fishmeal plant, the abattoir, and the city incinerator. The sooty smoke from coal and oil ranges was omnipresent from cooking or heating. The voices of neighbours, heard through the walls of the adjoining homes, joined the noises of barking dogs, church bells, the horns of ships, and the annual visits of gypsies and organ grinders.[60]

As in the semi-rural environment, disputes over the use of public space and the variety of smells and sounds of the urban periphery did not vanish with the construction of modern houses and garden suburbs. The influence of the British garden suburbs improved the standard of housing for many Hydrostone District tenants but did not alter tenancy patterns, and a high level of residential turnover continued. Better houses could mean better living conditions, but as Margaret Giles has noted in her study of British working-class suburbs between the wars, they did not mean happy endings.[61] Within their lives, many individuals may have directly experienced the local cycle of industrialization and deindustrialization. The explosion and reconstruction may have forced Halifax into the twentieth century with the onslaught of experts and state intervention, but change did not occur as suddenly as the explosion or even in the much longer period of rebuilding the city. The built environment of Richmond Heights symbolized much that was new, but the people who lived in the houses cannot be so clearly defined, since they continued to face fundamental inequalities, such as a rigid gender division of labour and a vulnerable position in the labour market. Life was a simultaneous experience of change and continuity, and this apparent paradox meant that people's lives could not be reconstructed as easily as their homes.

2

Values and Daily Life

While the kitchen may have been the most important room in the working-class home, it was the living-room or parlour that projected the public persona of the family. It was there that the public and the private worlds met through the visits of clergymen, public-health officials, and neighbours. An unusually high degree of uniformity characterized the living-rooms of Richmond Heights, since many of the residents were among the 1,800 households to receive furniture from one of the relief agencies to replace belongings lost in the explosion.[1] But beyond the standard-issue round oak table and pressed-back dining chairs common to many of the houses, there also appears to have been a shared understanding of what was appropriate decoration for a living-room. Details signified degrees of limited affluence and a common notion of good taste. In other words, interior decorations affirmed an unstated but well-understood community standard.

Within the homes of Richmond Heights, the issued furniture was individualized by many personal touches. A potted rose might sit on a white lace doily in the centre of a bare table or upon a tablecloth edged with large tassels. Family photos adorned the walls, sideboards, and bureaus. In some cases these photos included that of a priest, or a young man in uniform, or perhaps even someone killed during the war. A jumble of ferns, conch shells, cut-glass water pitchers, vases, books, small dishes, large bowls, and clocks set on an assortment of bureau scarves or floral valances added further personal touches. In Roman Catholic homes, religious icons of the Holy Family or the Bleeding Heart, religious medals, and crucifixes hung beside elaborate insurance calendars and pastoral prints. On the floor of the living-room might be the only carpet in the house, an oriental, standard-issue covering further individualized by scatter rugs. Other attempts to personalize the furniture were seen in the lace antimacassars draped on the backs of armchairs. The need to use a room for multiple purposes might also be evident, since the living-room could provide extra sleeping space, with beds disguised as couches behind large decorated pillows.[2]

A common understanding of what constituted good taste was just one of the informal rules residents of Richmond Heights recognized as they negotiated daily life among family, neighbours, and employers. Although not everyone complied with established customs and beliefs, these unstated ways of behaving had an important hold over self-definition and interaction with others. Some rules were remnants of a distant traditional past, such as the prohibition of weddings on Fridays and the avoidance of 'unlucky' May marriages. Other practices protected the reputation of the family or the privacy of individual members and had real economic significance in the 1920s. The possession of a good name, for example, could be used almost like collateral in order to obtain credit or a promissory note.[3] Adherence to these unwritten rules determined whether or not a household had a good reputation and was therefore considered 'respectable.' The idea of respectability and the various characteristics that it described played a major role in the mind-set of the community, its ideology, and its workings. Certainly, within this category there continued to be a wide variance of behaviour, and even the respectable working-class residents of a single neighbourhood could not be considered homogenous.

Yet, despite the number of ways respectability could be interpreted, at its core was an adherence to community gender ideals as they dictated the sexual division of labour and appropriate sexual behaviour and allocated the spheres of influence. Respectability was similar, in fact, to the elaborate parlour decorations – how they appeared to others was as important as any functional use. Since respectability was largely concerned with outward judgment – with reputation as seen by others – it assisted in organizing social relations. Concern about outward judgment increased the value of privacy and helped define and heighten the significance of private life among the working class. The decision to place value on the interlocking triad of respectability, privacy, and consumerism had political ramifications, since it strengthened patriarchy within the household and the maintenance of the private household at the expense of community.[4]

Domestic and public culture in the 1920s was a contested terrain with political consequences. In her study of Chicago industrial workers,

Lizabeth Cohen has effectively challenged the notion that the stereo-
typical symbols – flappers, Fords, jazz, movies, radio, dances, religious
revivals, and chain stores – were apolitical.[5] As in the Chicago depicted
by Cohen, the victory of mass culture in Halifax was neither swift nor
all-encompassing. While working-class Haligonians did participate in
the emerging continental culture, they also managed to maintain local
customs and concerns. For example, residents of Richmond Heights
patronized both local shops and national chain stores. The advantage of
personal credit at the neighbourhood store and the focus these stores
occasionally offered for the community continued to be important.
Among the most flamboyant of these neighbourhood shopkeepers was
Fred Eld, whose 'Original Veteran's Store' on North Creighton Street
saw the arrival of Santa Claus on Christmas morning and the celebration of Eld's fifty-seventh birthday in the form of a massive party attended by more than 1,000 children and at which 1,400 bags of candy
and fruit were distributed.[6] The Casino Theatre on Gottingen Street
where neighbourhood residents attended the latest movies was also the
very same place where they sat through meetings of the local Labour
party. Dancing, often held up as a symbol of the decade, did take place
at road-houses and public dance halls, but Richmond Heights residents
were just as likely to be seen trying the latest dance steps, square dancing, or waltzing at functions hosted by a union, church, or neighbour
down the street. Mass culture and class culture could be experienced
simultaneously with no apparent conflicts for the participants, in the
same way that Richmond Heights residents had no trouble blending
the sacred and the secular. In June 1921, the newly completed United
Memorial Church celebrated its new set of bells with a twenty-four-
song Sunday concert that included such diverse tunes as 'Drink to Me
Only with Thine Eyes,' 'Swanee River,' and 'Jesus, Lover of My Soul.'[7]
Stores, movie theatres, dances, and even church bells could reinforce
and foster a sense of community identity that encouraged links beyond
the workplace and family networks. But the most important identity
that coalesced around the working-class neighbourhood of Richmond
Heights was expressed in the label 'respectable.'

Richmond Heights had a reputation as 'respectable,' in marked contrast to other Halifax working-class neighbourhoods such as the downtown area north of the Citadel. In a history of the Halifax explosion by
Professor Archibald MacMechan of Dalhousie University, the respectability of the area was emphasized to underscore the tragic nature of
the disaster. The 'industrial class' residents of old Richmond were de-

scribed as 'thrifty, industrious, self-respecting' in character; and in behaviour as regular in their school and church attendance.[8] MacMechan's
willingness to link church attendance to respectability is not without
significance.

At the heart of Richmond Heights' respectability was a shared belief
in a Christian God, or at least Christian ethics; and an understanding
of the distinct roles men and women were supposed to play in the
operation of society followed from these religious convictions. Christian ethics were connected to many attitudes and behaviours, as Elizabeth Roberts has pointed out in her study of English working-class
women during the same period. Roberts has noted the importance of
being a 'good' or 'Christian' person through the act of loving your
neighbour, an Old Testament concept of justice, and a belief in the work
ethic, in which labour brings salvation and idleness damnation. All had
roots in Christian moral training.[9]

The role of religion in constructing a world view is extremely difficult to determine, but the religious iconography of the household and
the number of crucifixes and scapulars found upon victims of the 1917
explosion suggests it was central in many people's lives.[10] In the railway community of Allendale, Ontario, as Mark Rosenfeld has noted,
lectures and sermons under the auspices of the Methodist, Presbyterian, and United churches during this period specifically addressed questions of the proper roles of men and women. Lectures such as 'The
Need for Hot-Stone Men,' 'Men in the Making,' and 'A Challenge to
Manhood' attracted good crowds, as did sermons addressing 'domesticity, suffrage and the changing role of women.'[11] Similarly, in Halifax
at St Joseph's Church a parish priest recommended a series of articles
on the obligations of members of the Christian family – father, mother,
husband, wife, son, and daughter.[12] Furthermore, in Catholic homes,
the importance of the Virgin Mary and the Holy Family may have
provided additional important gender role models.

Language and the ways that people expressed themselves also reflected the importance of religious beliefs. Several of the thank-you
notes from explosion victims closed with a blessing for the people who
had donated money. Patrick Wylie, a tailor who lived at 17 Kane Place
throughout the 1920s, wrote, 'I trust and pray that God will bless them
all their lives.'[13] The religious sentiments expressed in these notes are
particularly interesting, since they are completely absent in similar notes
from the various religious institutions or professionals such as the minister of Kaye Street Methodist Church. In addition, the sheer numbers

involved in religious activities were impressive. Before the explosion, St Joseph's Church claimed a membership of 650 families or 3,300 souls, and despite the tragedy and later outmigration the congregation still required several large buses to take seventy-five altar and choir boys to their annual picnic in July 1927 at Silver Sands Beach.[14] The same parish counted more than 1,000 communicants on Easter Sunday 1928, and offered the sacrament of confirmation to 300 children and 31 adults in June 1929.[15]

While religious beliefs were somewhat elusive, the connection between respectability and gender ideals was more obvious since they were evident in the gender division of labour, behaviour, and responsibilities. Ideally, men and women had distinct areas of control and separate spheres of influence. 'Separate spheres' was an extremely potent bourgeois ideology that managed to touch nearly all aspects of society, but the transition from ideology to daily life meant that it was reproduced and adopted with significant class variation.[16] Even where the idea of separate spheres had the greatest hold, the division was always tenuous and artificial, since no one lived his or her entire life under the influence of the workplace or home. The division between public and private was constantly being negotiated as men sought refuge in the home and women expanded their horizons beyond the threshold and as they both came to grips with shifting definitions of masculinity and femininity.

For working-class men, manliness was associated with many facets of paid work: the physical strength and skills necessary to undertake it and its remuneration as the basis of a man's ability to support a family. Across the continent, urbanization and new consumption patterns consolidated the male-breadwinner ideal, displacing a pattern of combined household earnings where the income of older children was needed to support the household. The shift in ideals was particularly acute in centres like Halifax, where by the 1920s, as a result of economic and technological change, fewer men were able to identify with a manhood based solely on production, strength, danger, or skill. Consequently, great importance was placed on the ability to support a family and immense pride was taken in the role of the breadwinner.[17] The ideal, however, contrasted sharply with the realities of underemployment and poor pay. The belief that the wage of one male was sufficient to support a family was an illusion given life by skilled men, the state, trade unions, and some employers who either affirmed or desired the realization of the illusion by sanctifying the 'family,' 'living,' or 'basic' wage. They held that an adult male was responsible not only for himself but also for supporting his family and should be remunerated based on that assumption. In case after case, Halifax freight handlers, carpenters, teamsters, and labourers pleaded for the right to a 'living wage,' always in the context of 'domestic responsibilities' or the difficulty of supporting a family.[18] At a meeting of freight handlers in 1928, it was argued that 'By the time they [male labourers] buy coal, clothing for the family, pay insurance and rent, there is little left ...'[19] The notion of the family wage was also reinforced outside the workplace and the home. In 1928, the newly introduced offering envelopes were distributed only to male members of the United Memorial Church congregation.[20]

Men's role as primary breadwinner was the way in which they achieved status not only in the family, where their wages legitimized their position as head of the household, but also in the wider community. The pay package justified access to women's unpaid domestic work and, according to sociologist Stan Gray, offered labourers the perception of the property they lacked. In a sense, the primary wage-earner became the owner of the family.[21] The ability to support a wife and children marked the man, yet while men may have been under increasing pressure to provide, the pay itself also offered satisfaction. Beyond the home, community status, reputation, and hence respectability rested upon one's proven ability to support a family.[22]

While married men's lives had a dual focus of home and beyond, most adult married women found their identity within domestic life. Women were responsible for being good wives, mothers, and daughters. Being a good wife meant 'making do' – performing the difficult task of surviving on the husband's often inadequate wage. This involved using the available finances cleverly in order to ensure the adequate provision of food, shelter, fuel, and clothing, and stretching the money in order to make it possible for the family to get by.[23] Women were also important wage-earners, both as daughters before marriage and as wives in times of illness, underemployment, unemployment, and widowhood. Past work experience varied with age. Older women in the neighbourhood would have been employed at the cotton mill on Robie Street or as domestic servants in their youth, a work experience markedly different from that of their single granddaughters, who might be working as telephone operators or shop clerks in the 1920s.

While working-class men based their authority and respectability upon the ideology of the family wage, respectability was less tangible but more important for working-class women. For women, respectability reinforced their household identity, and they rarely had an alternative role to fall back upon. Yet the notion of respectability was not forced upon these women, since it offered many women status in their community and pride in its attainment. The connection between pride and respectability makes little sense unless we openly acknowledge that perfected femininity, like perfected masculinity, was a skill. This skill required years of apprenticing and could be destroyed by a single unfeminine or unrespectable action. Richmond Heights women, therefore, generally personified respectability, giving life to the ideal by their adherence to specific codes surrounding dress, public conduct, spending habits, and sexuality.[24] Respectability was not only an important feminine skill to uphold but was also a survival strategy, since the judgment and opinions of neighbours, shopkeepers, churches, and social-service workers played a role in the distribution and availability of assistance, credit, and charity.[25]

The achievement of respectability often depended on the achievement of privacy. The fact that physical and personal knowledge of a neighbour could easily become a form of power partly illuminates the value residents of Richmond Heights placed on privacy. Respectability was largely concerned with external judgments that had real consequences for people in vulnerable situations. As a result, paramount importance was placed on the ability to control who had information about the household. In fact, one might argue that the right to privacy was perceived as a kind of property right. The assessment of neighbours formed an important component of life in Richmond Heights. Neighbours regularly reported neighbours to the Halifax Relief Commission (HRC) which had enormous power over everyone's life as landlord and pension source.[26] The sexual propriety of women, the behaviour of a neighbour's children, and the standard of a neighbour's housekeeping could all be issues. In fact, in the original design of the Hydrostone District some people expressed concern that with row houses 'they did not know the kind of people [who] will be sharing the house with them.'[27] Neighbours who informed the HRC of the unrespectable behaviour of their fellow tenants distanced themselves from disreputable behaviour and enhanced their own reputations because they condemned the behaviour of the offending households. The desire for privacy was connected to pride and respectability. Minnie Smithers of Cabot Place took offence when a lawyer she had hired to sort out the intimate matter of a domestic financial dispute with her husband investigated all her financial transactions. Accordingly, she complained to the commission that the lawyer had no business contacting it, as 'Mr Kenny was not employed by me to pay my bills or rent bills. As far as Mr K. was concerned it was none of his affair what we owed.'[28] The need for privacy from a lawyer acting on her behalf suggests the extent to which residents tried to protect themselves from those with knowledge about their affairs. This was not so surprising, for when people are vulnerable, knowledge is power.

Adherence to respectability built the social 'fences' of distance that created the proverbial 'good neighbours.' These fences could be literal, taking the form of hedges, gates, or bordered gardens, or they could refer to the social space people tried to create. Space was important because the violation of the codes of respectability was often at the root of trouble between neighbours. Such breaches of etiquette may have occurred more often than the commission liked, for strife between neighbours was relatively common. Problems with neighbours could emerge as a result of abusive behaviour, but also over noise, garbage, and the tension of having to live together so closely – all invasions of a household's right to privacy. In one instance, a woman on Stanley Place wrote in 1927 requesting that the commission 'could put a stop or warn those people next door [the] Bradshaws [as] they fill my garden with paper every night.' The indignant tenant went on to explain that she had 'done nothing to them [but] when I sit out on my veranda they come out trying to pick a fight. We cant use our front if we want peace.'[29] Other residents complained about the way their neighbours discarded garbage and ashes, shook out their mats, or disposed of waste water from upper flats. The response to a neighbour's complaint could also invoke the right to privacy. A bewildered Cabot Place woman wrote in response to a neighbour's complaint to the commission: 'I dont enterfear with any off my neighbors and I dont [know] why any one would report stuff about me.'[30] In this case the woman seems to have considered that neighbourly relations were reciprocal and were based on a principle of non-interference.

The degree of non-interference of neighbours in the neighbourhood was actually somewhat ambiguous. Neighbours certainly were involved in 1921 when Mrs Annie Hutchinson allegedly assaulted Mrs James Lennox on the front veranda of her Stairs Place home in 1921. Six witnesses claimed that they had seen the attack and another three denied that anything had happened. Mrs Lennox had supposedly dragged Annie Hutchinson out of her house, and Mrs Lennox's husband, while holding Annie down, had instructed his wife to 'give it to her.'[31] Verbal assault was probably more common than physical assault. In 1919, a man in the temporary housing was charged with abusive language against his neighbour when he was quoted as saying 'your a ———— immigrant' and 'your a ———— Newfoundlander.'[32] Conflict and strife between neighbours seems to have been a normal aspect of life in Richmond Heights. In 1929, George MacInnis, a resident of Richmond Heights and a tenant of the HRC, received a letter at his workplace regarding his wife's behaviour at home and the consequent reaction of their neighbours. The commission reported that it had received 'complaints about the objectionable remarks and abusive language used by Mrs MacInnis towards her neighbors on Merkel and Cabot Places' and that 'this trouble has developed to such an extent that several of our tenants are considering moving away.' According to the commission, a similar 'state of affairs developed when you were at Sebastian Place which only died down on removal to your present address,' and 'it was then hoped that the difficulty would not re air but, unfortunately it is again being repeated.' The letter went on to state the possibility of eviction, but first offered to discuss the situation with the husband.[33] By sending the letter to the Nova Scotia Light and Power Company and addressing the complaint to the husband, the commission was pointedly avoiding the involvement of Mrs MacInnis about whom the complaints were made. It was also significant that they invited George MacInnis to discuss the matter without his wife. The antagonism between neighbours, often played out by women who spent a great deal of time around their homes, such as Mrs Lennox, Mrs Hutchinson, or Mrs MacInnis, is an important, though little studied, aspect of female working-class culture. The legacy of verbal or physical assaults among working-class women survives in the unusual form of a skipping rhyme, still chanted by little girls, about mothers who meet while hanging laundry and draw blood from a punch in the nose.[34]

Despite the best efforts of the architects there was very little physical privacy from neighbours, a fact that made social privacy all the more important. Did neighbours call each other by their first names? Did women pop over to drink cups of tea in the kitchen to break the isolation of housework? Did households actually use their front porches, and did neighbours gather there on warm summer evenings? We know many households were frequent entertainers, but were the guest lists based on family, work, or church connections or could they also include someone in the same housing block? These questions remain unanswered, but we do know that not all relationships with neighbours were antagonistic, and it is the nature of evidence that unrespectable behaviour is much more likely to be recorded than cooperation or assistance. The activities of women who helped with the sick, brought food after a birth or death, or minded a neighbour's child to permit the mother to run an errand go unrecorded. Dramatic gestures survive, such as the actions of Mrs Bert Black of 23 Hennessey Place, who experienced eviction herself in 1932 after harbouring homeless former neighbours who had 'no other asylum.'[35] The assisted family had been tenants in the neighbourhood since 1923 and had succeeded in achieving a good name and at least one neighbour's loyalty.[36] Mrs Black's actions offer rare testimony to the positive side of neighbourly relations.

Respectability needed privacy, but it could also be put into jeopardy by poor housing conditions or poverty.[37] The link between poverty and femininity was particularly interesting, since there was the inference that 'good women' were partially defined by a certain level of material success. In a letter written by a Mrs Richards after she had left her tenancy, she repeatedly referred to the idea of respectability. Her family owed the HRC considerable back rent in 1926 and was about to face legal action to recover the long overdue sum. The letter not only rings with her desire to remain 'respectable' but also emphasizes the overwhelming nature of debt, lack of family support, and how these worries fell upon the wife. This is a remarkable letter, worth quoting at length. Mrs Richards wrote:

I'm paying my way honestly a[nd] straight forward a[nd] unless a miracle happens a[nd] Mr Richards gets a better job it seems to me impossible ... I've *one bed* and Mr Richards sleeps in that with 3 children, I sleep on a mattress and broken spring with the baby with 3 blankets and 3 sheets between both beds ... It has been pretty hard to be respectable a[nd] to keep up under the conditions we are living.

We were living on *scraps* from the Priests' table at St. Thomas Aquinas Church Glebe House for 2 whole weeks before Xmas ... When I wrote to Mr Richards' father Columbus Pl a[nd] ask him if he would help us he wrote a[nd] said no ... We never have had any help from Mr Richards' people at all never. He would help my husband if he would go away. He would *put* my two eldest boys in the Roman Catholic orphanage a[nd] look after *me* my baby and my little girl on one condition that *I would be a wife* to him. I am not lying. I'm an *Englishwoman* and I'd not touch one cent of money belonging to that man. Thats why we are having to *pay* our own way. My Goodness Mr Tibbetts [Tibbs] if you knew just how hard it is to make both ends meet a[nd] to keep the children neat a[nd] tidy for school. I'd come up a[nd] see you but i've no *clothes* at all only me housedress ...

I'll willing pay you when *I can* see my way but just cant you understand that debt is worrying all the time then I've got to have meal milk bread coal and *I've* got to pay rent here or where will we go but it is no good saying June 1st get a judge a[nd] try me now if you want but I'm not going on the streets to earn money to pay back rent. I'll go to prison first.

I'm trying to live a[nd] pay my way a[nd] keep respectable a[nd] I cannot do any more.[38]

The Richards family was clearly in disastrous financial straits. Concern about paying grocery bills and rent were uppermost in Mrs Richards' mind, since the maintenance of reputation for any credit was essential for her family's survival. Clothing and housing conditions endured by the household were clearly unacceptable, and the need to protect her reputation meant that Mrs Richards, through lack of a good dress, was in effect held hostage in her house. The necessity of accepting charity from the Catholic church wounded the Protestant family pride, since seeking charity meant disclosing private household financial matters and was resorted to only in preference to her father-in-law's scandalous proposition. The only method of raising money available to Mrs Richards, beyond becoming her father-in-law's mistress, was to engage in prostitution, a consideration that made her reiterate her claim to respectability. As a former tenant with a poor credit rating and facing legal action, Mrs Richards had little to gain from her claim of respectability to the HRC except the important preservation of her own pride. Poverty did not destroy pride or respectability, but it certainly made it much more difficult to maintain.

According to Mrs Richards, cleanliness and proper dress were also important to respectability, since they reflected how one appeared in the eyes of one's neighbours. The proper presentation of children appears to have been particularly important during a period when mothers were increasingly being judged more harshly. A widow wrote to the HRC requesting suspension of her rent one September so that she could purchase school clothes for her children: 'If not my children will not be sent to school until I get money enough to clothe them properly to send them.'[39] Similarly, a mother wrote to the commission in April 1926, stating her predicament of 'just how hard it is to make both ends meet a[nd] to keep the children neat a[nd] tidy for school.'[40] Neighbours' and school officials' opinions of how their children looked were obviously important to these women.

Women were aware of being judged not only by the HRC, their neighbours, and their children's teachers, but also by their friends. New forms of domestic consumption such as curtains, carpets, dishes, and silverware all increased the amount of housework that was necessary and elevated the standards of cleanliness.[41] One's ability to achieve these elevated standards was judged by a host of friends and neighbours. In the case of Mrs Smithers of 34 Cabot Place whose ceiling was destroyed by a leaking boiler on the second floor, she found herself having to 'make excuses when my friends came for the dirty ceilings.'[42] Many women in Richmond Heights took great pride in their housekeeping, as seen in the 'lovely white lace curtains in the windows' and the nearly annual requests that the ceilings be whitened or whitewashed.[43] But the standards of cleanliness were not universal. The commission reported in 1923, that it was 'having a little trouble with empty houses that had been vacated by some of our less satisfactory tenants, as they left them in a very dirty state. Mr Thorne had been fumigating etc etc and we hope to get rid of this shortly.'[44]

In addition to cleanliness, the ability to control her children was an important characteristic of a respectable woman. The commission adopted a policy of monitoring the relationship between tenants and their children through formal letters and, if necessary, personal visits. In May 1924 the commission drafted a letter to Mrs Hogan concerning complaints about her sons' vandalism, warning her that their current behaviour would land them in the juvenile court. The letter concluded: 'We quite realize that all children are mischievous and in these days control is difficult: but I am sure a few words from you pointing out their share of responsibility for the care of the city and all property, public and private, will have the desired effect.'[45] Although the letter was not sent to Mrs Hogan, the exact same text was sent to a neighbour at 18 Kane Place whose sons were accused also of delinquency as a result of their having broken windows in several empty houses. Mrs Hogan had probably reacted better to a personal visit from a member of the HRC and hence avoided the formal notification. The neighbour, Mrs Rose, on the other hand, did not react properly, and her indifference concerned the commission. J.M. Hire, the commission's housing agent, reported to the commission that after complaints about her sons he had called upon 'Mrs Rose and pointed out that it was incumbent on the father and mother to keep them in control.' To Hire's dismay, 'Mrs Rose was in no way disturbed, neither affirming or denying, but it was evident to me that there is great lack of control in that family as far as the children are concerned.'[46] It is interesting to note that the housing agent called on the mother, though he expected the father to become involved. This perhaps suggests the ambiguity in changing parental responsibilities.

Unrespectable behaviour was a label associated with specific families. Mary Owen had the dubious distinction of facing charges of creating a public disturbance, sharing her home with a divorced daughter, and, finally, being evicted in October 1931.[47] Throughout 1927 police were repeatedly called to her home at 18 Livingstone Place, the result of neighbours' complaints 'of unreasonable disturbances' involving Mrs Owen. Although women conducted nearly all the correspondence with the commission, after one particular incident, the HRC wrote to Mrs Owen's husband, and on the assumption that he had some authority in his family, instructed him to 'either arrange for more seemly conduct in your home or else arrange to vacate.'[48]

Respectability was a great concern of the commission, which always wanted to attract the 'best' of the working class as tenants. The commission secretary reported in 1927 'that the housing situation was improving and we were now taking references of every tenant, feeling that the time had arrived when we should take only first class tenants in our houses.'[49] The commission occasionally classified its tenants, either vaguely as 'not satisfactory,' or alternatively by giving specific evidence of their inappropriate character.[50] Albert Gray, resident of 2 Cabot Place, was asked to vacate after sixteen years when he was accused of disturbing neighbours.[51] The case against Daniel Barlow of 28 Stanley Place was more explicit. The commission described him as noisy when home, as suspected of intemperance, and as having a family of many 'ragged' children who were 'dirty, slovenly and unkept.' The final condemnation implied that his family's behaviour had breached community standards, as his 'family [was] collectively an offence to the tenants in that neighbourhood.'[52] HRC judgments could be wrong – a man it described in 1924 as 'a good respecting tenant' was charged with beating his wife in 1929.[53]

The continued importance of respectability, as a daily way of sorting out reality, raises questions about the extent to which new value had taken root in the community. Respectability was an older measure of social status or prestige. It was based on the value of how one behaved rather than of what one owned. Clearly, this community did not have the economic means or resources to abandon old community judgments and adopt a social value system based on material acquisitions. While there is evidence of the advent of new and competing belief systems, changes in values and perceptions were uneven in their influence and respectability remained important. In fact new values that elevated the status of consumption merged with aspects of respectability that had valued the privacy of the domestic sphere. The household became the site of privacy and the primary location of consumption.

Historian Cynthia Wright has recently argued that consumption is 'a key component of understanding class and gender relations in twentieth-century Canada.'[54] The consumer society of Richmond Heights in the 1920s was not the same as the disposable consumer society that later emerged with this century. Residents of the neighbourhood did not consume in the sense that something disappeared; rather, like some variation of the law of energy, where matter is neither created nor destroyed, consumption transformed wealth into a more tangible and immediately useful form. In the same way, while respectability did not disappear, it was certainly altered by new kinds of status-driven consumption, since material possessions could lend support to one's reputation. There is little doubt that aspects of domestic production were being replaced by the consumption of goods produced outside the home. Women who had embodied respectability were now also assigned the roles of chief consumers and must have experienced particular frustration generated by their inability to afford everything they wanted. Pressure, even from their children, to buy may have been increasing as department stores attracted customers via elaborate parades through public space, such as Santa Claus's early arrival at the Halifax Simpson's on 8 November 1929. Advertisers constantly linked goods to status, as in an advertisement for Johnson's Polishing Wax that boasted: 'a wax finish denotes refinement.'[55] Not surprisingly, consumer goods connected to cleanliness and the traditional domestic responsibilities of women were associated with respectability, but status was also available through the acquisition of modern technology. This link, too, was not altogether new. Whereas a piano was an important measure of refinement and respectability in certain working-class living-rooms or parlours before the war, the choice of goods available was now much more extensive. Therefore, when a Sebastian Place family sold its piano that 'no one really played' in order to buy a gramophone, they 'thought they were somebody.'[56] With new consumer patterns, as with respectability, status was conferred by external approval. Ownership of a gramophone did little for the household's status unless the neighbours knew of its existence, suggesting that privacy was not an absolute value.

Consumption was an activity that took place on an individual basis, and therefore it is difficult to generalize across the neighbourhood. One measure of household participation in a consumer society might be the decision to instal a telephone. Ninety-two households in Richmond Heights in 1921 had telephones, and the number slowly and steadily increased to 153 in 1929.[57] This meant that by the end of the decade, a little more than two out of every five households could be reached through Maritime Telephone and Telegraph (MT&T). The likelihood of telephone service in the Hydrostone District appears to have been largely dependent upon whether or not a neighbour had one installed and the number of wage-earners in the family. Telephones were generally concentrated in blocks with adjacent or diagonal neighbours. Later, as telephones became more common, their presence can be taken as a measure of an expected standard of living, as was the installation of furnaces. Telephone hook-ups appear to have been less a luxury than an increasingly standard piece of household equipment.[58]

The presence of consumer durables in the homes of Richmond Heights was partly the result of the expansion of credit and the extension of new ways of buying. Households bought many large items on instalment plans: sewing machines, dining-room furniture, radios, pianos, kitchen ranges, washing machines, and gramophones.[59] Some households appeared willing to undertake new financial commitments, despite their limited or at times non-existent resources. John Miller, a toolroom machinist at the Halifax Shipyards who earned thirty-five cents an hour, bought a radio in 1930 for which he had to pay $10 a month, while he was $393 in arrears on his rent.[60] Instalment plans did not always work, and retailers often had to repossess goods that they had allowed on credit. Furniture and a stove acquired by Mrs George Molson were 'retook' in 1924.[61] Repossession was naturally impossible when the item purchased on credit had already been consumed, as with fuel, groceries, or services. In such cases, it became usual to involve the courts. The names of Richmond Heights residents appeared frequently in the city's magistrate's court with regard to unpaid debts, as grocers, coal merchants, and the local telephone company attempted to force payment.[62]

Money was a private matter and, at least at the beginning of the decade, few people used banks for personal savings or loans, judging from the number of cash boxes found among the debris, the claims of money lost after the explosion, and the promissory notes collected.[63] The extension of credit to the working class was not new, and Paul Johnson has noted with regard to the English working class that 'The distinction is not properly between those who used credit and those who did not, but between those who used it deliberately to purchase luxury goods, and those who could not do without it if they were to fill their bellies and cover their nakedness.'[64] While credit may have been easier to obtain for luxury goods, it may have decreased for essentials such as groceries and rent, with the expansion of cash-and-carry stores and the increasing use of formal leases.

Increased consumer expectations and a general decline in domestic production meant that any means of generating money took on added importance. Cash was necessary for survival. In Richmond Heights in the 1920s, two of the most common methods of generating money were taking in lodgers or boarders and liquidating assets.

The Hydrostone District houses were not ideal for either the landlady or the boarder. Although they were close to the tram line, Richmond Heights homes were quite distant from many places of employment except the shipyard and the Willow Park roundhouse, employers that had been particularly hard hit by the depression of the 1920s. Halifax remained largely a walking city, and alternative housing options would have been available much closer to most workplaces. Furthermore, the houses of the subdivision were purposely designed as single-family dwellings and had little flexibility for space reallocation without the complete loss of family privacy. Nevertheless, in 1920 and 1921 at least twenty-four advertisements were listed for individual homes in Richmond Heights looking for lodgers, boarders, or persons willing to sublet several rooms. The advertisements suggest that males were preferred, as five homes specifically mentioned men or implied their preference by noting the proximity of the neighbourhood to the shipyards. Conversely, no advertisement suggested women.[65] The importance of what type of person you let into your home was seen in an advertisement for 27 Stanley Place that specified that boarders must be 'respectable.'[66] In the 1920 Nova Scotia report on the Mothers' Allowance, one of the primary concerns of the investigating committee was the effect on children of living with boarders. Children in 'Boarding House families' lost family privacy and were exposed to strangers in the most intimate setting of the family home. The committee concluded unambiguously that boarders were a 'real menace to normal family life and

[were] not in the best interest of the children.'[67] Finally, boarders created additional work for women at a time when many women were increasingly occupied with living up to the expanded ideal of wife and mother, and did not have the time to adopt the additional role of landlady.[68] The desire for access to consumer goods still had to be weighed against the need for respectability.

Working-class consumption, particularly of new consumer durables, was not simply blind obedience to the calls of middle-class advertisers but in many ways performed a similar role to saving. Goods purchased were potentially goods to sell. For example, in the expensive process of leaving the city, the disposal of household effects financed outmigration. The variety of goods advertised in the *Evening Mail* was extensive, running the gamut from parrots and canaries through commodes and mahogany sideboards to motorcycles. During the 1920s, with telephone numbers replacing addresses, vendors became increasingly difficult to identify, but before 1922 there were forty separate advertisements of household goods for sale with addresses in Richmond Heights. Items such as sewing machines, pianos, and gramophones clearly fit into the category of consumer durables.[69] Others such as a farmer's wagon, a blacksmith's iron vice, and a 'planer, surfacer, and matcher' were the result of new occupational needs.[70] Most items, however, were large pieces of furniture, furnaces, kitchen ranges, and heaters that would have been too expensive to transport any distance.

When a resident of 11 Stairs Place vacated with rent owing, there was no property to seize, since the family had 'sold off furniture to get away.'[71] Similarly, by the time Arthur Spencer was evicted from 28 Stanley Place in March 1929, most of the consumer durables had been disposed of and the 'house [was] almost bare.'[72] A widow at 20 Livingstone Place 'had to sell furniture' to meet immediate expenses of fuel and food,[73] while a temporary setback such as illness in the family could also initiate the disposal of goods. A woman at 26 Kane Place wrote to the commission that since her husband 'was sick I found it impossible to send the rest of the money this week. I sold some stuff but I could not get my money.'[74] Although selling possessions was a quick method of raising cash, it was seldom possible to receive full value. An unemployed tenant wrote: 'I hope I will not be compelled to sacrifice my household effects in this way, as possibly things will be brighter soon.'[75] Unfortunately, the situation did not improve and his possessions were sold to settle his debts.

The most extreme cases affected the few people on the extension streets who owned single-family wooden dwellings and who were forced to sell or lease their houses. In February 1922 a five-room house on Cabot Street was offered to let with all its furniture for sale.[76] Similarly, 22 Livingstone Street, which cost $4,800, was offered for $3,300 since the owner was leaving the city.[77] Many property owners rented their property when they temporarily or permanently left the city. Mortgages on the extension streets were being paid by men and women in Dartmouth, central Canada, England, and the United States.[78]

The need for cash and the inability to meet financial commitments highlighted the difficulty that residents had in participating in the new consumer society. Certainly, many people owned things that could be sold. Consumerism was also a real aspect of daily life in Richmond Heights, but that alone did not determine status within the neighbourhood. The importance that residents continued to place on the notion of respectability suggests the simultaneous existence of competing ideologies.

The long-term waning of respectability as a measure of status and the waxing of consumerism created special problems for women. Married women could attempt to practise respectability independently of their husbands if they chose to do so. Consumption, on the other hand, was much more complicated. Women were the chief consumers in their roles as household managers. In the words of one local labour man, 'women did the world's shopping. Almost every dollar earned by the wage earner was spent by the mother of the home ...'[79] This role offered some status but very little subsistence. Women were encouraged to spend, but rarely had access to money independently of their husbands. As Richmond Heights households began to purchase large items such as cars in the 1930s and 1940s, it would be interesting to know the wives' roles in the decision-making process. Through the value system connected to respectability, women had some degree of command. As new standards of consumerism emerged, women had to abdicate control of their status or break the old male barrier of respectability centred on the sanctity of the family wage by entering the workforce again themselves.

A complex series of codes of behaviour governed everything from the decoration of the family living-room to the raising of children in Richmond Heights in the 1920s. Standards of cleanliness or the installation of a telephone could establish or affirm the reputation of a household and its members. Actions, acquisitions, and taste were applauded or censured through community consensus. Of course, not everyone adhered to the rules. Neighbours fought with words and fists, and poverty could interfere with standards of decent public dress. Attaining respectability by recognizing and complying with the many community dictums was largely the responsibility of women and was often dependent on privacy and some degree of economic security. A few individual women failed in measuring up to the ideals around motherhood and housewifery, such as a Sebastian Place woman whose husband claimed 'she drinks, smokes and everything else; she never did it before I married her.'[80] The etiquette surrounding cash was comparatively recent, but this too seemed focused on the mother and wife, since she often managed household finances and made decisions about boarders and about the disposal of goods. At the root of many codes and customs was a mutual understanding of the way things should be and how one should act – whether by proper attention to the responsibilities, duties, and behaviour of a wife or by proper placement of a doily in the living-room. These codes, rules, and customs comprised an important part of working-class culture, and their persistence alongside mass culture encourages further examination of the world of home and neighbourhood.

3

Elderly Men and Women

Inside many of the modern homes of this up-to-date subdivision lived men and women who had grown up in a colonial city when Queen Victoria was on the throne and her army stationed at the Citadel. By 1921, one in every four residents of Halifax had been born before 1881 and had witnessed tremendous change in the first forty years of his or her life. Between 1881 and 1921 the population of the city increased from 36,100 to 58,372[1] – not a tremendous level of growth compared to other cities in Canada, but sufficient to encourage population expansion into the northern section of the peninsula. More striking than the change in size and geographic boundaries of the city was the change in Halifax's physical appearance. The combination of the passing of time and the explosion was, according to one visitor, so great that the North End had altered beyond recognition.[2] But even the magnitude of local change must have appeared insignificant in light of the changes occurring nationally and internationally. Concepts as basic as time and space were in flux, with such technological innovations as air travel, the automobile, the moving picture, and the radio transforming the way in which people conceived their world. As the physical world changed, so did its ideological foundations. Basic values across North America were challenged by what one historian has referred to as a crisis in cultural authority, in which politics, religion, economics, gender roles, and the psychic composition of the individual all came into question.[3]

In the very midst of this metamorphosis, the proportion of Haligonians who remembered the older city and an older world was increasing. In fact, the national trend of an aging population was reflected in Halifax to such a degree that in 1931 the age distribution of the population matched the Canadian average better than that in any other census district in the country.⁴ An important characteristic of twentieth-century Canada was an aging population; and Halifax, as a long-established city in a region generally suffering from outmigration, reflected this trend earlier than other urban centres. While Canadian cities generally had a more youthful population than rural districts, urban centres in the Maritimes exhibited overall national demographic trends of aging. Since its demographic breakdown foreshadowed general Canadian population trends in the twentieth century, Halifax is thus an excellent place to investigate an aging population.

Haligonians of different ages not only shared the city and the same neighbourhood, but in many cases they cohabited within the same household. Under a single roof, individuals coexisted with varying self-definitions, partially rooted in generational differences. Class and gender were experienced differently according to age, since identities formed in youth resonated in an individual's world-view throughout his or her life. Men and woman who came of age in the 1870s or 1880s experienced and interpreted class differently from their grandsons and granddaughters who entered the workforce in the 1920s. The meaning and definition of gender underwent a similar historical transition. Recognition of the role of generation in the formation of an individual's identity can prevent us from making careless generalizations about uniform and universal values.

The approximately 6 per cent of the population of Halifax over the age of sixty-five was central to the balance between change and continuity, yet this group has often escaped the notice of historians. The elderly of Richmond Heights were generally pushed to the margins of society during the 1920s, but the glimpses of their lives that remain reveal their efforts to maintain independence and participation in the labour market. Their presence in the households of Richmond Heights offered an immediate and personal link to the past as well as a measure to evaluate change.

It is difficult to define precisely the aged as a distinct segment of the population. Without access to the manuscript census, it is impossible to determine the actual age distribution within Richmond Heights, but qualitative evidence suggests that age played a critical role in the way individuals experienced home and the workplace. In some ways the definition of 'old' differed for men and women because it was based on a variety of economic, biological, life-cycle, or cultural criteria that differed by sex. In accordance with the definition of masculinity, men were old when they were no longer able to support their families financially. Most men continued to work as long as they were able and experienced a gradual decline in their incomes.[5] On the other hand, women were judged by biological criteria connected to their reproductive roles. Menopause was a common boundary for women, as medical or biological tradition held that after its onset women ceased their reproductive roles, rejected sexual desire, and began a long period of illness or decline.[6] The use of menopause as the start of old age fostered the belief that women aged earlier than men despite the fact that they lived longer. The discrepancy between the economic definition of old age for men and the biological definition for women was exemplified in the difference in the ages at which men and women could retire under the pension plan of Maritime Telephone and Telegraph (MT&T), the local telephone company. Although women were likely to live longer than men, women could retire five years earlier with a full, Class-A pension.[7] Another important marker for women was life cycle. As women had fewer children and these children were spaced more closely together, women were increasingly likely to be middle-aged grandmothers, with their own children grown. The image of a grandmother as 'aged' could conflict with the reality. In other cases, old age was signalled by widowhood, a common experience among women who lived long enough.[8] Finally, old age could also be generally associated with women, since they numerically dominated the age group. Chris Gordon has claimed in his study of London's working-class elderly during the 1930s that when we speak of the elderly, 'we are talking mainly about women in later life.'[9]

While many factors were responsible for the different definitions assigned to men and women, there were some categorizations that measured age in gender-neutral terms. Both men and women were classified by an arbitrary bureaucratic definition of old age as beginning at seventy years of age. This chronological point was used by the Nova Scotia government in its study of the old-age pension and its collection of statistics under the provisions of the Workmen's Compensation Act, and by the federal government in its introduction of an old-age pension. James Struthers has recently made the important argument that the old-age pension was Canada's first '"gender inclusive" social program,' since payments were to be awarded equally to both men and women at the same age.[10] The fact that 'gender inclusive' legislation was first associated with the elderly was surely not a coincidence. Despite the differences in the ways that men and women experienced old age, their vulnerability and perceived redundancy emphasized and highlighted a number of shared characteristics that could overcome important gender distinctions.

Of all the groups in the community the aged were the most invisible to the social historian. Older people were more likely to be housebound by poor health and inclement weather, and so were less likely to be involved in activities outside the home that left historical evidence. In the 1920s in Halifax, the elderly were not yet considered to have any particular residential, social, or consumer needs. Glimpses of their lives can be caught in the rare announcement of a golden or diamond wedding anniversary, or the family celebration of an important birthday. The elderly in Halifax appeared most visibly at death, in obituaries that indicated age, marital status, religious affiliation, number of children, and their children's place of residence, and in accounts of funerals. The difficulty of capturing historical insights into the lives of older men and women is compounded by the difficulty of classifying them in other than broad chronological terms. Because of the variance in the definitions of old age, the category included a wide and heterogeneous group. The use of a broad chronological category, therefore, has methodological advantages; for example, as Tamara Hareven has noted, 'transitions of the later years – the empty nest, widowhood and loss of household headship – followed no ordered sequence, were not closely synchronized and took a relatively long time to complete.'[11]

The vague historical and disparate contemporary methods of classifying old age contrast with the intense interest in the aged that developed in the early twentieth century. Some American historians have claimed that between the First and Second World Wars, old age was increasingly regarded from a negative perspective and eventually came to be seen as a 'national problem.' Those who have wished to emphasize long-term continuity rather than change in the devaluation of the elderly have also focused on the early twentieth century as an especially important period in their research.[12]

In Halifax, as elsewhere in Canada in the early twentieth century, interest in the elderly centred on an awareness of their poverty. The Halifax Labour party actively supported the introduction of the old-age pension as part of its platform, a goal later adopted by both the Liberal and Conservative parties.[13] Concern expressed by the Labour party contained at least some degree of immediate self-interest, since many workers faced the expense of caring for elderly parents. In Labour's promotion of an old-age pension during its 1925 campaign, it claimed that a pension would not only 'keep the worker that is thrown on the scrapheap by industry from going to the poorhouse,' but also prevent him 'from becoming a charge of his dependents.' Political groups were not the only associations to notice the condition of the elderly. The local Society for the Prevention of Cruelty specified 'old people' as a segment of the population that needed the 'attention of our officers.'[14] Research conducted by a government commission into the introduction of an old-age pension in 1929 confirmed the widespread poverty among those in the population over the age of seventy. The financial and living conditions of the 929 Haligonians interviewed were shocking. More than one-third reported having no income at all, and more than half had an income of less than $199 per annum. Poverty among aged Haligonians would have been much more severe than for their rural counterparts, as the 1930 Commission on Old Age Pensions noted the importance of informal sources of income and home production such as the raising of hens and pigs and the cultivation of vegetable gardens; such activities did occur in the city but were more feasible in rural areas. The commission concluded that the province's aged had either successfully accumulated a moderate income and found themselves able to live off savings or were 'practically destitute and dependent' on others.

Poverty among the elderly had several roots. Explanations can be found in the lack of employment opportunities for older women, the death or illness of a wage-earning husband, and the gradual withdrawal of men from the workforce. American historian Andrew Achenbaum has linked deteriorating economic conditions for the elderly in the early twentieth century with the forced withdrawal of older men from the workforce. But according to Brian Gratton, caution is required in any discussion of workforce participation, since the level of employment among the elderly declined very gradually, with the result that scholars have exaggerated the poverty and dependency of the aged prior to the creation of the welfare state. This discrepancy between the very real poverty of the aged and the important role many elderly men continued to play in the workforce was reflected in Halifax in the 1920s.[15]

The question of the place of elderly men in the workforce was part of a general discussion that emerged across North America concerning the suitability of older male workers as employees. In the nineteenth century, workers had expected to have been employed as long as they were able to work. Despite the fears of older workers and the presence of efficiency experts, old age did not result in widespread dismissals. Fifty-five per cent of males aged sixty and above had some type of income from wage earnings in 1921, while the remaining 45 per cent had no access to such revenue. Comparable statistics for 1931 are not available, but men over the age of sixty-five continued to compose approximately 5 per cent of the total male population and approximately the same percentage of men over the age of ten who were gainfully employed. Although large numbers of men continued to work, the fear of job loss was not unfounded. Many older male employees found themselves working at different, less lucrative jobs as watchmen, janitors, and sweepers – less physically demanding work that they were judged still able to perform. Factory workers and industrial labourers who were less likely to keep their jobs probably composed the bulk of men in these occupations for 'old men.' Of the 608 men over the age of sixty-five listed in the 1921 Halifax census as still working, nearly half were employed in the trade, service, and finance sectors. Examination of the city's manufacturing sector in 1921 reveals few opportunities for older working-class men, since nearly 40 per cent of men over sixty-five were listed owners, managers, and superintendents.[16]

Local economic conditions, with high levels of unemployment and underemployment, may have made keeping a job particularly difficult for older men. During the Halifax Shipyards strike of 1920, a prominent elderly socialist ignored the strike call and crossed the picket lines to continue working. A younger contemporary looking back with the advantage of more than fifty years of hindsight analysed his motivation by referring to his age, attempting to reconcile the elderly man's socialist politics and his strikebreaking activity. He noted 'for a man of his age to have any job, let alone a rather good job was unusual. Did he fear that he would be fired and never get another?'[17] This was a relevant question for aging workers across the country.

The impact of limited economic opportunities was exacerbated by illness or declining health, thereby accelerating aging workers' shift to less demanding and less lucrative positions. Patrick Ross of 27 Stairs Street spent fifteen years as a groundman, lineman, and finally loop crew foreman with MT&T before becoming a janitor at its central office in 1921. Ross worked only three years in his new position of janitor before his death at the age of fifty-nine.

Occupational adaptability was an important factor in survival. An army pensioner was able to support himself and his wife by supplementing his pension with earnings from his position as caretaker at Joseph Howe School. John and Barbara Green, an aged couple who owned a house at 60 Stairs Street, made their living by taking in boarders. Others, such as sixty-four-year-old David Schultz, who was crippled, may have felt they had no option except illegal activities. Schultz, a Richmond Heights resident, pleaded guilty in February 1924 to keeping a gaming house at the corner of Agricola and Almon Streets. The newspaper report of the sentencing condemned his actions in terms of his having encouraged 'young men going into the house and gambling away earnings.' But after years as a boilermaker and ironworker at the Halifax Graving Dockyard, he may have felt entitled to some of the employed young men's money. Older men in Richmond Heights rarely formally retired. During the entire decade, not one name in the city directory listed occupation as retired, and only six retired men were recorded on the municipal voters' list.[18]

The most obvious explanation for avoiding formal retirement was the economic consequence. Some workers at both Canadian National Railways (CNR) and MT&T were eligible for retirement or pension programs, but these programs were not generous, nor were they guaranteed. Harry Walters had been employed with the railway for more than twenty years, yet found himself at the age of sixty-nine working as a caretaker at one of the waterfront piers.[19] Railway pensions varied according to position, length of service, and age of retirement. Engineman Norman Prince, a homeowner at 19 Kane Street, was employed intermittently with the Intercolonial, Canadian Government Railways, and the CNR from August 1890 until his retirement in March 1934 at the age of sixty-one years after a total of thirty-three years with the railway. His length of service, occupational classification, and age entitled him to a generous pension of $96.24 a month. Less fortunate was co-worker James Karl of 39 Livingstone Street whose poor health forced him to retire early on a pension of only $44 a month.[20]

Employees at MT&T received 1 per cent of their average annual pay for ten years multiplied by the number of years of employment. There was a minimum monthly pension of $25 for men and $20 for women, but this did not apply to employees who had worked for less than twenty years. The pension was also at the discretion of the Employee Benefits Committee, which was capable of suspending pensions to any employee it judged to be involved in activities 'prejudicial to the interests of the Company.' MT&T admitted to the inadequacy of its pension program when it introduced an Employees Stock Savings Plan in 1927 with the dual purpose of encouraging thrift and providing 'competence for old age.'[21] Poor private pensions and limited opportunities to save meant that voluntary retirement was a luxury that few people achieved.

Pension plans were an important component of the corporate welfare policies that flourished in Canada during the 1920s. Craig Heron has connected the steel industry's need to secure a dependable and stable labour force to the introduction of pension plans in that industry in the early 1920s. Similarly, Joy Parr in her study of the workforce in an Ontario knitting mill noted that the knitting company introduced 'a discretionary pension plan' around 1922. Parr claimed that the unstructured and arbitrary nature of this pension plan placed long-term employees with a potential stake in pension earnings in a particularly vulnerable situation that reguired 'aging employees and their kin' to take care not to jeopardize good relations with the company.[22] Personal and arbitrary pension plans bound long-term employees to the subjective whims of their employers as they approached the most vulnerable stage of their lives.

When private industry was newly experimenting with pension plans, the federal government had long attempted to encourage saving for old age through Canadian Government Annuities. This savings program was, significantly, transferred from the Post Office to the Department of Labour in April 1923, but was largely unsuccessful despite its claim to provide safe old-age pensions. Throughout the early 1920s, only several hundred Canadians undertook contracts; but a Department of Labour advertisement campaign through newspapers, periodicals, and radio talks increased sales to more than a thousand in 1928 and 1929.[23] The 'hard-sell' nature of this campaign is illustrated by an item in a Halifax newspaper that played upon the working-class fear of unemployment among the elderly with a drawing of a rejected older man and the caption: 'Everywhere they say too old. What a tragedy – to be turned away from all chance of earning one's living.'[24]

The attempt to play on fear of unemployment was obviously directed at male workers, for female employment opportunities diminished much earlier with marriage or motherhood. Employment for elderly Richmond Heights women did not differ from that of their middle-aged neighbours. The loss of youth – defined by physical attractiveness, marriage, or reproductive capacity – meant that employers discriminated against them. Their choices were often limited to domestic service or low-wage work that could be conducted from their own homes such as dressmaking, washing, or operating a rooming-house.[25] Few women over sixty-five were engaged in waged employment in Halifax in 1921, less than 7 per cent of the total age group, reflecting similar circumstances across the country.[26] The limited role of women in the paid workforce did not mean that old age brought relief from work. Women with homes continued to work within their houses and contribute domestic labour as long as they were able. In this respect old age was experienced differently by men and women. Men gradually withdrew from the workforce, while the work of women continued.

While the approach of old age for men was associated with a withdrawal from participation in the labour force, the greatest change in most women's lives was the death of the husband. The 1930 report on old-age pensions in Nova Scotia found that men over the age of seventy were much more likely to be married than women. Based on research gathered in the city of Halifax and the counties of Cape Breton, Richmond, and Shelburne, the report concluded that 55.7 per cent of men compared to 25.1 per cent of women were likely to have a spouse living.[27] This dramatic difference was explained by the dual impact of women's longer life expectancy and the tradition that men married younger women. For example, those over seventy who had a spouse under seventy accounted for 19 per cent of the men interviewed and only 2.3 per cent of the women.[28] This meant that the loss of a spouse was a more common experience for women. Mrs Fleck, the extraordinary grandmother described at the beginning of this book, was one such widow who found a home with her adult daughter.

The death of either spouse could mean the loss of household independence, since most women depended on a male wage to operate their home and men depended on unpaid female domestic labour. A rare glimpse of a woman who did not want to give up operation of her own home was evident in an enterprising widow's 1922 classified notice advertising for 'correspondence with gentleman 50 years of age or more. Protestant preferred.'[29]

American scholars have suggested that elderly men were more likely to face institutionalization than women.[30] A study of a slightly later period in Ontario by James Struthers, in contrast, has found that while men predominated in institutions in rural districts, women formed the majority in urban institutions.[31] Findings for Halifax are similar to American models. In Halifax, the impoverished aged were admitted to the City Home, where they composed a substantial proportion of the residents. An analysis of the number of deaths of residents at the City Home who were over sixty showed that, although women composed a greater percentage of the general population over that age, more older men than older women died in the City Home. These older men were not transient labourers or itinerant seafarers without local kin. Among those admitted to the Halifax City Home during the 1920s were five men from Richmond Heights but not a single women. All these men, who were between the ages of fifty-six and seventy-seven, listed sons and/or wives who continued to live in the subdivision, with their fami-' lies divided between the tenants in the Hydrostone District and the residents of the owner-occupied wooden homes on the extension streets. Their religious affiliations also reflected the neighbourhood's composition. Three of the five men were Roman Catholic, one was Anglican, and one was Presbyterian. In fact, the only unusual feature of this group was that four of the five were born in either Ireland or England, thereby making them somewhat atypical of the native-born majority of Haligonians.[32]

Why did more old men find themselves in the City Home than women? This discrepancy was probably the result of a number of factors. Most obviously, women in good health continued to make a valuable contribution to the household through their domestic labour. Older women babysat, cooked, and cleaned. Secondly, in a culture that sentimentalized motherhood, there may have been more social pressure on adult children to keep their mothers from the poorhouse than their fathers.[33] Finally, examples of Richmond Heights men who resided in the City Home may reflect individual circumstances. Institutionalization may have been the result of deteriorating mental or physical health rather than financial exigency, as their families may have been unable to cope with senility or provide full-time care.

For households dealing with this problem, there were few institutional options for working-class Haligonians apart from the poorhouse. In addition to the City Home, local charities operated the Home for Aged Men and the Old Ladies Home on Gottingen Street, but the clients of these institutions were elderly middle-class people in declining circumstances. The Sisters of Charity opened a home for aged women in 1886, but this institution evolved into the city's Catholic hospital. Apparently the work of the Sisters locally among the elderly must have been limited, since Roman Catholic women resided in the City Home, and the Catholic benevolent society, the St Vincent de Paul, regularly cooperated with admissions to the secular civic institution.[34] In fact, the St Vincent de Paul Society agitated for reforms within the City Home, including provision of married couples' quarters. The society claimed that it frequently had to maintain, for long periods of time, 'old married couples who when advised to enter the City Home, refuse to do so because it would entail their separation.'[35] In the absence of alternative institutional structures, at least some people preferred the insecurity of accepting direct charity, if it meant staying with their spouses and maintaining their own homes.

Many older people surveyed by the commission did manage to keep their own homes and maintain residential independence. Of the 2,767 persons who were over the age of seventy and had incomes of less than $400 a year, nearly half lived in their own home and more than a third lived with their children. The remaining 17 per cent, in declining order of frequency, lived with relatives or friends, in charitable institutions, and as boarders.[36] Once again, without a manuscript census, it is impossible to determine the exact household composition in Richmond Heights. Certainly, the relatively small houses of the neighbourhood did not encourage multigenerational co-residency. Nevertheless, many elderly people resided with their children. We do not know if elderly parents were more likely to stay with the eldest child than with the youngest, if daughters had more responsibility than sons, if those who stayed in Nova Scotia had more responsibility than those who left, or if there was any difference based on rural or urban origins. Based largely on obituaries, we do know that many parents and in-laws lived with their adult sons and daughters in Richmond Heights.

Living with an adult child could take a large variety of forms. Sometimes the accommodation was seasonal, as in the case of a Hennessey Place retired military man and his wife who spent the winters with their son in Massachusetts. It could also be permanent, as in the case of Richmond Heights resident John Ryerson, who was 'unable to earn a living through age' and whose only option was that of moving in with his married daughter's family a few blocks over.[37] The experience of those who had grown old in Halifax was different from that of those who moved into the city when they were unable to maintain their independence elsewhere. Moving in with an adult son or daughter may have been a terribly lonely and bewildering experience, as people were uprooted from the place where had they lived most of their lives. In 1922, at the age of eighty-five, George Milroy moved from Newfoundland to live with his son at 27 Columbus Place, where he died five years later. The impression that the stay in Halifax was only temporary and quite separate from their past was also suggested by the number of older men and women who died in Richmond Heights but were buried in outlying fishing villages such as Terrence Bay or Ketch Harbour.[38]

The loss of household independence in some situations was averted through the generosity of adult children. An elderly couple on Duffus Street was able to get by, since the husband earned $10 a week and

TABLE 1
Sources of support and income of persons over seventy years of age in the city of Halifax
and the counties of Cape Breton, Shelburne, and Richmond

	Number of people	Per cent Self-support	Others	Per cent others			
				Children	Relative	Friend	Charity
Total elderly	2767	29.7	70.3	71.2	13.2	8.0	7.6
Total annual income ($)							
300–399	228	78.5	21.5	91.8	4.1	4.1	0.0
200–299	306	80.4	19.6	78.3	15.0	5.0	1.7
100–199	469	62.2	37.6	73.5	10.7	7.9	7.9
< 100	385	27.0	73.0	63.7	11.7	9.3	15.3
none	1379	0.0	100.0	71.4	14.1	8.0	6.6

SOURCE: Nova Scotia, *Journal of the House of Assembly*, 1930, Appendix 29, 'Report of
Commission on Old Age Pensions,' 7, 9, 11. All numbers are based on people seventy
years of age and over with incomes less than $400 per annum and living in the sample
areas of Halifax city and the counties of Cape Breton, Richmond, and Shelburne.

their son paid their rent.[39] While some of the elderly managed by drawing on the principal of their savings or generating income from property, the report of the Nova Scotia government concluded that 'by far
the greatest number were supported by their children' (see table 1). The
importance of adult children as providers of financial support to the
elderly raised fears that the declining birth rate would place the same
responsibility on fewer family members.[40] More than half of the sample
group received full support from their children – with the likelihood of
full support increasing with the number of children living (table 2).
This conclusion conforms with traditional wisdom that children formed
the best old-age policy, but casts doubt on the findings of American
historian Daniel Scott Smith, who concluded that in 1900 the number of
children did not affect the likelihood of support in old age in America.[41]
Family commitment in Nova Scotia to the elderly may have been higher
than elsewhere in Canada. After Saskatchewan, Alberta, and British Columbia, Nova Scotia had by far the lowest ratio of institutionalized
elderly to overall population, despite its older population and the existence of county and municipal poorhouses.[42] Care for an elderly parent
or family member may have been required by the definition of Maritime respectability. In L.M. Montgomery's *The Tangled Web*, eighty-five-

TABLE 2
Sources of support and number of children of persons over seventy years of age in the city of Halifax and the counties of Cape Breton, Shelburne, and Richmond. Extent children can aid as a percentage

	Full	Partial	None	Unstated
Total	51.0	13.4	32.4	3.2
1 child	51.4	27.2	17.4	4.0
2 children	70.7	16.3	8.7	4.3
3 children	69.2	15.0	8.6	7.2
4 children	75.3	15.9	6.3	2.4
5 children	70.7	16.5	7.8	5.0
6+ children	72.7	16.6	7.8	2.9
none	–	–	100.0	–

SOURCE: Nova Scotia, *Journal of the House of Assembly*, 1930, Appendix 29, 'Report of Commission on Old Age Pensions,' 7, 9, 11. All numbers are based on people seventy years of age and over with incomes of less than $400 per annum and living in the sample areas of Halifax city and the counties of Cape Breton, Richmond, and Shelburne.

year-old Aunt Becky lived on her own in two rooms she had rented within a friend's home. Montgomery wrote that this housing arrangement had been Aunt Becky's own choice, for the homes of any number of her relatives 'would have been open to her, for the clan was never unmindful of their obligations.'[43]

But children were not always available to give the needed assistance. Approximately one in four of the septuagenarians interviewed had no children living, and in the remaining group, nearly a third of their adult children had left the province.[44] While many of these adult children may have provided material support through remitted wages, they would not have been immediately or regularly available for physical assistance. Care and support for elderly parents fell hardest on single-child families, and this appears to have influenced the life options of these children in adulthood. Even in large families, however, responsibility could fall unevenly on one or two adult children, since the size of a family appears to have been connected to the overall likelihood of sibling outmigration. Children in large families were more likely to have siblings living elsewhere in Canada or the United States (table 3).

Adult sons and daughters regularly assisted their elderly parents, but occasionally this relationship was reversed. In at least three cases in the neighbourhood, mothers financially or materially assisted their married

TABLE 3
Size of family and place of residence of adult children for persons over seventy years of age in the city of Halifax and the counties of Cape Breton, Shelburne, and Richmond

Families	Number of families	Nova Scotia (%)	Elsewhere in Canada (%)	United States (%)	Other (%)	Total number of children
1 child	313	86.6	2.9	10.5	0.0	313
2 children	346	77.5	3.3	19.2	0.0	692
3 children	320	69.4	4.7	25.7	0.2	960
4 children	306	69.4	6.3	23.7	0.6	1224
5 children	184	65.0	5.2	29.5	0.3	920
6+ children	319	64.6	4.4	30.7	0.3	2270

SOURCE: Nova Scotia, *Journal of the House of Assembly*, 1930, Appendix 29, 'Report of Commission on Old Age Pensions,' 7, 9, 11. All numbers are based on people seventy years of age and over with incomes less than $400 per annum and living in the sample areas of Halifax city and the counties of Cape Breton, Richmond, and Shelburne.

daughters and grandchildren. Thea Buckles married a man with an 'indisposition to work, a state of matters which has existed since her early married days.' As a result, she and her four small children relied on the generosity of her mother to supply the family with coal and fuel.[45] Another example of a mother who offered material support to a married daughter became evident when the Halifax Relief Commission was unable to place a lien on William O'Reilly's furniture, since it was not his own and had been loaned to him by his mother-in-law.[46] Probably, the most common means of support was offering shelter to a married daughter moving home with or without her husband. When Edna Farmer left her husband shortly after her marriage in 1919, she moved into her parents' Duffus Street home.

Examples of couples living with parents could be more complicated, since the balance of who was supporting whom shifted over time. Young newlyweds who could not afford either separate housing or the expense of setting up housekeeping occasionally moved in with parents. In the case of those families in the extension streets who owned their own homes, this pattern was prevalent, and appears to have been worked out in intergenerational negotiations in which housing was exchanged for regular contributions of money to the household.

The economic vulnerability of the elderly and their sometimes dependent state meant that the aged, along with widowed mothers and orphans, were at the forefront of the development of the welfare state. The federal Old Age Pension Act of 1927 provided the possibility of an income of not more than $20 a month to British subjects seventy years of age and over who did not have an annual income of more than $365, who had lived in Canada for twenty years and in the province for the preceding five years before payment. The pension act was a shared-cost program between the federal and provincial governments that Nova Scotia could not afford to enter into until 1934. When Nova Scotia began issuing cheques in March 1934, 11,685 Nova Scotians received an average monthly grant of $14.10. The hens, pigs, and woodlots were still needed, since poverty was not eliminated even from the lives of those who qualified.[47]

Gender was experienced in old age differently from how it was lived in youth or middle age, and younger men and women did not generally hold up the elderly as role models for gender-appropriate behaviours in their own lives. There were, of course, exceptions. The local Catholic church, which engaged in a battle against modern forms of sexuality as expressed in dancing, regularly hosted such events as 'old time' dances like those of 'grandmother's day.' Similarly, some union men clung to the probably false notion that their grandfathers had been better able to support their families than they could now. More typical were the complaints of local public-health officials about the detrimental influence of old women on efforts to modernize child-care practices.[48] Michael Roper and John Tosh have recently noted with regard to masculinity that 'one of the most precarious moments in the reproduction of masculinity is the transfer of power to the succeeding generation.'[49] For the elderly men of Richmond Heights, with this abdication through the loss of the status of breadwinner, the albeit limited social power they possessed as men was gone.

Men and women experienced old age differently, though they shared a common vulnerability and dependency on children. As with most women, old men were often caught in inferior and low-paying jobs. Old age, like gender, influenced the employment options that were available and limited the possibility of economic independence.[50] Just as old age took away those characteristics that defined men – their physical strength and their ability to support a family – so it defeminized women. Women reaching menopause lost some of the physical traits that society used to define women as feminine. Older women looked different, a change that went beyond natural attributes such as grey hair, stooped posture, wrinkled skin, and false teeth. Peter Stearns notes that the dress of older women was distinct – shapeless and black and often covered with shawls, in sharp contrast to the colourful fabrics of youth.[51] In the 1920s, this contrast must have been particularly visible with the increased cultural emphasis on youth. Older women also occasionally wore their hair short, but without the disapproval that marked the discussions about young girls who cut their hair short in the fashion of the 1920s.[52] Perhaps short hair on older women did not matter, since in many ways they were no longer considered to be feminine. Older women, however, remained entitled to be female through their roles as mothers and grandmothers. The Mother's Day attention paid by a local newspaper to Livingstone Place resident Mrs Fleck, the proud grandmother of 105 grandchildren, offered one example of a positive portrayal of old age.[53] Because old age was associated with dependency and vulnerability, gender connotations were less relevant. Men and women were perhaps equally disadvantaged by the scarcity of pensions and exclusion from the formal labour market. It is ironic that, in the final years of their lives, the men and women who probably possessed the clearest polarized and class-based understanding of male and female gender ideals were treated and perceived as very much the same.

4

Domestic Responsibilities: Husbands and Wives, Fathers and Mothers

The primary attraction of Richmond Heights for those who moved into the subdivision after the explosion was the appeal of working-class suburbia. As the words 'home' and 'family' became increasingly interchangeable and their use became almost synonymous, the physical characteristics of the family residence took on increased importance. With this in mind, the Halifax Relief Commission (HRC) promoted the advantages of the Richmond Heights development, describing it as a 'Healthful location, [with] excellent transportation facilities, close to churches and schools' and with 'ideal surroundings especially suited to householders with children.'[1] In the photo that often accompanied notices of available houses, three young children happily played on the park-like boulevard, safe from the heavy traffic of urban streets. The appeal to family was a marketing approach that struck a chord with many residents and was articulated succinctly by one father and husband whose desire was to rent in the Hydrostone District, 'as it is very suitable for my family and near the school for the children.'[2] Other households were also attracted to the neighbourhood by domestic amenities. The lighthouse keeper and his wife at Pope's Harbour on the Eastern Shore brought ten of their eleven children to 29 Hennessey Place during the winter of 1924–5 so that the children had the opportunity to attend school.[3] As a working-class suburb, Richmond Heights, with its carefully planned domestic architecture, and its proximity to schools, offered families conveniences that were regarded as conducive to the achievement of a happy home life.

Working-class suburbia was a product of the twentieth century made possible by the extension of public transportation, the decentralization of employment, and the increased physical and intellectual separation between the worlds of home and work.[4] These new suburbs were not idyllic; Kareen Reiger in her work on the Australian working class has noted that the 'stories of parents mistreating children, of neighbours squabbling over noise and livestock and many accounts of the suffering of deserted wives show something of life in working-class suburbia.'[5] These tales also form part of the reality of Richmond Heights in the 1920s. It must be acknowledged, however, that at the heart of this new suburbia was the ideal, and to some extent the practised reality, of an increased home and family centredness in the culture of the respectable working class.

The move towards private, compartmentalized, self-contained dwellings was physical as well as emotional. Domesticity was an ideology with an important material component. Poor material circumstances such as inadequate housing conditions severely limited the ability to achieve a comfortable domestic life. The value placed upon domesticity by Richmond Heights residents in the 1920s was not completely new or universal, but within some households it had taken firm root.[6] The connection between the ideal of domesticity and the household's physical environment was expressed unconsciously by a couple who after the explosion thanked a relief organization for furniture that helped 'to make our house look once more like home sweet home.'[7] This search for personal fulfilment through material conditions and family life simultaneously reinforced gender roles within the working class and assisted in changing them. The home-based roles of husband and father or wife and mother took on increased importance in defining the individual's purpose. Family provided a source of identity, security, and strength, while at the same time it also generated new tensions and established impossible objectives.

Despite tensions, the family continued to provide the most important economic and emotional support network. The centrality of this support network suggests the difficult choices facing many individuals as economic dislocation forced both rural migration to the city and outmigration from the region. In hard times people left their kin in rural Nova Scotia, moving either to Halifax to take advantage of urban opportunities or directly to the United States, central Canada, or the West. In the 1920s many families dispersed in the search for something better. Between 1921 and 1931, Nova Scotia experienced an actual decline in its population; and in Halifax, though the population of those over the age of ten increased, the impression of growth was deceptive, for 309 of the 350 additional men in the city were sixty-five years of age or older.[8]

In a period of high outmigration, the persistence of family was perhaps all the more striking; and in the community of Richmond Heights, even during the transient 1920s, neighbours and kin were for some interchangeable. The case of one railway family illustrates this point dramatically. A young married man, Noble Tinsdall, lived between Stanley and Columbus on Agricola Street, close to his parents and younger brothers and sisters at 14 Duffus Street and his uncle's family at 24 Duffus Street. Noble Tinsdall had three brothers who had also left home and remained in the immediate vicinity. The first brother moved around to tenancies at 8 Hennessey Place, 29 Sebastian Place, and 32 Duffus Street, never far from his wife's mother at 28 Hennessey Place. The second brother, who at various times lived at 8 and 27 Sebastian Place, had a mother-in-law and sister-in-law at 20 Sebastian Place and a second sister-in-law at 55 Livingstone Street. The third brother lived at 7 Columbus Place and his father-in-law a few doors down at 30 Columbus Place. In his own immediate family, Noble Tinsdall's in-laws lived a few doors away at the corner of Columbus and Agricola, and he had a sister-in-law on Cabot Street. This one family would doubtless extend beyond these twelve interconnected households if cousins and all in-laws in Richmond Heights could be traced. This extended network of kin also reached across religious boundaries. Three of the four brothers married Roman Catholic women, though they had been raised Presbyterian. The case of the Tinsdall's might be extreme, but there were certainly other large kinship networks in the subdivision. A women who grew up in the neighbourhood remembered that 'Most people ... who had relatives stayed – if you were brought up in the North End you more or less [stayed] there. I suppose 'cause families then were more clannish than they are today.'[9]

In Richmond Heights during the 1920s, 'family' could still stand for both an extended and a nuclear relationship. For those who lived away from kin, or had severed the relationship, the responsibilities and expectations of a larger family became concentrated upon fewer and fewer people. Strain was perhaps inevitable. As the structure of the family changed for some, so did the identities of the people who composed it. Men and women, uncertain of what type of husband or father, wife or mother they were supposed to be, rarely had the luxury of real privacy to experiment with new ideals, duties, or roles. Under the watchful eye of neighbours, who could also be family, a good reputation and the maintenance of the veneer of respectability continued to be of central importance. Indeed, if the working class retreated to the home in order to escape the defeats of industrial capitalism in the 1920s, it did not find the peace and tranquillity for which it had hoped. The disruptions that were touching every facet of life did not stop at the domestic threshold.

One of the obvious explanations for the attractiveness of domestic life in new subdivisions such as Richmond Heights was the comfort the houses had to offer. Electricity, water, and sewage connections all improved the standard of living for every household member. Throughout the 1920s, even the winters became more comfortable as furnaces were installed in many homes to replace the dirty and somewhat inefficient stoves and heaters. Although living conditions could still be crowded, they were probably better than those available before the explosion. In the new houses, separate space was marked for eating and relaxation. Improved housing conditions meant that it was no longer an imperative for family members, particularly men, to escape from the squalor of working-class housing as they pursued leisure activities.

The physical improvement of the homes was accompanied by new technology such as the radio, which encouraged working-class men to stay home by providing leisure activities within the household. A number of people in Richmond Heights built radio sets, and the *Evening Mail* noted that many workingmen were now 'spending a quiet evening at home.' The radio was a good example of the complexity of working-class adoption of mass culture, for while on the surface radios and their mass-culture programming appeared to be readily embraced by the Halifax working class, on closer examination we see that governmental licensing of radio operation was an area of conflict. Under federal legislation, all radio operators in Canada had to purchase a licence for an annual fee of one dollar. Many radio owners apparently ignored their legal duty, since the Department of Marine and Fisheries published a number of notices in the labour newspaper, the *Citizen*, warning 'users of radio' that all receiving sets must be properly licensed. A radio owner who described himself as 'only a poor working man' always having to pay for extras complained about the injustice of the additional expense of a licence. According to this radio owner, it was unjust that 'when a man purchased a radio set to entertain his family and his friends he had to pay for the pleasure.' Home-centred mass culture did not necessarily conflict with a distinct working-class culture. Even the radio, the virtual symbol of homogeneous taste with programming that entered every home, could provide an opportunity to resist the intrusion of the bureaucratic state into the home.[10]

The increased importance of home was reflected in discussions at the male workplace. An employee of Moirs voiced his concern about the company's corporate-welfare recreational program in terms of the separation of the employee from his family. The employee complained that participation in the work-based recreation program meant less time for the workingman to spend with his family. 'Such plans do not benefit a man's family,' the Moirs employee wrote. 'We are not asking for charity or amusements. All we want is a living wage, one that will pay our honest debts, and we will choose our own amusements.'[11] The inference, at least for the purpose of the newspapers, was that at least part of these amusements would be in a domestic setting. Similarly, the debate surrounding the evening working hours of barbers was presented in the context of the effect long hours had on family life. With the end of evening hours, a North End barber explained that it was now 'possible for me to enjoy myself with my wife and family in the evenings, whereas under the old conditions, by the time I got home the children were to bed, and my wife was patiently waiting to dish up my supper and wash up the tea things.'[12] During the long printers' strike for the eight-hour day from 1921 to 1924, the conflict between members' duties as fathers and husbands at home and the demands of work appeared in the strike propaganda. One case described a man with long working hours who was 'unfitted for fatherhood.' Long hours on the job meant that 'his overtaxed body sought relief in alcoholic drink and in the excessive use of nicotine and narcotic poisons.' The result, according to the striking printers, was that 'he could not be the good husband or the good father, or the good citizen that he might have been with less work and more leisure.'[13] The belief that work could infringe upon family life implicitly placed the home at the centre of workers' lives.

Home may also have been attractive to men because of higher expectations about how they were entitled to be treated. The popular advice books distributed to mothers by the federal Department of Health supported the elevated status of husbands and fathers. Nothing could be clearer than the book's admonition that a man carried 'the big responsibilities of life' and that he needed to come 'back to his home to rest.'[14] The political and economic defeat of labour after the First World War might have directed some men to find prestige and status anywhere they could get it.

The primary duty of fatherhood continued to be performed outside the home in the man's task of providing financially for his family. As the chief family breadwinner, a man was supposed to achieve status and respect within the home. Fatherhood took a variety of forms in Richmond Heights homes, and one type appears to have brought men greater involvement emotionally in their children's lives. In an exploratory essay on the history of fatherhood, John Demos has suggested that in the early part of the twentieth century, fathers emerged as 'chums' as they shared non-work activities with their children in an admittedly 'more contrived, and self-conscious and altogether more confined' manner. Demos claims that the leisure-based relationship between fathers and sons grew, while contact between fathers and daughters had 'no clear focus and little enough substantive content.'[15] Certainly the special relationship between fathers and sons was assumed by some Haligonians. The important role fathers were supposed to play in their sons' development was suggested by the concern the Halifax Rotary Club expressed about the fate of boys who had lost their fathers during the explosion.[16] This concern was not necessarily about economic consequences, for fatherless daughters would have suffered similar material repercussions.

Assorted glimpses of Richmond Heights fathers in interaction with their children suggest a variety of roles fathers could adopt, including disciplinarian, chum, indulgent provider, and moral counsellor. In a Sebastian Place home, the father implemented punishment. Stella Shore remembered that her mother postponed any punishments until her father arrived home from work, and that her father had revealed later in life how it had upset him to beat his children, though he had not been present when the incident occurred. The same father, a seasonally employed carpenter, made certain that each of his children received a dime every payday – five cents for a movie and five cents for candy. Other fathers spent at least some of their leisure time with their children. A widowed father with three young girls never sent them to Sunday school until they were older, since 'he thought more of taking us out ... on a Sunday.'[17] Fathers engaged in outings such as berry picking with both sons and daughters, but most organized leisure activities were restricted to their sons. Fathers and sons, if they chose to do so, had ample opportunities to participate in organized leisure activities, such as the father-and-son banquets at United Memorial Church, the 'youth work' of the churches, the wide range of sports, and formal associations like the Boy Scouts. Concern for the material happiness of their children was demonstrated by the men employed at the shipyard who in 1928 held weekly dances and card socials to raise sufficient money to 'give the children of Shipyard employees a real treat at Christmas time.' The plan was a success, and 530 children's parcels were distributed.[18]

Within the community, relationships between fathers and their children varied widely. A motor-boat operator was apparently unaware of his children's improper behaviour and, when confronted by a representative of the HRC, responded in what might be considered a traditional manner. The father, 'looked surprised but answered me he would not stand for any irregularity and would call his household to order and see that children behaved.'[19] The authoritarian father could be distinct from fathers who saw themselves as responsible for their children's moral education. When the son of a Royal Canadian Mounted Police (RCMP) officer was accused of breaking a neighbour's window, the father defended the boy's claim to innocence on the basis that he himself had 'provided child with general principles' of morality.[20] The varying patterns of fatherhood in part related to the long-term general shift in working-class families from traditional patriarchy to a child-centred orientation. As working-class children became less likely to engage in waged employment, many of their parents appeared to adopt the attitudes of nineteenth-century middle-class parents towards their children. Increased importance was placed on childhood and the role fathers played in raising children.[21]

As fathers became more involved with their sons and daughters, there was a concurrent increased emphasis on the mother-child relationship. The expanded responsibilities surrounding mothering were just one of the areas of the household that increased to fill the time made available by the decline of domestic production.[22] New and elevated standards of consumption, housekeeping, home management, mothering, and marriage continued to make the duties of the wife/mother almost indispensable.

Some households simply could not get by without the work of the mother, and important expenses such as rent had to be put off to pay for temporary help if no family member was available. In January 1923, Mrs Kyle of 32 Duffus Street requested more time to pay her rent because her children had been sick and 'I have been under the doctor's care ever since July and I am not able to do my own work yet but I expect to be alright in a few weeks and therefore you see I had to pay for a woman to look after the house for me.'[23] The economic decision to pay for domestic labour at the expense of rent emphasized the importance of this labour in the operation of a household.

Women not only performed the physical labour of the home but also played a managerial role. Correspondence with the HRC was often one of their responsibilities, since it involved financial transactions and household operations. When the HRC contacted Mr Richards at his work, Mrs Richards responded quickly to point out that 'I look after the money part of this house a[nd] handle all Mr Richards' business and when you write again will you please send mail here so as not to cause any upset with Mr Richards' work. I don't want him to lose his job.'[24] The fear of mixing the operation of the household and the workplace is interesting and suggests both the perceived vulnerability of some men's employment and the tension women experienced in the impossible task of trying to keep the private and the public artificially separated. In at least some cases this left men completely unfamiliar with household finances. A tenant at 33 Columbus Place was surprised to find rent in arrears, since he 'thought [it] was being paid by my wife monthly.' Women in their role of household manager also made decisions to fit their family's financial and space needs. They negotiated for larger or smaller houses based on changing family size and money available for housing.[25]

The labour and the management duties of women were complicated, since in most cases they were undertaken simultaneously with the demanding responsibilities of motherhood. This distinction was suggested in the frequency with which women appealed to the commission in their maternal capacity. A young woman whose husband had been unemployed throughout the winter of 1927–8 and did not pay any rent requested mercy and flexibility in the face of eviction: 'I have a young baby 4 months old and 3 other young children and as I'm not very strong myself it will be quite difficult for me to move so soon.'[26] In response, the commission delayed the eviction of the family from April to the end of August.

It was not surprising that women made appeals based on their roles as mothers, for the ideals and responsibilities surrounding motherhood were growing stronger. As middle-class reformers sought to better the working-class mother by focusing on public health, infant welfare, social purity, education, and child welfare, they created a new restrictive ideal for 'the good working-class mother.'[27] The antithesis of this ideal was personified by the ignorant and neglectful working-class mother common in British literature on 'the deterioration of the race' in the early 1900s and present in Halifax through stereotypes in the courts and the press.[28] The increased expectations of mothers and the corresponding negative images were evident in the 1920 remarks by a judge of the Halifax Juvenile Court, who placed much of the blame for juvenile delinquents upon mothers. Judge J.J. Hunt wrote: 'There are scores of homes in our City where the father of a family is compelled to be away all day earning a livelihood, and where the mother neglecting her family duties is found too often spending her time in some of our many places of amusement.'[29] From the same perspective, the *Evening Mail*'s 'shocking' headline for a North End domestic stabbing read: 'Mother Admits to Playing Cards Five Nights a Week.' Earlier in the same year, a reporter had spoken with a woman who claimed 'she knew mothers who either locked their children up at nights or let them roam the streets,' since the only thing 'women of this class cared about was playing cards.'[30] As noted in the discussion of respectability, issues of child care and mothering were of public concern for Richmond Heights mothers, and most individual women tried to live up to demanding community standards.

Criticism of mothers was not restricted to those easily dismissed as incompetent or negligent. The issue of public health is an excellent example of the complicated way in which experts entered the private home and challenged the authority and knowledge of the mother. Certainly, public health was a problem. In Halifax, as a result of the explosion, existing organizations were expanded and new organizations were created to deal with immediate health problems. These included the Victorian Order of Nurses (VON) and the Massachusetts-Halifax Health Commission. These institutions remained in Halifax after reconstruction and were influential in the development of public-health programs. As a female-based organization, the VON was particularly concerned about the ignorance of mothers. Its Halifax president, Agnes Dennis, noted in her report for 1919 that 'ignorance on the part of mothers and children of food values and the elementary conditions of health all help to make our death rate high' and questioned 'why give such care to mother and infant the first month and allow the child to die through ignorance or lack of care during the first year.' Dr W.D. Forrest, in congratulatory comments in the same report, was much more explicit as to the class of mothers to which this education must be directed. Forrest wrote that in reference 'to the child welfare nurses, I am firmly convinced that this work, which is really a work of education among the women of the poorer classes, must be most beneficial.' To educate mothers, the organization instituted 'Baby Saving Week,' 'Better Babies Contests,' weekly prenatal clinics, a Little Mothers' League, and a Mothers' Club. The work of the VON with mothers was far-reaching. Nurses conducted a weekly clinic at Bloomfield High School for new mothers on Friday afternoons and, during the winter months of 1926–7, attracted twenty-two young women to a home-nursing class at United Memorial Church.[31]

The VON was not alone in its concern about the competence of working-class mothers. The Massachusetts-Halifax Health Commission, a temporary public health agency financed by Massachusetts donations, employed fifteen public-health nurses and two visiting housekeepers who in July 1924 paid 4,745 house calls in the metropolitan area: 'Each nurse ... no matter what may be her reason for contact with the family, becomes responsible for the health standards of each member of the family.' According to one health commission nurse, Halifax, as a well-established community, posed special public-health problems, as 'for ever is one met with the argument that the mother or grandmother or great-grandmother did thus and so – hence it is right.' The health commission set about a vigorous program of re-education through weekly visits to every baby under six months, followed by visits every ten days until the child reached the age of one, on the grounds that 'the mother needs frequent advice as to her habits.' Prenatal contact was also stressed, so 'that the unborn child may not suffer throughout life because of any deficiency in the mother's diet' during pregnancy.[32] The health of children was one specific area in which the ignorance of mothers, particularly working-class mothers, needed to be exposed.

Discussion of mothers and motherhood during the 1920s took place within the context of a rapidly declining birth rate. The birth rate had been falling since the 1870s, but during the 1920s the decline grew particularly drastic as the Canadian crude birth rate dropped by 20.8 per cent.[33] The reduction in family size was obviously more significant for young families starting out than for the many older families that constituted the residents of the neighbourhood. Large families lived in the relatively small space available in homes in Richmond Heights, and there appears to have been little difference in the size of Catholic and Protestant families. In fact, two of the largest families identified, with fifteen and fourteen children respectively, were both active in the Protestant United Memorial Church. Through obituaries and notes in rental correspondence, twenty-one families have been identified with more than five children; seven had ten or more. Large families were often the poorest. Michael and Mary O'Brien lived with their eleven children in a seven-room house at 17 Kane Street. A note of explanation on their poor record of mortgage payments indicated that only one of the eleven children was earning. In another neighbourhood household, there was 'visible evidence that the home is not very prosperous,' since 'six children, none of wage earning ability' lived in crowded conditions, as several rooms had been sublet. Often these families had trouble meeting their rent, and the commission occasionally marked 'large family' as an explanatory note in the rent ledgers of families in arrears.[34]

Of course not all children born lived, as disease and accidents regularly claimed children's lives. Throughout the 1920s levels of infant mortality remained high, although the number of deaths per thousand live births declined from 135 in 1921 to 76 in 1929. This placed the Halifax rate midway between levels in Montreal and Toronto. Children who survived their first year were vulnerable to a number infectious diseases that occasionally proved fatal. During the 1920s, the Health Board registered 152 instances of infectious diseases in the neighbourhood and many cases can be identified as children. In February 1923, scarlet fever killed eight-year-old Frank Bailey of Merkel Place, while in November of the same year infantile paralysis was listed as the cause of death for a four-year-old living at Robert Daw's Cabot Street home. Of the fifty-five people who were buried in the new Protestant cemetery between May 1919 and December 1929 and who had addresses in Richmond Heights, eighteen were under the age of ten. Many Richmond Heights families were also familiar with a different sort of tragedy through having lost children in the explosion. Eight of Vincent Macleod's nine children from his first marriage were killed in the disaster; following his remarriage, he fathered an additional two.[35]

Child-care responsibilities in both large and small families meant that many women were isolated in their homes with young children. Discussion surrounding vaccination exemptions noted that it was nearly impossible for many women to visit the downtown Health Board office, 'especially when there are little children in the home, and the breadwinner is on hand for his supper shortly after five.'[36] Some women simply felt more comfortable in their own home environment. A widow who was having trouble meeting rent requested the postponement of rent negotiations until 'you get time [to] come up and I'll talk matters over as I can talk to you better in the house than in the office.'[37] That this woman would be more comfortable in her own home discussing such a delicate matter as family finances was not at all surprising, but it appears that other women did not always have a choice and were largely confined to their homes through various responsibilities. From an early age children acted as their mothers' feet, delivering messages and running errands. These little messengers, together with increasingly affordable utilities, gave women less cause to leave the home. Indeed, historian Christine Stansell has remarked that the solitary housewife emerged among the urban New York working class in the 1920s with the advent of inexpensive utilities.[38] Indoor water, electricity, sewer connections, and consumer durables such as iceboxes and washing-machines removed the necessity for frequent ventures into the streets and may have confined women to their homes to a much greater degree than their mothers or grandmothers.

Although wives' and mothers' time was likely to be divided among mothering, housekeeping, and consumption, domestic production also took place. Home preserving appears to have been relatively commonplace. Fruit was available from rural relatives, street hawkers, and berry picking, which appears to have been a common activity for fathers and children.[39] The volume of jams being produced in Richmond Heights was suggested by a North End teamster who reported in July 1928 that he had hauled 136 bags and twelve boxes of sugar to the subdivision. Children also contributed to home production by picking dandelion greens in the spring, shovelling snow in the winter, gathering berries, fishing, and occasionally stealing coal from the railway yards.[40]

Not all domestic production was carried out by women and children. The manufacture of liquor and home brew was largely undertaken by men. The *Evening Mail* in 1921 noted the large demand in the North End for pumpkins and brown sugar, the main ingredients for the manufacture of this home-made beer. There were also stills in Richmond Heights, and at least two tenants, one an RCMP officer, were charged under the Nova Scotia Liquor Act.[41] This form of home manufacture may have benefited the household, since it prevented the diversion of scarce cash from housekeeping money, but did not in itself act directly towards improving the family's standard of living in the way that alternative activities such as maintaining a vegetable garden did.

The scarcity of cash in these households makes any sharp distinction between the extremes of female domestic production and full-time, public paid employment misleading. Women's work, inside and outside the home, was more often a continuum of opportunities. Few married women in Richmond Heights undertook formal waged labour. According to the 1931 census, in the 3,104 Halifax one-family households paying between $16 and $39 in rent per month, a category that would have included all renters in the neighbourhood, only forty-eight wives reported earnings. The small number of employed wives can be placed in better perspective when one also considers that in these same households, 1,268 children reported employment.[42] The census, however, underestimated the number of women earning money, since women participated in occupations that might not have been included in the census return. If married women were unlikely to be found in the formal wage economy, they often engaged in more casual forms of labour. For example, Mrs Smithers received a commission for collecting rent on properties held by her father, who lived in Bermuda, while other women took occasional day work to make ends meet.[43]

Women also had opportunities inside their homes to do paying work of both a casual and a formal nature. Advertisements appeared offering employment for writing show cards or colouring Easter or birthday cards.[44] Mrs Richards paid a dollar a week for a sewing machine, which she used for dressmaking, but claimed that the opportunity and returns were limited and 'it only buys a meal.'[45] Not all work in the home was of a casual nature. Annie Thomas operated a grocery store from her home until the store's bankruptcy in 1928. Thomas, a married woman forty-nine years old, had operated a general grocery, meat, fruit, and vegetable store at the corner of Livingstone and Robie streets since 1919. The venture began with $100 of her own money; she kept no bank account, no life insurance, and no books, and claimed she did not 'know income or profits.' Though the business eventually failed, at the time of dissolution Thomas was able to raise $8,814 to partially repay her creditors, and among her assets were four houses and three sets of flats in the North End of the city.[46] Despite the informal nature of the enterprise, Annie Thomas's store was a major concern and had been profitable. A less successful enterprise appears to have been Mrs Keller's tailor shop, but even this business warranted Mrs Keller's modifying the front part of the parlour in her Stairs Street house for the shop's operation.[47]

Even though only a small percentage of married women formally worked outside the home, the public perception was that their numbers were increasing dramatically. In fact, married women who were employed may have appeared more numerous than was actually the case since they so often met with hostility. A reader of the labour paper, the *Citizen*, wrote in 1927: 'we have a real fad now in Halifax and I think this should be put a stop to; that is married women working; nearly every second one that marries holds her job, with husbands having good salaries coming in.'[48] Criticisms of wage-earning married women were nearly always connected to the responsibility of the husband for providing an income. A wife who worked was considered an insult to her husband's masculinity. In a 1987 article, Bettina Bradbury pointed out that 'The pride of skilled male workers did not end when they left the workplace. For married men, the "manliness" so important to them as workers and strikers extended to their capacity to support a wife.'[49]

Supporting a wife was the hallmark of an adult male, but family economies were precarious and could be sent reeling by the unemployment of an older child, an illness, or a birth. Evicted families often had little choice but to move to 'the country,' where rent was even cheaper and domestic production could reduce the amount of cash required.[50] Sarah Shaw explained in an undated note to the HRC that her family had crossed the harbour to rent in Tufts Cove, since her husband had a 10 per cent cut in his pay and by moving she could reduce her rent from $40 to $15 a month.[51] Alternatively, James Eaton, a tailor at Tip Top Tailors who was attempting to support his wife and seven children on less than $100 a month, moved from good housing at 18 Stairs Place to a self-built 'shack' on Elm Street. In an effort to decrease housing costs, he sacrificed comfortable conveniences for a dwelling in the city's undeveloped West End that in the winter of 1926 finally had water but no sewage connection.[52] Tenant Bernard Boyle demonstrated how precarious life could be for those who could find no such alternatives; he had been twice imprisoned for debt and released under the Poor Debtors Act before being evicted from HRC housing in 1926.[53]

Although women managed the money, it was usually the husbands who carried home the pay packet. The trick often became getting the money into the household before it was spent. Mark Rosenfeld has noted that in an Ontario railway community, it was usual for wives to meet husbands at the station on payday to pre-empt any diversions such as drinking or gambling on the way home.[54] Mrs Smithers, a resident of Cabot Place whose husband was a member of the CNR dining-room staff, was forced to take more drastic measures to secure her husband's wages. In 1930 after unsuccessfully attempting to get the cheque directly from the paymaster, she employed one of the city's most prominent lawyers to attempt legal intervention and force her husband to sign over his paycheques. Minnie Smithers informed the HRC that she had asked her lawyer 'to make Mr Smithers sign his cheque to me so I could get it and pay the bills as [he] was drinking and some times did not bring it home.' Initially Mrs Smithers had approached the paymaster without success, but now had no choice but to hire a lawyer and 'to chance' her husband would keep 'his word ... to give me a certain amount of his money.'[55] Although women largely controlled the way money was spent, it was not theirs, and if their husbands chose not to hand over the pay, there was little immediate action they could take.

Poor local economic conditions could affect the conventional roles of husbands and wives. The failure of a husband to provide for his family could disrupt established patterns of interaction and interdependence. One such problem appeared in a local advice column when a women wrote explaining that, since she and her husband were 'not well off' and although she continued to pride herself on being a good house-keeper, she often took temporary work. The problem, she went on to explain was that, 'Lately, however, I have discovered that each time I go out to a bit of work my husband stays away from his on some pre-text or other. My idea has been to help; but it does not seem to work.' In this case, the woman saw herself as generally conforming to societal expectations, stating that she was capable in her primary role as a house-keeper and only worked outside the home because of necessity. How-ever, when she moved slightly beyond her role and accepted some of the responsibility for bringing money into the home, her husband appears to have abandoned his role and responsibility as breadwinner. In response, the *Evening Mail* columnist summarized society's expecta-tions when she advised 'Mrs H.' that she must make it clear that the money she earned was 'not meant to take the place of his slackness.' The columnist went on to counsel: 'If that doesn't have the desired effect, stop taking these temporary jobs of work for a while ... It is dis-graceful for any man to rely on his wife's earnings when work is within his own reach.'[56] Obviously, although the masculine ethic was strong in Richmond Heights, it was not universal. In a similar vein, a representa-tive of the HRC visited an unemployed tenant in March 1924 and 'im-pressed him he must provide for wife and family.' The disapproval of the representative was evident in his remarks that 'Thibeault said he would follow up at CNR but talked of his rights and was largely indif-ferent.'[57] Mrs H's husband and Thibeault are important reminders that the masculine ideal was not accepted by every father and husband.

Those who rejected the role of husband as breadwinner and provider were exceptional, for it was in this light that most men saw themselves.

In the less frequent correspondence between male household heads and the HRC, the failure to provide weighed heavily on men's minds. The tenant at 23 Kane Place in 1920 who was unable to meet his rental obligations informed the commission that 'it worries me as much as you.'[58] In another case, an employee at Moirs, residing at 6 Kane Place, wrote in November 1924: 'I really don't know sometimes which way to turn with already two judgments against [me], no furniture anymore and my wife in the hospital. Certainly a bad year, this 1924 for me.'[59] Husbands who felt responsible for the family income did not prevent wives from making real contributions. An unemployed unskilled labourer related that he had 'held out as long as he could' before his wife had to go and do day washing to keep the family afloat.[60]

Conflicts within families between husbands and wives were likely to result from the almost inevitable failure of one partner to live up to the community's gender ideal. Men could not always be reliable breadwinners in an unstable local economy. In the same manner, many women also were unable to perform to high expectations as perfect mothers, efficient housekeepers, and loving and supportive wives. The result of this failure was perhaps evident in a rental report that noted an additional fee was charged to Albert Avery upon the completion of his tenancy since the storm door and cellar window had been 'wilfully' broken by his wife in her attempt to gain admittance into the family home after being locked out. A later addendum noted that his wife eventually left him in 1929.[61] Avery had been employed as a motorman with the street railway and, after a layoff, moved around to a series of unskilled jobs such as freight handler, porter, and employee of Vetcraft.[62]

The broken window alludes to the physical violence that could underlie relations between husbands and wives. Glimpses of this underside of domesticity emerge in the rare cases when women charged their husbands with assault.[63] In the nineteenth century, the Nova Scotia Society for the Prevention of Cruelty had offered its services to local women, but with the emergence of more specialized associations such as the Children's Aid Society in the early twentieth century, women were generally left without assistance. In Halifax in the 1920s, animals and children had special agencies, but little aid was available for women beyond the municipal policewoman.[64] While there was little institutional support, Nova Scotia was the sole province in Canada where marital cruelty was considered grounds for divorce. James Snell has noted that the number of petitions for divorce based on alleged cruelty peaked at approximately one-quarter of all divorce petitions in the 1920s.[65]

Domestic violence and economic non-support were at odds with community expectations. But even in less extreme situations, living up to gender ideals was difficult in light of the widespread hopes for domestic happiness within marriage. Heightened expectations of the private sphere were corollaries of the new home-centredness among working-class men. Marriage and the relationship with a spouse were expected to provide greater satisfaction than in the past. Yet there was not a single consolidated ideology surrounding marriage that young Richmond Heights couples could adopt. The new perceptions were apparent to Robert and Helen Lynd in their 1924–5 study of Muncie, Indiana. They found that most people believed that 'romantic love' was the only legitimate basis for marriage.[66] Romantic love certainly did not conjure up the traditional image of a holy hierarchy ordained by God. In its place, romantic love suggested a loss of control and the diminished desire to defer gratification to a heavenly afterlife. Like consumption, romantic love focused on immediate self-gratification and fun. While the modern perception of marriage gained strength, traditional views remained present. In the North End of Halifax, the rector at St Mark's Anglican Church articulated the older view in the 1922 debate surrounding the use of 'obey' in the Anglican marriage service. Rev. George Ambrose defended the use of 'obey' as integral to the preservation of 'the patriarchal government of the home.' Ambrose stated that 'Let the word "obey" be omitted and the word "honor" naturally follows it into oblivion; whilst "love" in its true sense cannot exist in a family without a head, without respect and without obedience.' He admitted that all men were not worthy of this government, but held that maintaining the ideal encouraged men to realize their responsibility and 'the very high position in regard to their families, in which God has placed them, and to make themselves worthy of honor and obedience.' Ambrose's vision of marriage did not coincide with contemporary thought, but may have been present among the older generation. For example, sixty-one-year-old Jane Anderson was noted for her faithful attendance to her dying husband. Certainly, there had always been households in which genuine affection bound husband and wife. In two of the rare wills left by Richmond Heights residents, wives were referred to as 'beloved.' Nonetheless, the purpose of marriage had partially shifted from procreation and the raising of children to personal fulfilment and the promotion of happiness for the spouses.[67] At the same time, working-class marriage to a large extent continued as a financial partnership. Wives were necessary to transform and extend a husband's wages into a form that could sustain the family.[68] This mutual economic dependence did not conform to either Ambrose's image of a family patriarchy or the modern goal of 'romantic love.' In the North End of Halifax, the romantic ideal and the economic function of marriage coexisted uneasily.

Although the romantic and the economic could not be reconciled, the idea of companionate marriage made inroads into Richmond Heights. Companionate marriage stressed the friendship and compatibility between husband and wife over the marriage as an economic unit. While it is impossible to measure the growth of the companionate ideal, changes in leisure activities confirm the presence of the new ideals surrounding companionate marriage. In her study of American fraternalism, Mary Ann Clawson has noted that social relations between men and women shifted in the early twentieth century with the expansion of mixed-sex commercial activities such as dance halls, amusement parks, and movies. Companionate marriage also encouraged a sexually integrated social life and the rise of married-couple leisure activities.[69] In Richmond Heights during the 1920s, though men continued to participate in exclusively male social activities, there appears to have been an emphasis on shared leisure of the couple after courtship and marriage. Indeed, an important aspect of the rise of domesticity among the working class was the increased likelihood that men and women would engage in leisure activities together.

Card playing, dances, sleigh rides, and church social events brought married men and women together outside the home. Public card socials could occupy more than 800 men and women on winter Saturday evenings in the five halls in the North End offering card games of '45s.' The Ways and Means Committee of the CNR hosted a Grand Armistice Thanksgiving Dance in the South End Railway Station rotunda that attracted 600 couples. Similar functions were held by other organizations such as the Tram Employees' Union. In 1929, for the first time railwaymen and their wives together attended the annual convention in Moncton, with the women holding simultaneous meetings.[70] In other Canadian industrial centres, women's auxiliaries for unions such as the International Machinists' Association promoted social activities such as children's parties, picnics, and socials, although Sylvie Murray has suggested that union men could be reluctant participants. There were also opportunities for mixed social activities outside the union. Church drama clubs at all three churches included both married men and women. Among other church-based recreational activities encouraging interaction between men and women were events such as the St Joseph's annual garden party and the St Mark's fair, choirs, and church suppers. 'Jiggs' Suppers' – inspired by the character in the popular comic-strip *Bringing up Father* and his love of corned beef and cabbage – and bean suppers were regular events at St Mark's near the end of the decade.[71]

The most prevalent form of leisure and entertainment involving men and women probably took the form of house parties. Despite increasingly greater opportunities to participate in commercial leisure activities, it appears that the residents of Richmond Heights continued to 'make their own fun' through mixed-gender home entertainment. In the limited space available, Mr and Mrs A.H. Grant of 2 Cabot Place managed to fit fifty guests into their home on a Monday evening in October 1925 for a card tournament. House dances, Halloween parties, whist drives, bean suppers, and singing all managed to crowd as many as thirty-five couples into the small houses.[72] Mixed-gender home entertainment also entered the debate on temperance, for one critic argued that prohibition brought alcohol into the home and thus made it accessible to women. The labour newspaper printed this argument before the 1929 provincial plebiscite, claiming that 'In the days of the saloon only men drank; but now the women are drinking.'[73] Mixed drinking or entertainment among married men and women suggests that a form of companionate marriage was emerging and was altering homosocial leisure. That the home was the centre for much of this new type of married entertainment reinforces the notion of the growing influence of domesticity. Leisure activities outside the home continued to be primarily male, but though married women were still tied to the home, they were no longer always there alone, and for better or worse they probably had their husband's company more often.

The appeal of home meant that many working-class men and women turned to their families and expected more personal fulfilment from the private sphere. At the same time that spouses had an increased emotional expectation of home, the household and the domestic economy continued to be much more fragile and precarious than was generally acknowledged. Heightened expectations and the vulnerability of the household economy were felt by all adult men and women. The roles of mothers and fathers changed: fathers appeared to become more involved with their children, and at the same time higher standards were set for mothers. Mothers in particular were exposed to increased criticism. The expectations of motherhood became more demanding even as maternal control was in decline, with power being lost to schools, the juvenile courts, and, in the case of Richmond Heights residents, the increasingly interventionist HRC. In addition, women appear to have lost some of their power and influence as mothers and heads of the domestic sphere with the increased participation of their husbands in the home. With more responsibility and less power, it became much easier to fail. Sharper definitions of ideal motherhood and fatherhood around a core of images varying little across class generated not clarity of focus but confusion.

In the Richmond Heights of the 1920s, at least three ideologies surrounding the purpose of marriage competed for ascendancy. The economic partnership of marriage and the traditional recognition of the distinct economic roles played by working-class husbands and wives continued to have very real resonance. Marriage as a blessed state ordained by God for procreation was still propounded by local clergy but was less obvious in residents' daily lives. The third and most modern ideology, marriage as a romantic and companionate union, was evident in the leisure activity of married couples. Married people in Richmond Heights, depending on age, economic security, and religious beliefs, probably lived some combination of all three.

Compounding this confusion, many women found that the rigid definition of motherhood contrasted with the variety of ideals presented to them as wives. Was it possible to reconcile and embody in a single person the competing images of devoted mother, efficient house manager, life companion, and sexual partner? The domestic role of men, though not as strained or demanding as that of women, was perhaps even more ambiguous. The involved loving father, the detached disciplinarian, the marriage partner, and the breadwinner whose connection to the household was primarily through his wage packet were all possible roles to adopt. Domesticity made gender roles more rigid and restrictive even in the privacy of the home, at the very time that men and women experienced increasing uncertainty as to how to act. As the emotional importance of home expanded, so did the many and sometimes contradictory roles men and women embraced within its walls. The roles created under the titles 'husband' and 'wife,' 'father' and 'mother' were not consolidated; nor were they by any means uniform. The ideal tranquillity of domestic life depicted by the play of small children on the subdivision's boulevards could be suddenly broken by an outburst of drunken screaming, the shattering of a window in a domestic dispute, confrontations about money, or the frustrated tears of generational tension.

5

Single Mothers and
Female Household Heads

When her husband died in December 1919, forty-three-year-old Jessie Muir had seven children under the age of fourteen and was pregnant again. Left without the earnings of her husband, who had been a yard foreman for the Canadian National Railways (CNR) repair shops, Mrs Muir faced an uncertain future, with a six-room house at 14 Stairs Street and personal property and effects totalling less than $2,200.[1] The house was an important source of income for Mrs Muir, and throughout 1920–2 classified advertisements appeared in the *Evening Mail* offering board and lodging. When work at the shipyard was plentiful, board at Jessie Muir's home was advertised at $8.50 a week, but the dramatic decline in local employment opportunities drastically affected the rates Richmond Heights' residents could charge prospective boarders. By the fall of 1920, the local shipyard had laid off employees, tenants were scarce, and Jessie Muir was advertising five furnished rooms to be let in whole or in part. Advertisements until the late summer of 1921 offered a varying number of rooms for light housekeeping. In August 1921, an advertisement appeared for lodgers, offering single accommodation at $2 a week and shared rooms at $1.50. The turnover in boarders was high, and three furnished rooms were again advertised in November of that year for $5.[2] Mrs Muir did not give up her house to live with friends and relatives, since her home was never rented out in whole. Advertisements offering up to five of the six available rooms, such as those appearing in October 1920 and January 1922, indicate that the living arrangements of the children must have been flexible. Perhaps the children spent time with relatives or friends or temporarily resided in a local orphanage. After the 1917 explosion, while Mrs Muir was recovering from injuries, the five eldest children stayed as students at the Convent of the Sacred Heart and St Joseph's orphanage. St Joseph's orphanage, an institution with historic links to the neighbourhood, housed ninety-five such 'half-orphans' in 1919.[3]

Jessie Muir thus survived the way most widows did before the welfare state: she used her home to generate income, and perhaps also accepted occasional day work in the critical period before she could depend on her children's labour. In 1925, John, her eldest son, was working as a call boy with the CNR. The fact that he was able to find employment in a period of layoffs with the company that had employed his father suggests one way that informal community networks were utilized to assist distressed families. In the same year, Mary, the eldest girl, was also employed as a cashier. Circumstances for the family must have improved further in 1927, when the second son was employed as a clerk.[4] While the older children may have had no choice about leaving school and earning for the family, Mrs Muir, unlike other women in her circumstances, does not seem to have forced all her children to work as soon as possible. Teresa, born in 1914, was able to attend St Patrick's High School.[5]

Mrs Muir also received support from her community and neighbours. During the late winter and early spring of 1923, a card social and dance, and a card social, dance, and pie social were held to raise money to assist the widow and her family.[6] While support from friends and relatives was typical, the broad community support offered to Jessie Muir was the only such example uncovered. This in part reflected her extreme circumstances as the sole support of eight children, but community support may also have been indicative of at least three other factors. First, there is no record of relatives, despite the fact that her husband had been born in the city.[7] Second, while Richmond Heights had a large transient population, at its core was a remarkably stable group, composed of families who had lived in the old industrial suburb of Richmond. This group could be subdivided along occupational lines and church affiliation. Jessie Muir, as the widow of a railway worker and a member of St Joseph's Church, had strong connections to both groups. Finally, Jessie Muir was the epitome of respectability. She was a devout Catholic with at least one of her daughters a member of the Sodality of the Children of Mary and another daughter entering a religious order.[8]

With the important exception of Bettina Bradbury, few historians of the working class and the family have examined the ambiguous position of single women with families. These women rarely appear on the

Canadian historical landscape, except as passive recipients in the story of the development of the welfare state. American historians such as Tamara Hareven and Susan Kleinburg include widowhood as a life-cycle stage, but do not look at deserted or separated women. Even the inclusion of widows can be problematic. Although both Hareven and Kleinburg note that widowhood was a life stage that did not conform strictly to age, their discussions of widows appear in chapters entitled 'Later Life Transitions' and 'Aging, Widowhood, and Death.' The association of female household heads and old age – or worse, death – denies the accomplishments and marginalizes the life experience of Jessie Muir, who lived for fifty years without a male breadwinner after her husband's death.[9]

The death or departure of a spouse affected men and women alike, regardless of class, but had a particularly devastating economic and emotional impact on working-class women. Society defined the ideal family as a male-headed household supported by a male wage, but families led by women that did not fit this model constituted a significant proportion of households. Most woman-led households were headed by widows, but women who were deserted, separated, or married to migrant workers also composed important groups of those left temporarily or permanently in charge. While the latter group of women might expect limited financial support from remitted wages, they nonetheless faced the challenge of managing without a husband. 'Going away' in search of employment was a standard strategy for riding out bad times among the Canadian working class in the nineteenth century, and it continued to be an important alternative in the Maritimes during this period. Working away from home occurred as a result not only of poor economic conditions but also of specific occupations, such as the military or the merchant marine. Women who found themselves temporary or permanent heads of households were economically and socially vulnerable, and their circumstances reveal some of the inequities resulting from a male family-wage economy. First, the disparity in male and female wages meant that it was almost impossible for women to earn sufficient wages to support themselves, let alone their children. Second, women were caught between the social ideal of a mother removed from the public labour market and the economic reality of life without access to an adult male wage. Respectable working-class culture was firmly based on the expectation of a male wage capable of supporting a family. And the contemporary definition of family was restrictive, supported by assumptions of natural roles, duties, and obligations. Female household heads therefore posed a challenge to the existing economic system and ideological framework.

While attesting to the flaws in an economic system that encouraged dependency on a male family wage, female-headed households also exhibited the strength and courage of individual women, and the flexibility of the household unit. The necessity for these women to move beyond traditional gender roles and the strain they placed on existing survival strategies and networks compelled the state to intervene. Concern was expressed for their economic vulnerability and poverty, but fear for their moral vulnerability, as sexually experienced women who now lived outside marriage and male supervision, was seldom far from the surface. These women did not fit any of the contemporary categories used to label women, and their presence was regarded as an awkward social problem.

The visibility of female-headed households was heightened after the First World War. During the 1920s in Richmond Heights, as a result of concern for the plight of women widowed by war or the explosion, fear for the traditional family in light of a perceived changing sexual morality, and, specifically, the dismal local economic conditions that forced men to leave Halifax in search of employment, these women were especially conspicuous. The absence of a male wage-earner exposed the deficiency of the ideal to those who cared to notice.

In 1921 and 1931, approximately 16 per cent of all Halifax families with children were headed by a single woman. Of the 1,506 female-headed families in 1931, the large majority, 1,131, were led by widows.[10] Many of the children in these families were sixteen or older, but this did not necessarily mean they had access to decent wages. Boys learning trades did not earn sufficient funds to maintain themselves, let alone contribute to the family coffers. The case of an Agricola Street widow with two sons, sixteen and twenty-two, illustrated this problem. The older boy, Albert, was apprenticed as a printer for $12 a week while his younger brother, Maynard, brought home only $3.50 a week as an errand boy.[11] Without access to the manuscript census, there is no way of knowing the number of these women living in Richmond Heights, or the ages or sex of their children; however, within the subdivision 30 widows appeared on the municipal voters' list between 1920 and 1929, and 115 individual widows were listed in the city directory.[12]

Halifax did not have an unusual number of widows. In other Canadian cities with a female age breakdown similar to that of Halifax, such as Hamilton, Ottawa, and Moncton, widows composed the same percentage of the total female population.[13] The probability of widowhood increased with age and was slightly higher in Nova Scotia than the national average. In Nova Scotia in 1921, 2.2 per cent of all women between twenty-five and thirty-four were widows compared with 22.3 per cent of all women between fifty-five and sixty-five, and 49.9 per cent of all women over sixty-five.[14] The explosion, the First World War, disease, and occupational accidents were common causes of early widowhood. In 1926 alone, thirteen fatalities in Halifax County were covered under the Workmen's Compensation Act, and this number did not represent all work-related fatal accidents.[15] Richmond Heights women not protected under the Workmen's Compensation Act included Elizabeth Docherty, whose husband was killed in an American construction accident, and Maude Kenner, whose husband drowned at sea.[16] In contrast to the sudden tragic news of a workplace accident was the death of the wage-earner after an extended period of illness that interrupted regular income and took any household savings for medical expenses. Tuberculosis was an extended and expensive disease that forced households either to pay for costly sanatorium treatments or to witness a slow death at home. If men were in the last stages of the disease, wives could not undertake even day labour because of heavy nursing responsibilities at home. At the time of the July 1929 death of James Walker from tuberculosis, his family was already in considerable debt since he had been ill for a year and unable to work.[17]

In such vulnerable circumstances, insurance and property were the only two means young families had of protecting themselves against the sudden impoverishing loss of the primary male wage-earner. In most cases, these means would prove either impossible to adopt or inadequate in their provisions. Life insurance was one way of making the future less uncertain. In her study of Italian and Jewish women on the Lower East Side of New York City, Elizabeth Ewen noted that the American working class carried life insurance on every person from the age of two up, since the expense of funerals made coverage a necessity.[18] Three Nova Scotia widows who appeared in the Boston case notes in a 1910 study of widows and charity had insurance regardless of their financial situation.[19] The way in which these widows distributed their resources, particularly the large outlay on funeral expenses, offers insight into both values and customs. The first widow's husband was killed in an industrial accident and left her with five children under ten years of age. The woman received $280 from her husband's life insurance, $100 from the insurance of her husband's employers, and a collection of $94 from her husband's fellow employees. Of the total $474, over one-fourth, or $143, was spent on the funeral. In the second case, another widow with five children under fourteen whose husband died of Bright's disease was left $240 in life insurance and spent $140 on funeral expenses. The final case mentioned involved a woman with two children under three, whose husband's life insurance of $100 did not manage to meet outstanding debts and so the funeral expenses had to be covered by a private agency. All three women secured life insurance, even though the first widow's husband had earned only $12 a week and the last woman's family was heavily in debt.

Insurance was just as important in Richmond Heights. Minnie Smithers, wife of a dining-car waiter for the CNR, explained in an undated note to the Halifax Relief Commission (HRC) that her rent would be delayed, as 'We had forgotten about the Insurance coming due and I never like to leave it over as something might happen and I would lose everything.'[20] Paying insurance premiums took precedence over paying rent.

Insurance could support the notion of respectability in at least two important ways. First, insurance provided the resources for a proper funeral. The large portion of available assets that widows chose to spend on funeral expenses was significant. The three Nova Scotia women living in an American city were probably without an extended family or a supportive community, a circumstance that possibly explains their appearance on public charity case files, but also suggests the importance of maintaining public prestige even in a funeral amongst strangers. Proper funerals were also important in Richmond Heights. As Stewart Howell of 21 Cabot Place stoically explained a missed rent payment to the HRC: 'Owing to the death of our boy at the Oil works i am unable to pay my rent as it put us to quite an expense.'[21] Like the nameless widows in Boston, providing a decent funeral took priority over the most basic expenses of the living.

Insurance also offered the bereaved family some privacy from the intrusion of charity associations after the death of the primary wage-earner. The pride and dignity attained from looking after oneself and not accepting charity played upon at least two important aspects of respectability; privacy and independence. Insurance could mean that, in the initial period of transition, the widow's neighbours did not need to know her troubles. But this period of adjustment could not last long, for a 1920 Nova Scotia government report concluded that life insurance alone was inadequate, since 'it was found in practically all cases sufficient only to cover funeral expenses, doctors' bills, and clothing or at most to tide over a temporary period of adjustment when the real struggle would be faced.'[22]

While insurance alone would not suffice, the same 1920 Nova Scotia government report found that, in cases where savings had been invested in a home, 'a number of fatherless families were found to be self-supporting.'[23] Property played an important role in Jessie Muir's household strategy, but this was not an option for most residents of Richmond Heights. Tenants in the Hydrostone District, such as widow Ida Davis of Stanley Place, may have owned property before the explosion; but during the 1920s all residents rented.[24] In the owner-occupied wooden houses of the extension streets, however, widows were listed among property owners. By 1929, at least twelve properties on these streets had been or were currently owned by widows, most of whom had been widowed in the decade after resettlement. Thus property ownership was only available to a relatively small proportion of the residents of Richmond Heights, and even the widows who did possess their own homes were usually saddled with a large mortgage. Since both insurance and property were found wanting, or in the case of property just unattainable, most widows had to rely on alternative survival strategies.

The supposedly ideal family-based survival strategy was home ownership with one or two older children working; but most women had to accept less satisfactory alternatives. These options included participation in wage labour, the use of the home to generate income through boarders and lodgers, and the early school leaving of children. As Bettina Bradbury has found in the case of nineteenth-century Montreal, widows usually engaged in wage labour if the children were young, and in these cases preferred employment opportunities that kept them in their own homes. Alternatively, when young children were involved and work inside the home was not possible, children were temporarily or permanently surrendered. One of the obvious impediments to waged labour was the problem of child care. The Jost Mission operated a downtown crèche, but it would not have been convenient for women in Richmond Heights.[25]

The decision to surrender a child was the last line of survival strategies, an option for only the most desperate, such as deserted wives. In fact, desertion was the primary cause of surrendering all children to the Children's Aid Society. In 1925, the desertion of twenty-four fathers meant that nearly sixty children in the city were removed from their homes.[26] But the Children's Aid Society did not handle all surrendered children. Throughout the 1920s, local newspapers ran adoption columns in their classified sections. While inserts with box numbers may have been placed by the Children's Aid Society, others gave private North End addresses. Several of these adoption advertisements – 'Adoption – home for baby girl eight month, 833 Robie,' 'Home wanted for a baby girl six months old. Apply 76 Maine,' and 'Healthy Baby girl for adoption, aged one year. Apply evenings between 7 and 8, 49 Bilby' – suggest family dislocation or tragedy.[27] An offer of 'complete surrender' of a four-month-old baby boy of refined parentage or an advertisement specifying the religion of prospective parents cause one to imagine the desperate choices some women had to make. Women were not the only ones faced with the dilemma of surrendering children. The following 1920 advertisement from a father suggests a conjuncture of several family crises. Perhaps the death or desertion of the mother in combination with the dismal economic conditions in Amherst forced the father to contemplate outmigration, which he could not manage if accompanied by two young daughters.

Home wanted Good Christian home for two bright pretty girls, age 7 yrs and 12 yrs, oldest one good singer, Would like to have them in one home. Religion Baptist or Methodist preferred – Will give them away absolutely. Bedroom suite goes with them, also clothes for a year or two and $250 in cash to each one. Apply N.D. Atkinson, father of the girls, P.O. Box 532, Amherst.[28]

We may never know if the $500 promised came from the sale of his Amherst possessions, but the wording of the advertisement expressed concern for the girls' future and pride in their qualities. These feelings may have been shared by the many women who could not be so generous in their search for their children's new home. The surrendering of children was one of the tragic aspects of life for women on their own in a male wage economy.

Mothers looking for private homes to board their children also advertised in the adoption column. One woman asked, 'Will you give an eight month old baby a good home and mother's care for $12 monthly?'[29] Another wanted board for a seven-month baby girl, stating that she was willing to pay a reasonable price, while another was more concerned that the home should be 'loving.'[30] Offers to board children 'cheap' also appeared, such as that of the woman at 188 West Young Street, suggesting another house-based survival strategy by which women could generate income.[31]

There were not many options available to women to generate income. Formal employment opportunities for older women were not plentiful during the 1920s and with a few exceptions they were limited to domestic service. The expanded female employment opportunities in the service and clerical sectors were largely restricted to young, single women, so they in no way benefited older women.[32] Clara Brown, a tenant on Sebastian Place who was behind in her rent, was labelled in the housing records with the self-explanatory comments, 'widow in strained circumstances working for Dr. McDougall as [an] office cleaner.' Domestic service, even in the private sector, was characterized by low wages. Hennessey Street home-owner Melinda Graham, a cleaner at one of the Richmond piers, knew that even full-time work did not necessarily secure a widow's financial position, because in September 1925 she was nearly $500 in arrears on her mortgage.[33] In fact, with the sole exception of a widowed teacher, the death or absence of a husband did not open up any occupations for Richmond Heights women other than the limited opportunities available to their married counterparts.

Limited employment prospects for widows had little to do with community stature or respectability. Emma Ingram, a member of 'a prominent North End family,' was employed as a cleaner at the old North End railway terminal after her husband's death.[34] Regardless of a women's reputation in the community, there was also a general prejudice against wage-earning mothers. The Nova Scotia Mothers' Allowance Commission reflected this position in its criticism of 'Day work,' 'Service,' and 'Boarding House' widows for destroying family life. The report expressed concern for the children of 'Day work widows' who were left unsupervised, and, as was previously mentioned, the government commission was terribly anxious about the detrimental effect of boarders on the quality of family life.[35] At greatest risk were the children of widows in service who paid for their children's keep in institutions or 'scattered about with relatives who could provide a home as long as the mother could contribute from her earnings towards their support.'[36]

With poor employment prospects and limited child-care assistance available, remarriage for widows may have appeared as an attractive alternative.[37] Marriage records at St Marks Anglican Church show that 11 of the 135 weddings performed in the church between January 1920 and December 1929 involved widows.[38] These women ranged in age from twenty-two to thirty-eight, with a mean age of thirty. The widows who remarried, while older than first-time brides, were largely a youthful lot. Most women could not count upon the prospect of remarriage and the support of another male earner, however, so when they could not manage by themselves they turned to others for assistance.

Extended families were the most important support and survival network for women on their own. After the death of her husband, Mary Gracie of Cabot Place moved in with her brother's family, who lived several streets over.[39] Similarly, when fellow Cabot Place resident William Tilley went to the United States in search of work, his wife lived with her sister in nearby Kane Place until her husband was established in Rhode Island. Shortly thereafter, the assistance was reciprocated when the sister's husband suddenly died, leaving the Kane Place widow with three small children. The new widow sold her furniture and followed her sister to Rhode Island. The desertion of a husband also left women dependent on their families. When Thea Buckles of Stairs Place charged her husband for non-support in February 1930, she and her four small children were relying on the generosity of her mother. According to an HRC report, Thea Buckles's mother had 'put in the winter's coal and also provides food to stave off absolute want.'[40] Upon the family's eviction from the Hydrostone District, a married sister provided shelter.

The poverty that most women without access to an adult male wage endured made them particularly dependent on their children's earnings, no matter how meagre. The change in Christmas school holidays affected one widow with six young children because she depended on her fifteen-year-old daughter's part-time work on Friday and Saturday evenings and over the Christmas holidays. An early Christmas in 1928 meant that the daughter could work only two days before the holiday and there would not be sufficient money for presents. Not surprisingly, few children of female-headed households continued in school beyond the age of fifteen. In 1931, only 225 of the 1,850 children of widows in Halifax fifteen years of age and over, or about 12 per cent, attended school.[41] This was significantly different from the rate for the total population, in which approximately 25 per cent of the children fifteen years of age or older who lived with a parent remained in school. Early school leaving meant entry into waged labour, or perhaps for some young women full-time assistance at home. Between 1920 and 1925, property-owning widow Melinda Graham of 10 Hennessey Street shared her home with four women and one male with the same surname as hers, all of whom worked at Moirs. In addition to what appears to be her five children, Melinda Graham also housed a boarder employed at the same confectionery factory. Mrs Graham, with her own income, a boarder, and possibly five working children was still unable to keep abreast of her mortgage payments. While the wages of children might provide enough income on which to survive and keep the family together, unless the widow could depend on the full or combined wages of adult sons, the children's combined income did not compensate for the lost wages of an adult male worker.

Along with family, the community played a role in helping women survive. As in the case of Jessie Muir, specific assistance from outside the realm of church or work was unusual. Trade unionists and workmates might offer generous assistance such as the $1,300 collected by employees of the Halifax Shipyards for the widow of James Slater, the secretary of the Electrical Workers' Union Local 625 who had been electrocuted in a workplace accident.[42] The generosity in this particular case was noteworthy, since the collection took place during a strike that economically devastated many of its participants. Other efforts of support were less specific. A shipyard walking party took place in November 1925 and attracted 200 people, raising $50. Weekly dances and card socials held in the Mayflower Hall on Agricola Street raised funds that were distributed to community cases of need.[43]

The churches also played a role in assisting families within their parishes. During the Great Depression of the 1930s, Father Curran of St Joseph's Church paid the rent for at least one of his Hydrostone District parish members.[44] The St Vincent de Paul Society was also active at St Joseph's and presumably assisted local families. Beginning in January 1923, the members of United Memorial Church began contributing to an extra collection each Communion Sunday, the proceeds of which were to be distributed by the minister to needy families. While session minutes note success, as the fund collected $61, a number of parcels, and an order of groceries during a 'Poor Fund Gift Sunday' in December 1927, the same minutes also indicate that in January 1926 a motion was passed that wine for Communion Sundays should be paid for out of this fund. The diversion of 'poor funds' from their original purpose raises questions about the community's commitment to the problem and probably reflects the ambivalent attitude towards charity.[45] This mixed public perception surrounding charity was carried into public policy in the development of early government-assistance programs.

A new survival strategy available to Richmond Heights widows was pension income made available through the HRC, the Department of Soldiers' Civil Re-establishment, and the Workmen's Compensation Act. In the early 1920s, there were nearly 200 widows receiving pensions from the HRC. The HRC, like the federal Board of Pension Commissioners with its elaborate pension scheme, became an avenue by which a government body attempted to intervene in the lives of ordinary Canadians. Like the military's widow's pension, the HRC's widow's pension was based on the earnings of the deceased husband. The link between the deceased husband's wages and the widow's pension was particularly significant in a working-class neighbourhood where many of the widows would have been at the lower end of the scale. For example, under this scheme the widow of a ship's captain who had earned $170 a month might receive a pension of $60, while a labourer's widow who had been managing her home on $45 a month would receive only $25.[46]

Throughout the 1920s, the possibility of a new state-administered pension for widows hung over the community as an unfulfilled election promise. In 1920, when a Nova Scotia commission presented a report on the establishment of a mothers' allowance, five other Canadian provinces, Manitoba, Alberta, Saskatchewan, British Columbia, and Ontario, had already instituted what the commission described as 'a system of granting government aid to indigent mothers with young children deprived of a father's support.'[47] The Nova Scotia commission recommended that a mothers' allowance should be made available to only 'one class in particular as unquestionably deserving of state aid, the indigent widow with two or more children to support.'[48] Deserted women were not to be considered for state support, since the commission felt that the legal process should be strengthened to ensure that the absent father fulfilled his 'natural obligations to his family.' Similarly, support for the families of disabled men 'would be open to abuse.' While the commission acknowledged that assistance for families of men who had been institutionalized in mental hospitals had merits, families in which the father was in prison 'although recognized under some schemes, [are] of more or less doubtful character, particularly as prison labour with remuneration for the wife and dependents is being strongly advocated in many quarters and seems the more reasonable remedy.' No public money would be distributed to unmarried mothers; it was left to the legal system to establish paternity and financial responsibility. The commission's restricted vision of who would be entitled to state aid, and its tendency to recommend legal changes, ensured that even the limited help it offered would have no impact. The commission's recommendations remained largely intact in the Mothers' Allowance Act, which finally sent out its first cheques in October 1930.[49]

The findings and recommendations of the commission had no immediate effect on the lives of the women it set out to assist; the findings and attitudes revealed and reinforced contemporary stereotypes. Research was carried out by the province's teachers, who submitted names and addresses of all widows with whom they had contact. Obviously, from the beginning of the study there was no intention of including women other than widows. In Halifax County, which included the city and its rural environs, the commission found that there were 303 widows with 775 children under sixteen and that 78 widows and 234 children needed assistance.[50] Seventy-three of the widows had only one child, and the commission adopted the general principle, which was also accepted by the Children's Aid Society, that mothers should be able to support one child without public aid.[51] With this conclusion, the commission demonstrated the same gap in logic as the rest of society. While waged work outside the home and the taking in of boarders by mothers were regarded as inappropriate by the commission, it did accept the belief that a mother should be able to support at least one child. How a woman without access to a male wage was to do so without engaging in waged labour or taking in boarders was never explained. Not surprisingly, economic reality won over ideal definitions of motherhood; nevertheless, the commission determined that there was no way that these women could achieve the contemporary ideal of a good mother.

The initial report of the Commission on Mothers' Allowances was not only contradictory, exclusive, and rigid, it was also parsimonious. The report recommended an average pension of $35 a month, a sum below the pension granted under the Workmen's Compensation Act.[52] The meagre pension proposed, the restrictions placed on recipients, and the ten-year delay in implementation call into question the intentions of the government and its commission. Widows might be the most 'deserving' of the poor, but their ambiguous position meant that they were not above suspicion.

While widows such as Jessie Muir epitomized respectability and evoked community sympathy for their unfortunate circumstances, other widows were subjected to careful community scrutiny. The Nova Scotia Mothers' Allowance Act of 1930, sensitive to public opinion, further restricted those who could benefit by declaring that the act would assist only the mother who was 'in every respect a fit, proper, and suitable person to have the custody and care of her children' and make payment only for legitimate offspring.[53] HRC pensions could also be suspended for immoral behaviour. When a man was seen leaving Emma Lawson's home late in the evening, the man's wife filed a complaint that resulted in Emma Lawson's having her pension temporarily discontinued. Another widow, Lillian Kennedy, was permanently suspended after an illegitimate birth. Her immoral behaviour was reinforced by the fact that she had taken in boarders with 'undesirable character.'[54] Similar interference probably occurred with widows receiving military pensions, as these invoked morality guidelines.[55] The concern that the Mothers' Allowance Act, the HRC, and the military should support only 'respectable' women reflected general prejudices. Neighbours spied on widows and passed judgment on their activities. A Sebastian Place woman, for example, was concerned about the widow who was subletting the house next door and wrote to the HRC to inform them that Mrs Canning was keeping 'a proper cat house I guess you know what that is. now that Mrs George that you put out last fall moved in this morning, they have partys nearly every night including Sunday evenings and they get drunk vomiting over my veranda and backyard ...'[56] Widows had to be particularly careful of their reputation, since public opinion was fickle and there was little middle ground between compassion and condemnation.

It was not always possible to distinguish between widowhood and a broken marriage. The situation of deserted or separated women did not differ greatly from the plight of widows. Certainly, in this mobile community, some of the women who claimed to be widows were not. A separated woman who testified under oath at a Halifax divorce trial in 1923, when asked directly if she was a widow responded, 'Married woman; I am the same as a widow.'[57]

Desertion, which the Halifax Welfare Bureau described as 'The Poor Man's Divorce,' was the most common form of marriage breakdown. The Children's Aid Society and the Superintendent of Neglected Children, later Child Welfare, regarded it as one of the most crucial problems they faced.[58] Within the community of Richmond Heights there were many examples of the devastation it caused. Howard Wilson of 17 Cabot Place deserted his wife, leaving her with back rent owing. Another husband, James Bowden, abandoned his wife, who was ill with tuberculosis, and left her to be supported and nursed by friends and charity.[59] Desertion occasionally was temporary. In August 1929, Bart, a debt-ridden thirty-three-year-old shoemaker who lived at 29 Stairs Place, disappeared for six days. Upon his reappearance at his sister's home, Bart 'claimed to have been doped and robbed of $50.' Similarly, George Paul, a waiter on the Maritime Express who lived at 1 Livingstone

Place, 'disappeared' for a few days after picking up his paycheque in May 1929. At the time of George Paul's departure, he was at least $145 in arrears on rent.[60] The economic pressures of supporting a family in hard times must have made the possibility of escape attractive, even as the disappearance of a wage-earner would have sent panic through the entire family.

Sometimes separation was involuntary. Emma Jones, a woman with two sons who was renting at 60 Stairs Street for $12 a month, became a single mother when her husband was incarcerated at Rockhead prison. Her poverty and equally poor reputation were evident, for when authorities appeared in October 1925 to evict the family she was accused of 'bluffing the sheriff' by claiming to be ill in bed.[61] Other patient histories of the Halifax Visiting Dispensary, a charity organization that provided medical services for the city's poor, also reveal the devastating impact of desertion on the family unit. In case after case, the cause of poverty in the family is noted as, 'Father not with family' or 'Husband left her, does not know where he is,' linking the desertion of the primary wage-earner to the collapse of the family unit.[62]

The HRC was reluctant to accept deserted women as tenants in Richmond Heights because such tenants had the potential to burden it with responsibilities 'we should not be called upon to carry.'[63] During a high-vacancy period in the spring of 1925, the Halifax Welfare Bureau proposed that the HRC accept one of its clients. The Welfare Bureau would provide the women with $60 a month, and requested a special reduced rent from the HRC. The woman's husband had left her with their seven children in the summer of 1924 found work as a carpenter in Albany, New York. Until December of the same year, he regularly had sent $25 a week for the support of his family, but since that time he had not been heard from. According to the report made to the HRC, the deserted wife was keeping the family together by taking day work in wealthy homes in the South End of the city, but this created an 'awkward circumstance in that the children are young and leaving them alone all day presents a problem from our point of view.'

This example was in no way unusual. The 1925 report of the Halifax Children's Aid Society described the case of a man with eight children, who had 'been an average husband and father' until he lost his job a year earlier. After searching for work in Halifax, he left for the United States and stopped communicating with his family. Through social-service agencies, the man had been traced, but he continued to move about frequently. Meanwhile, in Halifax, the deserted wife tried to support her children through day work and left the eldest, a sickly girl of seventeen, in charge of the house. The report concluded that the children were 'undernourished, through insufficient food and unruly because of the absence of the mother.'[64] In this example, the mother surrendered three children to the Children's Aid Society and took out a warrant for the arrest of her husband.

Deserted women did not stand helpless in their fight for survival. In October 1928, George Swan, a former resident of Merkel Place, was sued by his wife for non-support. Thea Buckles of 30 Stairs Place also sued her husband for non-support in February 1930, but the action was too late to delay her family's eviction in April of the same year. The wife of Guy Thompson of Stairs Place and Hennessey Place succeeded in a dual conviction against her husband for profane language and non-support. If the deserting husband remained in Halifax, he could be forced to fulfil his financial obligations. In a period of high local unemployment, however, many men left to find work in the United States, and crossing international or even provincial boundaries made disappearing men much more difficult to trace and to prosecute. Obviously, not all women were familiar with their legal rights, but questions regarding the legality of desertion did appear in the newspaper, and agencies such as the Halifax social-service bureau did press women to exercise their legal rights. In fact, women used legal means not only to force their husbands to fulfil their financial responsibilities, but also to control physical abuse. A former resident of Stanley Place was summoned to court in April 1929 when his wife charged him with assault.[65]

Women were not always the 'victim,' as separation could come about by mutual agreement or female-initiated dissolution. Self-divorce, the mutual dissolution of an unsuccessful marriage, may have remained as a popular solution that rejected dominant respectable mores. Public notices appeared in newspapers announcing the names of wives who had left their husbands' 'bed and board' and whose husbands declared they would no longer be responsible for any debt contracted. Bessie Lewis's husband could not be held liable for her unpaid rent on Duffus Street, since they were living apart at the time the debt was incurred.[66] For a Cabot Place resident, his wife's departure meant the end to a home, since he was a navy cook, away for periods of time, and unable to maintain independent housekeeping without her assistance. The desertion of a wife may have been inconvenient or embarrassing, or may even have made it impossible to maintain a household; it did not create the same financial chaos as the departure of a husband, however.

While desertion was relatively common in Halifax in the 1920s, divorce was not. Nova Scotians had perhaps the most liberal access to divorce in the country; cruelty was designated sufficient grounds for termination of marriage.[67] But the 1931 census lists only seventeen men and seventeen women in the city of Halifax as divorced. Certainly the number of divorcees would have been greater than seventeen, since we can assume remarriage in some cases. While the total number of divorces would not have been large, the number of people personally touched by divorce might explain the perceived threat divorce posed to the institution of marriage. There could not have been many people in Richmond Heights who were not either a relative, a neighbour, or an acquaintance of someone involved in a legal separation. In one case, a twenty-two-year-old widow of a Hydrostone District family had married a twenty-five-year-old widowed machinist in April 1919, and both parties continued to reside in the neighbourhood after separation. This marriage lasted only four months, for the new husband had been found guilty in the City Stipendiary Court of fathering an illegitimate child. Between the court's decision and the 1926 divorce, Edna Farmer, the wronged wife, lived with her parents in Richmond Heights. At least two other Richmond Heights couples, both from 'old North End' families, were also involved in divorce proceedings in the 1920s, though the first of these cases seems to have been discontinued.[68]

Divorce was relatively infrequent, but female-headed households were more regularly created when men left Halifax in search of employment. Men who worked elsewhere were a fact of life in Halifax. Some occupations by their nature meant that long periods of time had to be spent away from home. The presence of the military and merchant marine meant that men had always had to leave their families in order to earn their living.[69] The economic crisis of the 1920s accentuated this trend, and while many families left the city, often it was just the men.

In addition to the larger economic cycles, there were the familiar seasonal variations in local employment opportunities. During the winter, men in the merchant marine sailed out of the port, and in the summer they were usually laid off. This seasonal interruption of employment forced migration from the city to find work. Ellen Conley of Columbus Place, whose husband was employed by the Canadian Government Marine, wrote in March 1923 that her husband had found work in Ontario and 'if all goes well' would earn $75 a month until October.[70] The case of Ellen Conley illustrates the importance of family assistance in keeping the house together while her husband searched for work, because she claimed her father's pension cheque and her sister's earnings as a means of settling her own debts.[71] A husband sailing out of port could also mean a long period without any knowledge of his whereabouts. Sarah Shupe had to explain to the HRC: 'My husband is gone away to sea, where, I dont know yet.'[72] The annual Harvesters' Excursion to the Canadian Northwest was another example of seasonal employment that took men away. Every August men left Halifax to work as agrarian labourers on the Prairies because of the attractive one-way fare to Winnipeg, which was set at only $26.10 in 1924. In November 1920, 115 lumbermen were recruited by a New Brunswick firm, and many Halifax men must have been involved in large construction projects such as the Sheet Harbour hydroelectric development, which temporarily employed 300 men along the isolated Eastern Shore.[73]

Men also left their families for employment elsewhere for reasons that did not reflect the demands of their occupation but were the result of the scarcity of local opportunities and large-scale layoffs. The layoffs at the Halifax Shipyards, at one point the largest employer of local labour, were devastating, as the payroll dropped from more than 2,000 in the spring of 1920 to a low of less than 100 in 1927.

The departure of a husband in search of work could mean an immediate expense for the remaining household. Mrs Sears of Merkel Place explained her failure to pay rent, since 'Mr Sears has gone to the States to look for employment and I gave him all the money I had.'[74] Remitted wages would not have been generous, since the male wage-earner was placed in a position where he had to support two households. Sometimes the separation was only temporary, as the family followed upon the establishment of a new home. One example of this two-staged migration was that of Mrs Sewell and children of 12 Stairs Street who in October 1924 left to join Mr Sewell after he had settled into a permanent position in Massachusetts.[75]

The decision to go away in search of work was difficult, but at times almost inevitable. Mrs Armstrong dreaded the future prospect of having her husband, a laid-off employee at the shipyard, leave Halifax, writing to the HRC that, 'I hope and trust there may be a job come in, before he starts to move.'[76] Once the decision had been made to move, a husband's departure to work away might take the form of an annual migration. Owen Isnor, a carpenter who owned a set of flats at 7 Hennessey Street, was back and forth to Boston with great regularity. The *Evening Mail* social column noted in March 1926 that after having spent the winter with Mrs Isnor and family in Halifax, he had returned to a permanent position in Boston.[77] At times, these migrations were unsuccessful: as noted in an undated memo in the HRC rent book, on one occasion Owen Isnor had been back from the United States for three months and was without work or money. While carpenters might move because of the seasonal nature of their work, family tragedy could also bring men home. In May 1926, John Mahar returned to his Livingstone Street home from Detroit, Michigan, where he had been working, to attend the funeral of his only child.[78]

It is difficult to comprehend the impact of long absences on family life. In June 1924, a former employee of Hagen and Company who had found work in Chicago visited his wife and children after a twelve-month absence.[79] Similarly, in November 1923, the North End social column in the *Evening Mail* remarked that a local woman had 'returned home from an extended visit to the U.S. where she remained with her husband who is working in Massachusetts, near Boston.'[80] Mark Rosenfeld, in his work on an Ontario railway community, has suggested the difficulty women faced in keeping a house and raising children on their own while managing the emotional stress of adjusting to the absences of their husband. Separation probably increased tension in the home, both before, during, and after the husband's absence. The closeness of kin would have relieved part of the loneliness, but would hardly have compensated for the absence of a husband.[81]

In March 1924, Ellen Conley hinted at the risks involved in having a husband working away by concluding a message with the information that he would be returning to Halifax in eight months, 'please god.'[82] Sometimes men did not return, the result of desertion or death. In February 1928 Frank Docherty died in a construction accident in Bath, Pennsylvania, leaving a widow and four children at 34 Merkel Place. Frank Docherty had worked at the Halifax Shipyards, but for the two years preceding his death had worked on building sites throughout the United States, largely in Florida.[83] With Frank's death, Elizabeth Docherty suddenly went from temporary to permanent household head.

The devastating loss of a partner and breadwinner, as well as the personal loss of identity as someone's wife, was somehow overcome by the surviving family. Yet the social position of these women who headed households was so ambiguous that, according to Linda Gordon, between 1890 and 1920 female-headed households were identified as a social problem.[84] Society's inability to reconcile the role of mother with that of wage-earner led to social assistance, in which we can see evidence of the nascent welfare state. As a stop-gap response, pensions were not only difficult to obtain and inadequate, but their very introduction and existence was a means to keep women in an economically disadvantaged position. Women did not have to earn an equal wage to men's, since this meagre income supplement could stave off absolute want – as long as they were willing to conform with restrictive moral regulation. In the absence of a male breadwinner, rigid adherence to the ideal based on a male family wage as the best means to preserve the family could require women and children to engage in low-paying waged labour and to share the home with outsiders.

Poor health, marital unhappiness, or unemployment could all easily undermine or destroy the domestic ideal of a household based upon a male wage. Yet any discussion of households in a male wage economy must keep in mind the large number of households without a male wage upon which to depend. Even households that survived on remitted wages did not conform with dominant stereotypes, since they made do without the presence of a man as the family head. For these women in the Halifax neighbourhood of Richmond Heights, the struggle for subsistence could be especially poignant, since they were paying the price of domesticity in the most obvious manner. The fact that so many chose and fought to reside in independent households among respectable neighbours in good houses reminds us that aspirations were not abandoned with the loss or absence of a husband. In the daily lives of these women, and with their heroic struggle to meet the rent, to put food on the table, to burn fuel in the stove, and when possible to keep their families together with as much pride and dignity as possible, we catch glimpses of their strength as they responded to the best of their ability in a economic and ideological structure that permitted very few choices and options. The Mothers' Allowance was introduced too late to help Jessie Muir during her most desperate period, but in 1930, by which time her older children were working, she was probably among the first women in Nova Scotia to receive a cheque.

6

Men

'Big Bill' Vallance lived at 30 Livingstone Place throughout the 1920s with his wife, Emma, and his four daughters and five sons. As a foreman for one of the line crews at Maritime Telephone and Telegraph (MT&T), he had reliable and steady employment. Vallance began his working life early when as a boy he went to sea, and as a result he probably had little formal education. A personal history published in his company magazine noted that he joined the telephone company in Halifax for the first time as a groundman in 1896, but four years later when the large steel mill in Cape Breton opened, 'like many another young, strong and – shall we say restless – man at that time, he joined the crowds then pouring toward Sydney and presented himself at the Dominion Iron and Steel Co.'s office.' After five years in the steel plant Vallance returned to Halifax and his job with MT&T. Though Vallance had a steady job and a large family, his activities beyond work were extensive. Vallance was a member of the Halifax Fire Brigade, played an instrument in the MT&T band, and made time for his favourite recreations – fishing and shooting.[1] In occupation, itinerant labour history, family, and leisure activities, 'Big Bill' Vallance was typical of many Richmond Heights men of his age. As a foreman, a volunteer fire fighter, a musician, and a sportsman, Vallance possessed a number of overlapping public identities beyond his private role of father and husband.

Male adults were likely to have multiple guises. Men were not only fathers and husbands but also carried an assortment of public identities such as employee, trade unionist, comrade, team member, and lodge brother. While men remained integrated into the household through expanded domestic responsibilities in their roles as husbands and fa thers, the most obvious examples of a distinct working-class culture remained exclusively male and removed from the home.

The text of men's obituaries often highlighted the diversity in their lives and richness of their experiences. Obituaries of working-class men recited employment and military history, the names of family members, and involvement in sports or hobbies, and often included remarks about social activities and affiliations. The importance of acquaintances outside the workplace or family was noted in the frequently repeated phrases of 'widely known,' and 'well known,' or comments about the bereavement of a 'wide circle of friends.'[2] Examination of men must extend beyond the household, since the domestic sphere, while encroaching on their time, was only one aspect of their life. The world outside the home as experienced in work, trade unions, labour politics, sports, and leisure activities simultaneously affirmed class and fraternal bonds.

Home, family, neighbourhood, church, and some leisure activities could unite men and women, yet there was much that kept them apart. The economic role performed by most males, as active participants in the formal labour market, meant that men were more class-bound in their outlook. Many men experienced a lifelong connection to paid labour as direct participants in the labour market. Women, on the other hand, usually attained a class position as the result of a relationship with male breadwinners, such as fathers or husbands. Unmarried daughters might also sell their labour, but they did so under different circumstances and in different sorts of occupations from their fathers and brothers. The position and attitudes of married women were even more difficult to determine. The majority of married women who did not undertake formal paid work were in a 'no man's land' located somewhere between married working-class women who worked for household survival and middle-class housewives.

Paid labour could provide men with both a class identity and an important component of the meaning of masculinity. As Andrew Tolson has pointed out, at the core of masculinity in Western capitalist societies is the importance of work.[3] Occupation, strength, skill, and the ability to support a family were value-laden qualities integrated into the construction of what it meant to be an adult man.

In contrast to the experience of women, work made a boy a man. In 1923, a Halifax man in his early forties remembered the way fathers were instrumental in the launching of a boy's career. One day, a father would declare, 'Jumbley, the junk man wants a boy; better go and "get the job,"' and with those words a boy would begin to earn a living.[4] Fathers continued to be important in finding their sons employment, whether through neighbourhood contacts such as the junk man or their own place of work. In the railway shops, apprentices were often the sons of shopmen.[5] Similarly, a number of non-railway Richmond Heights families had fathers and sons working in the same establishment. Oscar Mathers and his son Lauchlan of 28 Stairs Place both worked as repairmen for the tramway. William, son of foreman rigger Charles Myers, lived with his family at 22 Cabot Street and apprenticed in the same trade as his father. Despite dismal conditions in the shipyard, young William Myers was able to find steady work.[6]

Although some fathers were able to get their sons into good positions through connections and prestige, technological change and the rationalization of the labour force were rapidly changing the conditions under which production occurred and the skills required. Furthermore, as manufacturing became centralized in other regions of the country, the process of deindustrialization in Halifax meant that, in a relatively short period, fewer men were employed in making things. This shift in production took place across Canada at different times and at different speeds, but the rapid pace of local change meant that the changing economic structure of early-twentieth-century Halifax was especially difficult for men. Economic change within the regional economy threatened conceptions of masculinity, and this uncertainty was reflected in the nostalgic and romantic regional culture that emerged during the 1920s. The writings of F.W. Wallace celebrated the 'iron men' in Nova Scotia's seafaring past, while the prominence awarded to the *Bluenose* honoured similar masculine qualities through international sailing competitions.[7]

The changing nature of the regional economy, in which men were becoming less likely to produce things, was evident in the occupations of men in Richmond Heights. Between 1920 and 1929, according to the city directory, there was a shift in the occupations in which male residents were likely to find employment. In 1920 and 1921, construction was the most important sector, as it included employees still connected to post-explosion reconstruction efforts and the numerous employees of the shipyard. Throughout most of the rest of the decade, transportation was the largest employer. The combined employment at the Canadian National Railways (CNR) and the Dominion Atlantic Railway meant that railways were the largest employers in the area of transportation and communication, but the importance of the street tramway and the telephone company within this sector were daily reminders of the increased opportunity in the expanding urban infrastructure. By 1929, the service sector was the largest employer, with more than half of the 145 men employed in this category working in the public service, as employees within a branch of the military or at one of the levels in government.

Among the important service employers of Richmond Heights men was the military, an organization one might immediately associate with reinforcing notions of masculinity through discipline, training, and rewarding manly characteristics and values such as courage. In fact, however, Halifax's military in the 1920s was a military in peacetime, its soldiers as redundant as industrial workers from closed factories. Those who remained in the forces were not the virile combatants of the war, but were employed as handymen, orderlies, or to be in permanent training to defend Halifax and its harbour against no enemy. Even the city's maritime naval heritage appeared meaningless when the dockyard was closed. Those who remained in the navy escaped some of the feeling of redundancy, but long postings at sea away from home and family meant forgoing the rewards of domesticity.

The shift in important employers reflected changes in the local economy. The overwhelming importance of the shipyard in 1920 and 1921 was significantly different from Richmond Heights' employment profile of 1929 when employment was distributed much more evenly among the areas of transportation, trade, and service. The number of Richmond Heights men with occupations listed in the directory also varied dramatically, from a high of 643 in 1920 to a low of 345 in 1924. Some of this variance might be accounted for by inaccuracies within the city directories, but the numbers in any given year do correspond with general economic conditions. The numbers of men employed changed, and the economic sectors in which Richmond Heights men were likely to find employment altered, but the occupations as listed in the city directory did not change greatly from year to year. Excluding the numerous employees of the railway and the shipyard who were simply listed as 'employees,' carpenters, chauffeurs, labourers, and clerks were the four most prominent occupations in every year except 1926. The fifth alternated between sailors and police, with the exception of 1920 and 1921, when skilled metal workers filled this position. The prominence of semi-skilled occupations in Richmond Heights at least in part related to the broad way in which they were defined – the occupation of chauffeur, for example, included teamsters, drivers, deliverymen, and taxi operators. These occupations were more broadly defined than skilled trades such as bakers, barbers, blacksmiths, or boilermakers. It is important to clarify this point so as not to underestimate the number of skilled workers who lived in the neighbourhood (see appendix table A).

As the number of skilled workers rose and fell in relationship to activity at the shipyard and the level of building activity in the city, it is possible that the very definitions of skilled work changed. George Rountree, in his study of employment in the Canadian railways, noted that as new procedures were introduced, jobs continued to be performed by the same craft, though the actual work might be altered dramatically. In particular, Rountree drew attention to the blacksmiths, whose work had disappeared from the railway shops, yet without any recorded decrease in the overall number of 'blacksmiths' employed.[8] As technology changed, so did the definition of what it meant to be a blacksmith, even though the title remained the same. Thus, while the number of skilled workers living in Richmond Heights did not change dramatically, it is probable that the level of skill necessary to perform their tasks did. As reflected in the new census category of 1931, the decline in skill appears to have been complemented by an increase in employees in the area of warehousing, storage, and shipping. These men did not produce, but rather handled and distributed goods made elsewhere to be consumed locally. The city directory also indicates significant growth in two other occupations, clerks and police, neither of which was involved in production.

The increased emphasis on the role of a singular breadwinner may also have affected turnover in levels of employment. With high levels of unemployment, married men may have been reluctant to quit their jobs, as new work was difficult to secure and seniority was emerging as a valued principle. This reluctance was noted in an American study by David Montgomery, who concluded that during the 1920s workers were 'more likely to link their plans for the future to a particular company, and less likely to tie themselves to some particular occupation than their parents and grandparents had been.'[9] Long-term residents in Richmond Heights, unlike their transient neighbours, experienced practically no job turnover or changes in employer.

Corporate welfare programs introduced into male workplaces reflected the man's role as breadwinner. They stressed economic benefits rather than social programs. Companies that offered profit-sharing and stock-ownership plans, group insurance, pensions, and paid vacations all had continuous employment provisions, thereby encouraging a stable and loyal workforce. Death benefits payable to spouses at MT&T began after five years of service, but it was not until after ten years of employment that benefits reached the equivalent of one year of pay. Pensions, if awarded, began after twenty years of employment, while sick benefits were prorated after two years based on the number of years with the company.[10]

The focus on a man's role as breadwinner was also evident in the classified advertisement of an unemployed carpenter from 61 Columbus Street who had lost $25. Like the women who wrote to the Halifax Relief Commission (HRC) requesting allowances in their capacity as mothers, in this classified advertisement Simon Lewis described himself as a poor married man, on the assumption that the finder would have been more likely to return the money than if he had been single.[11] Similarly, in another advertisement, a North End carpenter looking for employment mentioned that he had a family of nine to feed.[12] This also presumed that the community's consensus on the burden of the breadwinner would capture the compassion of anyone reading the notice. General agreement on the male breadwinner's importance was also reflected by restrictions on employment in municipal relief projects that discriminated against unmarried men. Single men were not eligible to apply for work on city contracts and in municipal stone crushing; preference was given to married men with families, and especially workers with babies.[13] Family responsibilities were also mentioned during periods of wage negotiations, such as the 1929 effort to raise wages of labourers in the building trades. Trade unionists argued that labourers had 'the same domestic responsibilities as those enjoying better wages. They have homes to maintain, families to feed, rent to pay, children to clothe and educate, and at 35¢ an hour cannot meet the ordinary expenses of even a decent living.'[14] Through their responsibility as breadwinners, they believed they were entitled to better pay.

If the primary responsibility for men was to earn money and support a family, it is necessary to ask how successful Richmond Heights men were in this role. The 1920s were a much less prosperous time for most Canadians – particularly for Atlantic Canadians – than popular mythology suggests. American labour historians such as Frank Stricker, Irving Bernstein, and David Montgomery have successfully attacked the myth of universal prosperity among the American working class in the 1920s, but the twenties continue to roar within popular culture.[15] The discrepancy between myth and experience was also evident in Richmond Heights.

After the dramatic inflationary period of 1917–21, the cost of living throughout the 1920s was relatively stable. Except for rent, most expenses declined in the 1920s. For working-class Canadians this price decrease was most important in expenditures surrounding food, which in the early 1920s could consume more than half of a household's income.[16] The relationship between the overall decline in the cost of living and the standard of living can nonetheless be deceiving, as the greatest drop in prices came in areas other than food, rent, and fuel. In other words, those who benefited the most from the decline in prices were those who had money to spend beyond basic necessities. The Canadian Department of Labour published a monthly household budget for five persons based on prices in sixty Canadian cities. In this budget for March 1921, a date that roughly coincided with the federal census, a weekly minimal income of $23.83 was broken down into $13.23 for groceries, $3.98 for fuel and light, and $6.62 for rent. This budget based on national averages would have been inadequate for Halifax, as rent and the price of food were higher than elsewhere.[17] The Department of Labour's budget provided only the bare minimum for survival and did not include necessities such as clothing, insurance, and sundries. The same family budget published a decade later in March 1931 reflected general deflation over the decade. The necessary weekly sum for family survival had dropped to $19.44, with food down to $9.14, fuel and light at $3.24, and rent increasing to $7.06.[18] It must be noted that at no time did the Department of Labour claim that this wage was sufficient for the household, but rather that food, fuel, and rent composed about 65 per cent of the necessary expenditure of the average family, thereby bringing the $19.44 government budget to a minimum requirement of approximately $30 a week. Even the sum of $30 a week, however, was below a 1925 budget produced by the Canadian Brotherhood of Railway Employees for 'minimum health and decency.' This budget required an annual income of $2,202.37 or $42.35 a week.[19] If, depending on inflation or deflation, a household of five needed somewhere between $30 and $42.35 a week to 'make do,' it would be important to know where the majority of incomes in Richmond Heights households fell.

The 1931 census lists both the average annual earnings of male heads and the combined earnings of their households for thirty-four different Halifax occupations. At first glance it appears as if the 1920s were prosperous for the local worker. More than half of the thirty-four occupations listed had higher wages in 1931 than in 1921, and for two-thirds of the occupations, total family income had also increased. On closer examination, however, it is difficult to miss that in the most numerous occupations, where the male head of household was employed as a carpenter, chauffeur, unskilled labourer, longshoreman, or teamster, the 1931 average income was less than it had been ten years earlier.[20] These struggling occupations of carpenter, chauffeur/teamster, and labourer were among the most important occupations held by tenants of the Hydrostone District and the owner-occupants on the extension streets. The decline in wages perhaps explains why the number of households supported by these occupations declined towards the end of the decade.

The families of unskilled labourers and longshoremen in 1931 had total average family earnings of around $13.54 and $14.12 a week. Although longshoremen were among the most numerous occupations in the city, never more than ten were listed in Richmond Heights in any given year. It was even less likely that any of these men was the sole wage earner in the family. Longshoremen, or stevedores as they were called, tended to be boarders, have boarders, or, alternatively, to have a number of wages entering the household. For example, long-time tenant Hugh Zimmerman of 32 Stanley Place was a stevedore, but in 1929 the household was also supported by a son employed as an auto mechanic and a daughter working as a teacher. In the same year, stevedore Garfield Paige lived at 16 Kane Place with his widowed mother, two working brothers, and a sister-in-law. Stevedore households with only one low-wage earner could not contemplate the rents in Richmond Heights. While carpenters averaged only $17.83 a week, their slightly higher average wage was more easily supplemented with the small earnings of children. According to the census, carpenters' households in Halifax had an average accumulated family income of $23.39 a week. Not surprisingly, therefore, they were more common among the tenants. Similarly, truck drivers, teamsters, and chauffeurs, whose families averaged nearly $19 a week, also took out leases regularly.

The most common occupations of male Richmond Heights residents paid in the income range of $23 to $33 a week. This range of incomes was composed of most railway employees, except the well-paid engineers and conductors, metal workers, skilled building trades, street-railway employees, police, salesmen, and clerks. If work was regular in these occupations, it was feasible to meet the rents in the Hydrostone District, which ranged from a low of $25 to a high of $40 a month, with a supplement of two dollars a month if a furnace had been installed.[21] Tenants whose households were bringing home between $23 and $33 a week met the minimum budget issued by the Department of Labour – but households at the lower end would have been struggling to provide more than food, rent, and fuel. Even when incomes were constant, however, they rarely proved to be sufficient to meet the highly variable expenses of most ordinary households. A doctor's bill, a pair of eyeglasses, or the need to assist a family member were expenses that households could not always anticipate.

The income level of most households in Richmond Heights was perilously close to poverty, and under fragile local economic conditions many families, through illness, unemployment, or reductions in wages or hours, descended sometimes temporarily and sometimes permanently into its grip. Families evicted for an inability to pay their rent were often struggling under the combined stresses of low wages and insufficient hours. In 1926, Bernard Boyle was a sectionman with the CNR earning thirty-five cents an hour. The most generous estimate might calculate that throughout the year he was able to work 300 nine-hour days, but certainly the actual total would have been much less. This meant that Boyle had an annual income of less than $945 or $18.17 a week.[22] Similarly, attempts in the same year by the HRC to collect back rent from a former tenant were not promising, since the man was supporting a wife and seven children on less than $100 a month. Yet, the $25 a week earned by this tailor was more than what was earned by most unskilled and semi-skilled workers. Even employees with regular incomes fell behind on their rent. When RCMP officer William Calvin vacated 32 Cabot Place in June 1926, he was $294.50 in arrears. Men with less dependable work were that much more vulnerable. In 1926, as a result of the ill health and ensuing unemployment of Mr Richards, the former tenants of 22 Kane Place were unable to manage on just $9 a week. Mrs Richards explained in a letter to the HRC that although the rent at their current address had been paid, 'I cannot pay any on my grocery bill only 4 dollars and I've had more than that this week too that means a double payment next week.' She then went on to write down her weekly expenditure, stating that rent was $5, groceries $8 or $9 dollars plus an additional $2.30 for milk, coal $1.50, insurance $1, and, lastly, $1 went towards a sewing machine she had purchased. Although the family was taking in only $9 a week, it was spending more than twice that amount – $18.80 to cover the most minimal expenses. As for catching up on back rent owed on their former residence in the Hydrostone District, Mrs Richards asked, 'If you will just reckon that and than tell me just how a[nd] where I am going to get any money

... to pay.'[23] Part of the reason that providing for his family was so central to the male identity was that it was the wife's responsibility to make do. As in the case of Mrs Richards, it forced her to undertake the impossible, and it both revealed the failure and undermined the authority of her husband on a daily basis. In another example, Mrs Armstrong complained that because of lack of work in the shipyard, her husband was giving her only $16 a week, and hence meeting the rent was not possible.[24]

Rising consumer expectations increased the potential for disappointment and increased the likelihood of failing to meet more demanding consumption standards. In a study of divorce in California and New Jersey during this period, Elaine Tyler May has noted that failure to provide was at the root of a number of working class divorces. Similarly, Lizabeth Cohen in her study of Chicago industrial workers between the wars argued that economic dislocation took a toll in domestic tension and in the decline or fear of decline of patriarchy within the working-class family.[25] Evidence from Richmond Heights suggests that although economic stress was certainly felt within the household, working-class patriarchal culture remained standing. Women had to make do with whatever they had, but men were ultimately responsible for the household's financial management. When the Smitherses of 34 Cabot Place went into arrears on rent, Joseph 'claimed that his wife was running him into debt without his knowledge or sanction.' Smithers stated that he earned a good wage of $155 a month with the CNR and from that sum paid $5 in insurance, kept $25 for his 'privy purse,' and paid to his wife $125 for housekeeping.[26] The same responsibility ultimately fell on Michael Flynn, who when he signed the lease at 23 Cabot Place explained that he was a salesman 'making good money.' A business reorganization at Moirs in 1929, however, eliminated their confectionery sales team and Flynn was then placed on a delivery team with reduced wages. Under his new circumstances he admitted he found 'it impossible to make ends meet.'[27] Flynn, however, did not blame his wife or anyone else for his family's financial problem and alone shouldered responsibility for his inability to make do.

Failure to provide for a family and the inability to fulfil the duties of manhood affected individuals differently. Some men temporarily or permanently deserted their families. In the case of one Hydrostone District resident, it appears that severe financial stress and thwarted social mobility eventually led to an emotional breakdown. After the First World War, when he was discharged from the army, the forty-five-year-old

English-born William Wilks rented a house at 16 Stanley Place and established a china and crockery shop among the Hydrostone District stores on Young Street. Poor local conditions hastened its bankruptcy and put Wilks in arrears to the HRC. The Wilkses' pretension to upward social mobility – they had one daughter training as a music teacher and placed a rare engagement announcement in the newspaper – was firmly capped when the family's name appeared in the records of the Halifax Welfare Bureau and the Halifax Visiting Dispensary. By 1945, Wilks, at the age of seventy-one, experienced his third nervous breakdown and was reduced to selling newspapers outside the Majestic Theatre.[28]

All men, regardless of class, were to some extent experiencing what has been referred to as a crisis of their masculinity. According to Michael Roper and John Tosh, the term 'crisis of masculinity' may actually reflect the 1980s, but the anxiety around the gender ideal for men has been eternal because of the unresolved difference between personal experience and the expectation of social and economic power.[29] Around the turn of the century, as women moved into the public sphere in their fight for and ultimate benefit from legal, political, and educational reforms, many North Americans began to discuss the feminization of culture. The expanding public role for women had direct consequences for men. Female reform movements such as the temperance movement were specifically directed at changing the ways in which men behaved and enjoyed themselves in the world beyond the home. At the same time, the women were perceived to be curtailing the public activities of adult men, while in their roles of mother and teacher they also dominated the early development of boys.[30] Discussions of the 'crisis of masculinity' have located this turning point at various times from the mid-nineteenth century to the present day, making it appear as a perpetual state of mind. While the inherent contradiction contained in the idea of perpetual crisis may annoy the historian who desires a precise concept of when something happened, the ambiguous and vague periodization actually underlines the very nature of gender identity and its expression within a specific context. Since gender identity is socially and historically constructed, it is always undergoing change in accordance with specific circumstances, and this change is often experienced as crisis. The reassessment of masculinity that took place by Haligonians in the 1920s during a time of economic dislocation made many working-class men feel particularly vulnerable and hence created anew the experience of a gender crisis.

Though the 1920s saw consolidation around the idea of a single male breadwinner for each family, specific evidence reveals time and again the continued necessity of several economic contributors in many households. Not surprisingly, the appeal of a single male breadwinner at a time when it was simply not feasible in many households led to frustration, and at times women were held responsible. On the front page of the *Citizen*, the local labour newspaper, the question was posed in November 1922: 'What will be Man's Place in Society of the Future.' According to the paper, 'Every sort of clerkship and factory job is done nowadays by a woman or a child where a man used to earn double the pay and support a family.' In light of this change, the article asked, 'Where are the men to go if this keeps on? What is to become of family life? Many towns in the United States are already known as "She-towns."'[31] The false perception of an expanded economic role for women and the imagined belief by many men that they were less able to support a family than their grandfathers contributed to the view that men's position in society was jeopardized.

Yet men's uncertainty over their role and the tensions of economic instability provided the foundation on which men could build a new and far-reaching power. The fear of 'She-towns' encouraged men to reach across class boundaries to recognize cross-class bonds. These cross-class bonds were reinforced as many working-class husbands and fathers adopted what had been the middle-class ideal of domesticity that supported their own feelings of importance as primary wage-earner. Men in Richmond Heights adapted these general principles to fit the context of lives in which it was nearly impossible for families to exist on one wage. Ideas about home and work were not the only links between men that reached across classes. Many young men shared the experience of the First World War and took away notions of masculinity as a result of that conflict.[32] The restlessness that caused Bill Vallance to leave his Halifax job for the steel plant in Sydney was characteristic of men regardless of class. Noted businessmen had also worked in the Canadian West or the United States during some period in their youth. Finally, regardless of class most men were able to participate in leisure activities outside the home since they were relatively free from domestic responsibilities such as child care. For working-class men, economic downturn brought unemployment and underemployment, expanding their free time and permitting them to pursue a greater variety of activities.[33] Although participation in these activities was usually restricted by class, the 1920s brought greater uniformity in the type of activities undertaken.

Richmond Heights men were involved in many cross-class activities. Although they were certainly not invited into the upper-middle-class Rotary Club, many neighbourhood men formed important connections with Rotarians in their shared roles as scoutmasters and church stewards. Michael O'Brien of 17 Kane Street, leader of the 2nd Halifax Sea Scouts, which operated out of St Joseph's Church, was assistant scoutmaster of the City Armoury Jamboree in 1927. One of his patrol leaders at this fund-raising event was a neighbour from Livingstone Street, William Warren. At United Memorial Church in 1925, four Richmond Heights men acted as stewards responsible for the financial and management decisions of the congregation. At St Joseph's, Leo Foot, a paint-mixer once employed as blacksmith, led a drama group. Other neighbourhood men accepted leadership roles in cross-class organizations such as the Acadian Société L'Assomption, the Knights of Pythias, and the Masonic Order.[34]

The assumption of leadership roles in church, youth, or ethnic organizations by working-class men contrasted with the experience of neighbourhood women – a finding also reflected in Lynne Marks's investigation of church culture in a small town in Ontario in the 1890s. At United Memorial Church, a woman from a middle-class family remembered that with only one exception the working-class women of the congregation were excluded from all leadership positions in women's church organizations.[35] The discrepancy in the leadership experience of men and women again reminds us of the different experiences of men and women and perhaps reflects the greater demands made of working-class wives and mothers, as they rarely had opportunities to undertake responsibilities beyond the home.

Public drinking, often associated with male working-class culture, was predominantly illegal in Halifax, after the 1886 liquor legislation restricted lawful drinking to private residences and hotel guests. Complete prohibition in Halifax finally occurred in March 1918 as a result of federal wartime legislation and was maintained after the war by a provincial plebiscite that swept the province of Nova Scotia, with the exception of Halifax itself. Nonetheless, alcohol continued to be available. As previously noted, two Richmond Heights men were found with stills, and the temperance inspector was occasionally called in with regard to 'certain tenants.'[36] Other Richmond Heights men, among them 'Big Bill' Vallance, appeared in city court and were fined two dollars for public drunkenness. Certain men, such as carpenter Ambrose Carl, had wide reputations as drinkers, but this did not prevent Carl from being granted a lease on two separate occasions for 4 Columbus Place.[37] While drinking created important social bonds amongst men, teetotallers could also find an active social life with like-minded men in the various chapters of the Catholic Total Abstinence and Benevolent Association or temperance lodges.[38] But even these associations demonstrated a stance distinct from that of middle-class reformers, as the society at St Joseph's Church exhorted 'voluntary self-discipline and self-control' over 'abstinence through compulsion.'[39] The strongest indication of the general consensus on the use of alcohol by the citizens of Richmond Heights was their overwhelming rejection of prohibition in 1929. In that plebiscite, more than 80 per cent of the Richmond Heights polling division favoured discontinuing the Nova Scotia Temperance Act and supported the availability of alcohol under government control.[40] The neighbourhood's support of government control echoed the opinion of the city's trade-union movement, which formed one of the most visible proponents in the fight to abolish prohibition in a cross-class coalition with men from other sectors of society.

As much as tensions surrounding changing gender ideals united all men, class differences remained important. The most obvious examples of class-based activity that attracted Richmond Heights men were trade unions and labour politics. Neighbourhood men joined and led unions, sat as labour politicians on the city council, and organized the unemployed. Robert Daw of Cabot Street sat as the labour alderman for Ward Six from 1922 to 1927, and his nomination forms indicate support from neighbours. Other Richmond Heights men were prominent in the short-lived Marine Trades and Labor Federation at the shipyard, and in the more permanent Carpenters', Barbers', Street Railway, and Firemen and Railway Engineers' unions.[41]

Involvement in the labour movement not only reflected political and economic interests but also met social needs. Local labour activist and radical Ronald MacDonald explained his involvement in a wide range of labour activities as a hobby. Before his permanent departure from the city in 1924, the machinist explained that 'He liked the Labor movement [and] it was a hobby to him. He had spent time and money on it, he had not been interested in much else.'[42] For some men, their commitment to the labour movement and labour politics took the form of involvement of fraternal organizations.

Union and labour politics in Halifax in the 1920s were marked by a cycle of strength, fragmentation, apathy, and resurrection. The leadership of the economic and the political organizations overlapped. A small cadre of men remained in permanent executive positions until removed by either death, departure from the city, or the revitalization of the labour movement during the Second World War. Even in the 1920s, this leadership was not composed of young men, and the generational differences were a recurring theme in the complaints of the older labour leaders. According to E.E. Pride, an organizer for the American Federation of Labor with twenty-three years of experience in the local labour movement, commenting in 1929, a typical young man in the union 'is quite satisfied with paying his dues, but that is as far as his interest in the Union goes.' In contrast, according to Pride, 'older men understand better the value of unions and because of their interest in all union matters, they, therefore, come in for the great share of the responsibility and work.' In the same manner, another trade unionist complained that modern urban living provided too many distractions and alternative ways of spending leisure time away from the union, and as a result the labour movement suffered. The combination of 'flivvers, flappers, and road houses, horse races and prohibition,' meant that it was 'a difficult matter to secure volunteer workers for the interests of the Union ... our members want increased wages and better conditions, but do not want to make any personal effort.'[43] This lack of 'personal effort' represented a generational split, as younger men did not step forward to take over union duties. Here, union duties and labour politics may have been connected to stages in the male life cycle, since young men setting up households in which they hoped to be the sole breadwinner were in a different position from the more senior union members who had access to their children's wages if the need occurred.

At the end of the First World War, Canada witnessed from coast to coast an extremely high level of labour organization. In 1920, Halifax boasted 8,000 unionized workers and had the fourth largest number of organized workers in the entire country.[44] The economic depression, which began in the summer of 1920, played havoc with local employment, and many workers faced unemployment and/or wage reductions that wiped out postwar union victories. Charters and locals lapsed and disintegrated as members left town in search of better prospects. By the end of the decade, however, there was a resurgence of organization as at least twelve Halifax unions reorganized and brought the total 1929 union membership to 3,000 in forty-three different unions.[45]

Not only did unions fall apart in mid-decade, but so did the umbrella organization, the Halifax District Trades and Labor Council. The brief integration of economics and politics in the postwar labour revolt created permanent schisms between radicals and conservatives on the council. In 1926, when the Communists finally succeeded in taking over the organization, nearly every major union in the city withdrew. The resurrected Trades and Labor Council of 1927 was very different. It was founded on an apolitical premise and able to boast that it knew 'no religion, no nationality, no politics and no color line.'[46] While this avowed departure from politics reduced the possible impact the council could have upon its members' consciousness, it would be difficult to deny that it had some organizational success, which was seen in the growth of union membership and the purchase of a labour temple in 1928. But this success had a cost. A central feature of the revitalized Labour Day celebrations hosted by the Halifax Trades and Labor Council in 1927 was the first 'Miss Nova Scotia Beauty Contest,' which attracted more than 1,000 spectators to nearby McNab's Island.[47] The Halifax Trades and Labor Council appeared no different from the city's other fraternal societies and service clubs. As part of the fund-raising drive for the labour temple, the council hosted an 'Industrial, Auto and Fashion Show' in November 1928. The show displayed a bizarre mix of contemporary gender-based commercialism and traditional regional culture. In a strange way this reflected the depth and breadth of Halifax working-class interests. Alongside the automobiles and the fashion show were demonstrations of old-time cloth making on hand-looms, a display of hooked rugs and mats, and a fiddlers' contest.[48] This jumbled exhibition is particularly interesting because of its potential appeal to all tastes regardless of age, gender, or class.

Like the service clubs of the middle class, unions also participated in community services. For instance, the tramway employees participated as a group in an unsuccessful search for a lost boy in 1921, and the painters' union volunteered to paint the old Dutch Church in 1927.[49] This type of public-relations activity was very different from the practice of self-help or mutual assistance. As unions abandoned politics and adopted activities with mass appeal, they appeared to be on the road to the secular union.

The concept of a workingmen's organization, an association without connections to work or politics, was raised several times in the attempts to form a workingmen's club for Richmond Heights residents. In the winter of 1921, the joy of domesticity seems to have been wearing thin, as it was suggested that one of the vacant stores in the Hydrostone District be turned into a club where men could 'gather for quiet evenings of cards, chess or dominos, away from home.' In 1924 this proposal was again raised 'by a number of Richmond Heights residents,' but the continued poor economy made cost a barrier. Unions had to serve as the workingmen's club, and in 1928 the labour movement was finally able to achieve the long-term goal of purchasing a labour temple that fulfilled a primarily social function.[50]

The other explicit working-class image of male leisure activities pertained to young single men and their actions as hoodlums and gang members. In this instance, class, gender, and age intersected to create an apparently unique culture based upon male bonding and exploration of the boundaries of masculinity through courage, cunning, and nonconformity.[51]

The sons of Richmond Heights were regularly noted as a bad lot. Juvenile vandals cut down a clothes-line on Kane Street and placed the clothes on the front step. A report concluded that 'the fact that the clothes were not stolen proves that this is the work of juveniles who seem to find pleasure from such mad pranks which cause so much annoyance to mothers of baby children.' Other regular pranks included stealing milk bottles and groceries left at back doors and stealing rides by jumping on the rear of tram cars.[52] A 'gang of hoodlums in the Hydrostone' between the ages of sixteen and twenty also annoyed residents by interfering with shoppers in the Hydrostone Block, breaking fences, throwing stones through windows, and congregating at nearby Fort Needham to 'sing and shout at all hours of the night ...'[53] The most persistent complaints, however, referred to 'garden vandalism.' Boys were blamed for stealing tulip bulbs and destroying trees. During the summer of 1921, garden vandalism in the neighbourhood was so severe that the HRC had to hire a watchman for regular patrol. Army pensioner William Colt of 2 Hennessey Place seems to have been a regular victim of the boys' actions. A person or persons unknown ignored his sign to 'Have a Heart and Keep off Grass' and removed all the plants from his yard in 1921. It was again noted in 1924 and 1929 that his garden was 'ravaged by hoodlums.'[54]

High unemployment would have been particularly hard on young boys who had finished school and were not able to find work. Unlike their sisters, who could always at least enter domestic service, teenage boys had little choice. Classes at Alexander McKay school were regularly disrupted during the winter of 1923 by the noise of 'large boys who do not go to school, who skate while school is in session.'[55] Several residents of Richmond Heights noted that because of the long unemployment of their teenage boys, they were getting behind in rent. The

Bothwells who resided at 22 Sebastian Place throughout the decade went into arrears when son 'Buster' lost his job. Similarly, Mrs Gunn wrote that 'the oldest boy has not been able to get work for a year,' and that this made it impossible to begin paying any of the rent owed. During William Gunn's period of unemployment, he had in fact been charged with assault after a snowball he threw knocked out two teeth of another boy. The frustration of being denied the opportunity to become a man, since poor economic conditions blocked access to work and made it impossible to express masculinity through wage earning, encouraged some Richmond Heights adolescents to express themselves in what was considered a deviant manner. Most of the activity was directed against property or violated the regulation of public space.[56] This behaviour alone appears to have had no cross-class equivalent, but this could be explained by the specialized group involved and the fact that middle-class adolescent males would be less likely to face youth unemployment because their education lasted longer. Vandalism and gang activities were only one aspect of working-class male adolescent culture. Teenage boys also participated in sports in much the same manner as men.

Absorption in sports, as athletes or spectators, was characteristic of men across all classes, though the activities were usually class based. Sport, such as the baseball games organized during the building trades strike of 1919, could reinforce class loyalties. The various building trades scheduled afternoon games to keep up the spirits of striking workers.[57] The popularity of sport among the city's workers was also evident in the central role it played in annual Labour Day activities.

Leisure and work were not completely distinct, since company teams and leagues were evident throughout the city. Bowling was a particularly popular company sport because the ability to participate did not depend on the age and physical condition of the employee. Moirs operated an interdepartmental bowling league and participated in the City Commercial League, which had twenty teams representing a wide range of businesses and factories.[58] Other commercial leagues were less successful. In 1921, the baseball league had only five teams and the hockey league only three. The Halifax Commercial Baseball League was reorganized in 1928 with six teams playing Tuesday and Thursday evenings on the Commons. Participation in commercial leagues and intramural sports reflected local employment levels. High levels of employment at the shipyard in early 1921 meant that hockey games between the boilermakers and the machinists could be organized. Company picnics, such as the annual events hosted by Eaton's, the CNR, or MT&T, always had a sports component such as the annual baseball game between the Eaton's furniture division and the employees of the main store. At the MT&T picnic, job skills and athletic competition merged as male employees competed against each other in job-related events such as pole climbing, cable splicing, and line throwing.[59]

Baseball was the most popular working-class sport, since it was inexpensive, with practically no special equipment or facilities needed, and took relatively little time to play or watch. Furthermore, as a game, it encouraged what Colin Howell has described as 'manly virtue' – the characteristics of courage, strength, agility, teamwork, decision making ability, and foresight.[60] In Halifax, spectator baseball was dominated by the Twilight League, whose games were played on the North Commons on Monday, Wednesday, and Friday evenings during the 1920s. The league was composed of six teams, all roughly associated with working-class neighbourhoods.[61] The Federals and St Agnes represented the West End, the Casinos and St Patrick's the North End, and the Willow Parks and St Joseph's the far North End, including Richmond Heights. The Catholic teams corresponded to parishes and were associated with the amateur athletic clubs that operated from their gymnasiums. Twilight League matches on the Commons were free of charge and attracted as many as 2,000 fans.[62]

In contrast to the success of the Twilight League was the decline of the Halifax Senior Amateur Baseball League. The league was organized in 1920 and was composed of four teams representing two of the city's amateur athletic clubs, the Wanderers and the Crescents, the Great War Veterans' Association, and a Dartmouth team. Games, held in the Wanderers' grounds, with twenty-five cents charged and an extra ten-cent fee to sit in the grandstand or bleachers, were barely able to attract 500 fans. In 1925, the Crescents dropped out of the league, and in the following season the league did not operate.[63] The Twilight League was able to attract the fans because of a combination of free admission, a high standard of play, and the fact that many of the players on the six teams would have been known to North End residents. Two Richmond Heights residents were among the baseball stars of the Twilight League. Leo Churchill of Livingstone Street was an athlete with the Shamrock Amateur Athletics Club and manager of the North End Soft Ball League. Similarly, Nelson Comeau, a fireman living on Stairs Street, played baseball throughout the twenties on both the Federals and the St Agnes teams before a work-related accident in 1930 ended his sports career.[64]

Even when sports were supposedly separated from work, employment could touch upon leisure.

Despite the tremendous appeal of organized sports, the popularity of hunting and fishing may offer the best insight into local notions of manhood.[65] Masculinity was tied not only to work and the ability to support a family, but, for the respectable working-class, to nature as well. Edward Rotundo has drawn attention to the relationship between the American popular misunderstanding of Darwin's theory of evolution and the widespread view of man as animal. Rotundo noted that some men literally accepted the idea that 'they were part animal. They left their civilized urban environment for the woods and the Western plains, hoping to cultivate their own "natural" masculine strength and aggressiveness.'[66] Total escape from their daily life was not an option for Richmond Heights men, but with the number of woods, lakes, and streams nearby, it was possible to have the experience of battling nature with a rod or gun in an environment totally removed from domestic responsibilities or the presence of women.

Hunting and fishing were the antithesis of work in a warehouse or shipyard and provided a welcome contrast to modern industrial capitalism, the de-skilling of work, life in the city, and the rise of domesticity. They played upon the nostalgic appeal of a rural existence, as seen in the very idea of the garden suburb, in which man conquered nature. At the same time, hunting and fishing, like the garden, offered an escape from widespread domesticity. They reinforced what was manly about men in the same way that the boy-scout movement hoped to do by teaching about nature and outdoor survival skills in the urban environment.[67]

Recreational hunting and fishing could be considered either work or play, and yet for men such as Bill Vallance it was their favourite leisure activity. Both sports had in fact many parallels with work, as they required a specialized skill or knowledge and could augment the pay packet by helping to feed the family. In addition, like most forms of male employment, hunting and fishing excluded women. The sports were generally a communal activity, yet it was the achievement of the individual in the kill or the catch that was important. In this manner, hunting and fishing transform some of the characteristics of an older form of work into play.

The popularity of fishing in Richmond Heights was suggested by the large assortment of fishing gear available at the Hydrostone Hardware store and the owner's annual advertisement of this fact.[68] Other advertisers in the labour paper indicate that the intended audience might be interested in fishing and hunting supplies. A chandlery on Water Street advertised tents, blankets, and kit bags, a grocery store suitable fishing food, and sporting-goods stores guns and ammunition.[69]

Fishing was particularly widespread, since Halifax was situated close to 'simply hundreds of lakes and streams ... and in nearly all of them trout are plentiful.'[70] Fishing also had the advantage of being inexpensive to practise; and, unlike shooting, it could be carried out on a Sunday. The trout season lasted from May to October, with the best catches in the first two weeks of May. The widespread practice of Sunday fishing was noted in the 1929 debate around Sunday tennis. The *Citizen* replied that 'There is no more harm in that than in going blueberrying or trout fishing, but it seems to me that the class who play tennis usually have time to enjoy the game every day in the week, while the other class have but one day and it is Sunday.' The catches of North End anglers were occasionally referred to in the newspapers, but the activity may have been so great a part of daily life that it merited little attention.[71]

Hunting would have been difficult for many Richmond Heights residents, since shooting was forbidden on Sunday, the primary day for recreation. However, rabbits and partridges could be shot nearby and did not require an entire day's outing. Moose were the ultimate prize, and throughout the decade, between 844 and 1,780 big-game licences were purchased annually by residents of Halifax County alone.[72] The perception of the sportsman as tourist appears to have been exaggerated, as non-resident big-game hunting was minimal, and only 100 non-resident licences were granted between 1924 and 1926.[73] Most sportsmen in the province were in fact local residents and were drawn from all classes.

Other hobbies were also connected to nature. Henry Sinclair, resident of 6 Sebastian Place, raised African owls in an owlery covering nearly the space of an entire lot on Gottingen Street. The expenditure of time and money on these birds must have been considerable. Sinclair owned approximately 125 birds in 1927 and had travelled to Toronto where he swept the bird competition at the Royal Winter Fair, winning twenty-six out of the twenty-eight categories, including best bird.[74]

Gardens were common and popular among men in Richmond Heights and were actively encouraged by the HRC, local newspapers, and the Massachusetts-Halifax Health Commission. The HRC, in fact, presented annual prizes of $15, $10, and $5 for the best gardens in the neighbourhood, and local observers noted that 'No sooner have fathers and husbands finished suppers than they are out planting, raking and hoeing.'

The assumption that men were responsible for the garden was also implicit in a criticism made of the Hydrostone development that appeared in *Social Welfare*. This report on housing in Halifax noted that the space allocated for gardening was too small 'for the new era of the eight hour day.' Men, after all, were most likely to experience the reduction of working hours, thereby gaining the extra time to work outside in the garden. Within the Hydrostone, the virtual absence of property meant that the tiny front yards were often completely dug up in order to provide either vegetable or flower gardens.[75] During the celebrations for the Diamond Jubilee of Confederation in the summer of 1927, Hennessey Place gardeners supplemented their elaborate gardens with flags, bunting, coloured electric lights, evergreen swags, and Chinese lanterns. The following summer, flower gardens on Livingstone Place were so attractive with their displays of dahlias, gladioli, and sweet peas that they attracted visitors to the neighbourhood and promoted ardent competition among male gardeners. The enthusiasm for gardening could also bring neighbours together, as the limited space available encouraged neighbours to cooperate and join their front plots. An excited gardener spending the winter with his son in Massachusetts ended a letter to the commission with a spirited, 'so roll on spring and then HO! for the Garden.'[76]

The popularity of gardening and the rise of domesticity for men poses an interesting question about the control of space within the household. The garden was a liminal area, distinct yet attached to the home, where men could exercise independence apart from their spouse. There were also connections between gardening and rural nostalgia, apparent in the concept of the garden suburb and the continued popularity of fishing and hunting, and between gardening and the independent-producer ideology held by many skilled workers. Through individual skilled effort, men were able to challenge nature and cultivate the urban environment.

There was no language available to recognize the male contribution to domestic production, so activities such as alcohol production, gardening, hunting, and fishing were described as hobbies or leisure activities. These activities in fact contributed to the welfare of the household and improved the standard of living of its members. Even puttering, an activity, that may have been restricted to the working class of Britain and North America, improved the living conditions of household members and reflected the presence of house pride that was by no means restricted to women. Indeed, the work of men and women was regarded as so distinct that there was no way of conceptualizing or expressing unpaid production by urban working-class men within the domestic sphere.[77]

A perception of society that completely separated the work of men and women distorts important connections within the household. At the same time, under the economic structure of advanced industrial capitalism all men had much more in common beyond the household. Heroes such as baseball star Babe Ruth, boxer Joe Louis, and pilot Charles Lindbergh continued to achieve their goals through the traditional qualities of masculinity such as bravery, skill, strength, and individualism. Nevertheless, the age-old characteristics of strength and skill were replaced with a new kind of manhood based on the ability to support a family; a test that depended as much on general economic trends and luck as on any abilities or qualities the individual might possess. It was no wonder that many men were attracted to the ideas of rural nostalgia.

Leisure and work established common links among all men, even though the actual activities continued to take place within and to reinforce class-based social groupings. This class-based sociability of men preserved if not a separate class culture then a distinct male working-class social environment. This masculine society had little problem co-existing with domesticity, since it did not touch upon the private world of home. The strength and importance of these social bonds should not be underestimated, for they did foster a feeling of community and shared experience and they were able to preserve a male working-class identity against the onslaught of mass culture. Yet the relationship between working-class men and mass culture was not exclusively oppositional. On the basis of a male working-class social environment and through conscious effort, the workers, fathers, husbands, sportsmen, and lodge members were instrumental in instigating or promoting some of Halifax's most obvious examples of what might be considered mass culture: the beauty pageant, the auto show, and the baseball game.

7

Young Women

The enduring icon of the 1920s in North America is a young woman. Class does not easily adhere to images of flappers, 'business girls,' or boyish athletes, and though class by no means disappeared, a new identity based solely upon the appearance of young working-class women seems to have emerged that eclipsed class and focused upon age and gender. In fact, one English contemporary noted that the most important change in female fashion in the 1920s was not the bobbed hair, short skirt, or 'boyish' figure, but rather the increasing difficulty of determining 'what class someone belonged to by looking at their clothes'.[1] Certainly 'the girl of the new day' looked dramatically different from her mother, to say nothing of her grandmother. But were the fashion trends, the new ideals of feminine beauty, and the veneer of classlessness indications of merely superficial change or of a more profound societal transformation? For the daughters and female boarders of Richmond Heights, the changes in their appearance represented the most immediate effects of the new opportunities available to them in the expanding lower levels of the white-collar sector as well as their personal integration into mass consumer culture. As a result, young women from St John's to Victoria looked, acted, and perhaps even spoke differently from other members of their households.

Leisure activities of young women received a disproportionate amount of attention from the press and social commentators. Most young women in Canada did not spend the majority of their time dancing or challenging community standards. The young, single women who lived in Richmond Heights were not flappers, but rather an assortment of factory workers, retail clerks, and 'business-girls.' While national statistics revealed an increased percentage of women in the total labour market from 15.5 per cent in 1921 to 19.9 per cent a decade later, in Halifax the perception that women were increasing their importance in the Halifax labour market cannot be supported numerically. Locally, women composed 25.5 per cent of the labour force in 1921, and the numbers increased to only 26.9 per cent ten years later (table 4). In fact, the Halifax experience for wage-earning women between 1920 and 1930 is consistent with the conclusions of American historian Lisa Duggan, who has stated that during the 1920s the numerical expansion of the female workforce slowed to a virtual stop and destroyed the possibility of continuing growth towards economic self-sufficiency for women.[2] Historians have emphasized female participation in the labour market during the 1920s, but the Halifax example suggests an actual decline in the number of young women under twenty-five years of age who were working for wages. Although young workers remained the most important constituency of the female labour force, any visible or recorded growth in Halifax was achieved by women over the age of twenty-five.[3]

Attention to numbers of employed women has obscured the more important change in the occupations where women were likely to find employment. In 1911, 23 per cent of Halifax wage-earning women were employed in manufacturing, a sector that by 1931 accounted for only 8 per cent of all wage-earning women. This drop coincided with an admittedly less dramatic national shift from manufacturing, which employed 27 per cent of the Canadian female labour force in 1911 and 18.4 per cent in 1931. This sector included women employed in offices within manufacturing, so the actual number of women involved in production would have been less. When the 1931 census provided for the first time a distinction between employment in economic and occupational sectors, the new category 'clerical' immediately claimed 23.9 per cent of Halifax female wage-earners.[4]

By 1931, new opportunities emerging in the clerical, retail, and service sectors did not dislodge domestic service from its long-established position as the single most important female occupation.[5] Private domestic service continued to be the largest employer of women, and it accounted for nearly a third of the under-twenty-five female Halifax workforce in 1931. This prominence lasted longer in Halifax than in other cities such as Toronto, but its tenacity did not necessarily reflect the actual employment opportunities available for urban working-class daughters. It appears that few women from Richmond Heights were actually involved in domestic service. Of the 690 female occupational listings that appeared in the city directories between 1920 and 1929,

TABLE 4
Female labour and the Halifax workforce, 1911–1931

	1911	1921	1931
Population of Halifax	46,619	58,372	59,275
Total workforce	13,784	23,063	23,017
Total female workforce	4,487	5,888	6,188*
Females as per cent of total workforce	32.6	25.5	26.9
Female workforce < 25	2,320	3,053	2,565
Per cent of female workforce < 25	51.7	51.9	41.5

* An age breakdown is available only for the 5,236 women who reported their earnings in 1931.

SOURCES: Canada, *Census*, 1911, vol. 6, table 6: 326–35; 1921, vol. 4, table 5: 382–99; 1931, vol. 2, table 12: 31, vol. 5, table 36: 572–5, vol. 7, table 43: 267–77, and table 57: 739–45; Veronica Strong-Boag, *The New Day Recalled: The Lives of Girls and Women in English Canada, 1919–1939* (Toronto 1988), 43.

only fifteen women were listed in the largest female occupation. This figure was undoubtedly low, since some women engaged in this type of work on a part-time or temporary basis, or resided with their employers in other districts and so would not have shown up in the count. Women in domestic service in Richmond Heights were most likely to be resident housekeepers for unmarried male relatives. Together with the six women listed as 'maids,' they represented only the smallest proportion of neighbourhood wage-earning women.

Most young women employed in domestic service were probably migrants from rural areas of the region and were without family in the city. Like other urban centres in Canada, Halifax attracted young women, and females between the ages of fifteen and thirty outnumbered males in the same age group. No doubt this female majority was further inflated by urban male outmigration. For young migrants from the country, domestic service was often the only possible form of employment. Low wages for women meant it was difficult and at times impossible for young working women without family to subsidize room and board to support themselves. On the other hand, domestic servants who received room and board could subsist on their 1921 average annual salary of $230.[6] The paltry wages, low prestige, and isolation of domestic service, however, did not appeal to young urban women who had the option of living inexpensively with their family and surviving on low wages.[7]

The decline of domestic service as the most prominent occupation for urban working-class daughters contributed to the appearance of their classlessness, since wage employees could claim an independence unattainable by those in service. The transfer of women from domestic service also elevated women as consumers because as wage-earners they received all their earnings in cash rather than in a combination of cash and board. Finally, occupational change permitted the development of a collective workplace culture.[8] New employment opportunities were physically less isolating, and the communal nature of most wage-work positions inadvertently promoted a sociability impossible in the solitude of private homes.

If the daughters and boarders of Richmond Heights families were unlikely to be found in domestic service, where were they employed? Did the employment of female labour in a residential working-class neighbourhood differ from that in the city or the nation as a whole? To answer these questions we must turn to an unsatisfactory source – the annual city directories. Undoubtedly, these directories missed many male heads of household among this transitory population, and their records on young women were probably even less complete. Nevertheless, the directories do provide the names, occupations, and addresses of 327 individual employed females between 1920 and 1929. The largest number of women, approximately one in three, were engaged in trade or retail. Employment in manufacturing was concentrated at the Moirs confectionery factory, which over the decade employed sixty-six women from the subdivision. In addition, thirteen women were listed as employed in clothing manufacture, nine as laundry workers, eight in other assorted manufacturing positions, and six in the skilled trades of bookbinding or printing. The growing importance of clerical positions was clearly demonstrated by the thirty-one women listed as stenographers, twenty-five as operators, and seventeen as assorted non-retail clerks. Not all women were employed in traditional working-class occupations, since the directory lists seven teachers, six nurses, and one doctor. These occupations indicated specialized training and possible upward mobility, but perhaps more importantly the continuing residency of young women with their families.

A breakdown of directory listings on a year-by-year basis provides

TABLE 5
Female employment by economic sector, 1911–1931

	Halifax			Canada		
	1911	1921	1931	1911	1921	1931
Primary	0.1	0.0	0.1	4.4	3.8	3.8
Manufacturing	23.0	13.0	8.3	27.0	21.6	18.4
Electric light and						
power	0.0	0.0	0.3	0.0	0.1	0.3
Transportation	1.7	5.7	5.0	1.9	3.4	4.3
Construction	0.3	0.6	0.6	0.1	0.1	0.2
Trade	16.5	21.6	22.5	11.6	15.6	16.5
Service	58.4	51.7	62.7	55.0	50.4	56.8
Other	0.0	6.4	0.5	0.0	4.1	0.6

SOURCES: Canada, *Census*, 1911, vol. 6, table 6: 326–35; 1921, vol. 4, table 5: 382–99; 1931, vol. 2, table 12: 31, vol. 5, table 36: 572–5, vol. 7, table 43: 267–77, and table 57: 739–45.

683 listings. The number of women listed in the directory in any given year varied from 92 in 1921 and 1929 to 44 in 1924 (see appendix table B). When these are further broken down into occupational sectors, they suggest the growth of service and trade at the expense of manufacturing. These service occupations ranged from waitresses and laundry workers to government clerks, teachers, and nurses. For every year in the second half of the decade, clerical and sales occupations composed more than half the identified female occupations. These numbers suggest that national long-term trends in the female labour force were exaggerated in the local context of Richmond Heights. Rapid regional deindustrialization meant that the speed of transition in female employment from manufacturing to service and clerical jobs and the timing were specific to Halifax, though the shift from manufacturing and domestic service was also reproduced to a limited extent in the national statistics in the growth of clerical, service, and retail work for women (table 5).

Despite local deindustrialization, a confectionery factory remained the largest employer of female labour in Richmond Heights throughout the 1920s. The factory warrants a brief examination, because of both its economic importance and the connection with traditional opportunities for working-class women that it offered. Moirs was not only the most important employer for the neighbourhood, but after the destruction of the cotton factory in the explosion, it became the most important employer of female labour in the whole city. This Halifax firm was originally founded in 1816 as a bakery, but at the turn of the century, progressive management steered the company into the manufacture of chocolates and confectionery.[9] This specialization succeeded, and in November 1927 Moirs opened a new factory that claimed to be the tallest commercial building in the Maritimes as well as the largest candy factory in the country.[10] The payroll of May 1929 listed a total of 1,100 employees, with a large number of women employed in candy and box manufacturing.[11]

Confectionery manufacture remained labour-intensive and was largely dependent upon inexpensive female labour. Low wages were compounded in the industry by unpleasant working conditions. Many found the unavoidable smell of chocolate sweetly sickening and the factory climate uncomfortable because the temperature had to be less than sixty-five degrees to create the optimal conditions required to harden the chocolate. Chocolate dipping was the most prestigious and skilled position open to women in the factory, and at Moirs a two-year apprenticeship was necessary. Employees worked for either an hourly wage or a piece-work rate with all being subject to fines of ten cents a pound for an imperfect product. Wages at Moirs were very low: nineteen-year-old Annie May Cunningham was reported to have been earning $5.23 a week in 1918. As well, the hours were irregular, and depending on the season, the factory either operated a night shift and demanded overtime work or was closed with temporary layoffs.[12] It is difficult to trace job turnover, but in addition to the many Richmond Heights women who passed through Moirs and then disappeared from the record, at least six young women from Richmond Heights left positions at Moirs for alternative employment in retail, and one woman left the firm for waitressing.[13] The directories indicated only two instances of women who left other places of employment for work at Moirs, and both of these women did so to escape the declining millinery trade. Like domestic service, employment at Moirs was not desirable. Although a job at Moirs was less isolated than one in domestic service, the poor pay, tedious work, and uncomfortable working conditions made it generally unattractive and definitely less prestigious than employment in retail.

As a large employer during the 1920s coping with a high turnover of employees, it is not surprising that Moirs became involved in the welfare-capitalism movement. But the particular flavour of welfare capitalism adopted reflected its largely young female workforce.[14] Welfare programs, such as discretionary pension plans, were largely designed for men in order to help them acquire property or provide benefits for their families when they were unable to fulfil their roles as breadwinners.[15] The argument went that property and security would create a stable workforce. Women, on the other hand, were less likely to hold property and were not supposed to be responsible for dependents. Therefore, Moirs concentrated on the third component of welfare capitalism – recreation – providing a library, first-aid room, and company orchestra and planning a lunch room where women could eat hot meals at cost. As with the large employer of female labour in Joy Parr's study of an Ontario textile company, social activities formed the heart of the corporate-welfare plan. Moirs emphasized cultural activities and ignored the type of programs for providing sick benefits and pensions that were adopted at MT&T. Dance classes for employees were held weekly in the recreation rooms of the Moirs Welfare Bureau. On Saturday afternoons during the summer, the female employees of some departments were taken on outings.[16] Within the company were 'clubs' whose membership was based on gender and occupation. The females who constituted the Pyramid Builders (Paper Box Department) and the Triangle and Merrymakers clubs hosted theme dances and participated in athletic events. The Young Women's Christian Association (YWCA) offered its camp at Hubbards to the Moirs Welfare Bureau for the Dominion Day weekend of 1927, and forty young women participated in the weekend events on the South Shore.[17] Perhaps by emphasizing recreational activities and creating a factory-based social life, Moirs was trying to offset its unattractive working conditions and compensate workers for the low prestige of the job. Dances and picnics, however, were not sufficient counterweights, and women left the factory when sales or clerking positions became available elsewhere.

An exception to the women employed in the usual narrow range of occupations was Dr Florence J. Murray. Dr Murray was a recent graduate of the Dalhousie Medical School, who set up housekeeping on Sebastian Place while she was trying to save money to repay her family for educational expenses before leaving as a medical missionary to Korea. The presence of Murray in the neighbourhood illustrates the complexity that family often brings to generalizations about class. Although Murray was a physician and employed at Dalhousie as a demonstrator in anatomy, she had two brothers employed as labourers at the Halifax Shipyards.[18]

The case of Murray reminds us of the multitude of connections that link women's work outside the home to domestic responsibilities and family pressures. The young women of Richmond Heights were not 'women adrift.' Indeed, daughters tended to be anchored to family in such a way that mutiny or continued pressed service were the only two courses available. Female boarders who chose to live in Richmond Heights consciously accepted reduced independence and privacy in exchange for superior housing conditions. While some young working women in Toronto in the 1920s may have opted to live away from home or outside a family environment, this form of lodging was not widely available in Halifax, so that young women not living with kin were nevertheless usually in a family environment. As a result, few women in Richmond Heights were free from domestic responsibility, whether this was in the form of financial assistance or labour. According to the number of hours worked, the seasonality of employment, and particular family circumstances, some female wage-earners were burdened with a great deal of domestic responsibility, while at the opposite extreme, others may have escaped such responsibility entirely.[19] Most young women probably fell somewhere in the middle.

The death of a mother or the disruption of household operations due to childbirth or illness affected the domestic responsibilities of young women. Glady McTier's mother died from complications after the explosion, and an accident in the railway yard killed her father when she was twelve.[20] Thereafter, Glady McTier was raised by her mother's spinster aunt. As the eldest girl with two younger sisters, she had already begun housework at an early age, but the death of her father increased her responsibilities dramatically. Glady McTier remembered that though she had some responsibilities before her father's death, he had done most of the housework. Once she lived with her great-aunt, Glady McTier lost the freedom to play when all the scrubbing 'was slapped on.' Annie English bore a similar burden of household labour when her mother's death affected her career opportunities. English had left high school for MT&T where she rose quickly to become chief operator of the North Halifax exchange. The death of her mother, however, made it necessary for her to resign her position and return home as a full-time housekeeper. Presumably, it was when her brothers and sisters became older that she was able to return to work as chief night operator of the other city exchange.[21] Childbirth or illness also placed additional responsibility on young women. In 1922, a Yarmouth Victorian Order of Nurses (VON) maternity nurse noted the involvement of the eldest daughter in assisting the mother with infant care and household responsibilities. While these examples might be unusual, they cannot be considered exceptional. The work of daughters could also pall beside the domestic labour of their mothers. Stella Shore, an employee at Simpson's whose family lived on Sebastian Place, recalled that while everyone was expected to 'pitch in', her own contribution was small when compared with the arduous labour performed by her mother.[22] Even for those few young women who did not live with their family and therefore had full responsibility for their own laundry, cooking, and cleaning, the 'double day' of waged employment and domestic upkeep was probably not as demanding as the work day of their mothers, who usually had many responsibilities beyond their own personal needs and, in the words of Stella Shore, were always 'slaving.'

It is impossible to determine the number of women in the neighbourhood who were boarders. For example, it is difficult to identify lodgers who were related and shared the same surname as the household in which they stayed. In addition, a different surname did not necessarily indicate a non-kin relationship with the household. Rural female relatives would have been an important part of the urban influx.[23] Richmond Heights women with different surnames from the household head were likely to be employed in retail or at Moirs. Twenty-five of the 112 women listed as retail clerks or saleswomen and 21 of the 66 employees at Moirs fell into this category. The likelihood that Moirs employees were also boarders is consistent with a report from the company that it drew workers from across Nova Scotia and Prince Edward Island. The Employment Bureau reported in 1927 that there were 'quite a large number of work seekers from outside points applying at this office ... [and] the major proportion of those looking for employment are girls, seeking work in factories.'[24] Although independent young women constituted part of the community, their numbers were significantly less than those indicated in Joanne Meyerowitz's Chicago study, where one-fifth to one-sixth of the non-servant female population did not live with family in the 1920s.[25] Ultimately, Richmond Heights was not an attractive location for most boarders, because it was too far away from both employment opportunities and the downtown core.

Many girls had no choice but to stay at home and take advantage of the inexpensive lodging that only their family could provide. Miss Palmer of the YWCA informed the 1920 Nova Scotia Minimum Wage Commission that the average board in Halifax was between $5 and $6 a week. The YWCA had been charging $6.50 but was losing money and had recently increased its rates by $2 a week. The same commission con-cluded that the high cost of boarding meant that many factory girls lived at home, paying no room and board or only a fraction of the usual cost, and that in many cases these young women depended 'on their parents for a living, [and](in part or in whole) work for wages that provide them with little more than spending money.'[26] Such an ar-rangement existed for Sebastian Place resident Stella Shore, since living away from home would have been unthinkable on the $5 a week she earned at the Simpson's warehouse. Instead, she lived at home and paid her mother $3 a week in board. This amount was considerably below the going rate.[27] While she received room and board at a reduced rate, she also contributed money to household coffers that were often low because the family was dependent on the seasonal wages of her carpenter father. Family support was a two-way relationship in which dependence and independence, advantages and disadvantages existed on both sides.

The earnings of young women were a common part of household financial strategy. The importance of their relatively meagre contribu-tion was noted by a columnist in the local labour newspaper when he praised young women for 'contributing to the budget and making life a little easier for a worried father ... helping younger sisters and brothers with their education,' and 'aiding the children of a brother who married young and who hasn't seemed to be able to get a real start.'[28] The earnings of young women were extracted for the use of the entire fam-ily. In one specific example, the low wages and irregular hours of her husband led Mrs Wetherington of 22 Columbus Place to initiate a job search for her daughters. 'I took my 2 girls down to Moirs, Bauld Bros, Tobins, Morses, Wentzells and Jensen and Mills and Mr Wilks['] store on Young St and put their name down at the 13 cents store also the 25 cents store,' wrote Mrs Wetherington to the Halifax Relief Commission (HRC). Emphasizing her own role in this attempt to pay the rent, Mrs Wetherington concluded 'I have tr[ied] everywhere I took them my-self.'[29] Whether or not it was usual for a mother to undertake the search for work on behalf of her daughters cannot be determined; however, in times of financial crisis such as failure to pay the rent, all available resources were explored.

The role of Mrs Wetherington in her daughters' search for work is suggestive of the many ties that linked the family and the workplace. Family connections could secure a position, interfere with work rela-tions, and even terminate employment. Many young women worked for the same company as their fathers. Dorothy Vallance, daughter of an MT&T foreman, worked as an operator at MT&T, while Florence Foot found a position at her father's firm, Brandram-Henderson. Sisters also provided a contact for employment. One Hennessey Street family had three daughters employed consecutively at Moirs. Beyond acquiring the job, parents could also intrude into the workplace on their daughters' behalf, as in the case of the father who wrote to the company for his daughter regarding her entitlement to sick benefits at MT&T. Molly Artz, also an employee at MT&T, resigned from her position because of 'the desire of her parents, now resident in the U.S.A. who wish to have her beside them.' Family exerted a great deal of pressure on daughters, and this control has been cited as a prime motivation for escape, whether through early marriage or outmigration.[30]

The pressure exerted by families on daughters was not always successful, and conflict reveals that the increasing intrusion of the state into family life could be at the request of family members. While concern over young men's delinquency usually related to vandalism and theft and the sanctity of private property, anxiety over young women was likely to focus on their sexuality. In April 1932, Mrs James of Columbus Place contacted the city's policewoman about her daughter, whose behaviour she could not govern. In this case, policewoman May Virtue approached the local priest, who explained the situation by labelling the girl as 'insane,' and thereby directly linking expressed sexuality with feeble-mindedness.[31] In a similar case involving seventeen-year-old Jessie Miller of Hennessey Place, the girl's aunt contacted Officer Virtue on behalf of Jessie's widowed mother, who could not prevent her from staying out all night.[32] Virtue issued a warrant for the girl and the case was processed through the courts. In both cases, a family member initiated the complaint and requested the involvement of the law in an essentially private family matter. Intervention of the courts into family life to control the behaviour of daughters was not unique to Halifax. Similar experiences or situations have been cited recently in a study of Toronto. Carolyn Strange has argued that legal action could be pursued when a daughter refused to balance 'personal pleasure with her domestic duty.'[33] Jessie Miller and Mrs James's daughter remind us that the responsibilities placed upon young women were not always accepted, and the forms rebellion took were varied and individually based.

Rebellion in the workplace was also varied and individually based. Intermittent work and low pay did not encourage self-sufficiency in the workplace. A 1920 survey of forty-nine employers who employed 2,032 female labourers in Nova Scotia reported that the women worked an average of 50.4 hours a week. The average, however, disguises great variations for the many women employed in jobs affected by seasonal fluctuations. While waitresses might work a seven-day week consisting of a total of between seventy-three and eighty-one hours, laundry workers' employment was seasonal and throughout the winter was based on a four-day work week.[34] The number of weeks of employment in a year also created significant variation in the total number of hours worked and the potential earnings available. While bookbinders and municipal clerks in Halifax were employed for the full fifty-two weeks in 1921, women employed at Moirs in the manufacturing of biscuits and confectionery worked less than forty-six weeks. Six weeks of unemployment throughout the year was devastating when the average weekly wage was $9.09. The irregularity of work, along with the extremes of overtime, night work, and unemployment, must also have affected young women's ability to participate in domestic labour around the household. Obviously, questions of the 'double day' for young women who worked both inside and beyond the home were complicated and related to specific employment circumstances.

Most female wage-earners were young and had short employment histories. Examination of ages, numbers of years of experience, and wage levels for women leaving employment at MT&T reveals that most women were concentrated at the lowest pay levels because of youth and relatively limited experience with the company. Ninety-nine of the 487 departing women employees in 1921 had worked for less than a year. Furthermore, those employed for two years or less comprised nearly half of the total female workforce. As a result of this frequent turnover, most women were between the ages of seventeen and twenty and earned $6 to $11 a week.

Youth and short employment periods did not mean that women accepted their low wages without question. In May 1919, unorganized women employed in the Moirs chocolate factory struck for the eight-hour day. A year later the box makers at the same company also struck for higher wages.[35] Waitresses in a downtown café walked off their jobs for a one-day strike in support of a provincial minimum wage in October 1920.[36] These actions were unorganized and spontaneous, but a few pockets of female workers finally did succeed in unionization. Male trade unionists occasionally mentioned the need to organize women, but no action was taken until the arrival in 1929 of Sophie Mushkat

McClusky. McClusky, a Polish immigrant, who had experience in the Socialist Party of Canada both in Moncton and Alberta, began to organize Halifax female retail clerks in March 1929 out of the Workmen's Circle at the Robie Street Synagogue.[37] Despite the tepid support of local trade unionists, her organizational campaign expanded towards the women at Moirs. As a result of this effort, by the beginning of December 1929, 150 women were organized. Her success brought the support of some members of the Halifax District Trades and Labor Council executive, but the argument for organizing women presented by old labourites such as E.E. Pride and William Halliday was that low wages for women exploited the male breadwinner. Pride and Halliday, in their attempt to attract labour men to the cause, argued that low wages for young women who lived at home really hurt the male breadwinner who 'can ill afford to keep grown-up daughters so that cheap labor may be supplied to earn greater dividends for stockholders and owners.' But even this appeal to the self-interest of union men did little to attract interest. This became apparent when a local police agent reported that the Halifax District Trades and Labor Council was 'Not enthusiastic about organizing the working girls while there are still so many labor men unorganized.'[38] Once again it was clear that, according to the male trade unionist, men formed the 'real' working class and the basis for any significant movement.

As a result, group action in general was atypical of women, whose protests were characterized by their individuality and spontaneity. Class identity, as far as it was connected to the local labour movement, was largely conceived to be a masculine trait. The reluctance of male trade unionists to incorporate women into male forms of labour organization further emphasized the exclusion of women from a collective identity beyond their age or sex. Women, therefore, used other means to protest their conditions. Letters to the editor of Halifax newspapers publicized the shocking conditions of long hours and low wages. A woman who identified herself as 'S.P.' wrote to the 'Question and Answers' column of the *Mail-Herald*, and asked if there was labour legislation to prevent employers from demanding up to six hours of overtime and 'if the Department of Labour at Ottawa has any control over this kind of slavery.'[39] Another woman used the same means to bring charges of sexual harassment against her employer, whom she accused of 'using improper language and acting indecently towards female employees.'[40] 'One out of Work' expressed her anger after investigating an advertised position in a restaurant kitchen. The restaurant desired a cook who would work seven days a week, twelve hours a day, for a wage of $6 a week. Linking the low wages for women to the presence of prostitution in the city, she concluded that if Halifax women had 'a chance to work at a fair wages and decent hours and conditions' 'ninety per cent of our night walkers would disappear.'[41] The use of newspapers by individual women to air complaints about conditions, wages, and sexual harassment may have been important in the formation of public opinion, but it seems to have resulted in very few specific changes.

Individual action by women might also include feigning illness in order to go home early;[42] but certainly the most common methods of protesting working conditions and low wages were quitting, changing careers, and outmigration. When one woman at Moirs was denied her request to be transferred from an hourly rate to piece work, she found a new position as a shop clerk.[43] With respect to outmigration, the MT&T *Monthly Bulletin* noted the departure of a number of Halifax operators and stenographers who were off to Massachusetts to train as nurses. An advertisement that promised jobs for qualified teachers in Saskatchewan and Alberta may have provided an escape from the poor local conditions. Certainly a number of young women from Richmond Heights left for the United States without their families. Mabel and Hazel Larch of Columbus Place found employment in Boston, Hannah Hixon of Stanley Place left home for Philadelphia, and Hattie Howard, whose parents lived on Merkel Place, nursed in Massachusetts.[44]

When possible, young women left their jobs and entered new areas of employment such as retail and clerical work. It was from within these sectors that important changes emerged that had an impact on working-class life. As Veronica Strong-Boag points out, high-school education offered the best chance at white-collar employment.[45] Young girls willingly stayed in school longer and, in order to get the jobs in offices and department stores, adopted the standard grammar, speech tones, and dress of the middle class.[46] In the North End at St Patrick's High School, girls' enrolment outnumbered that of boys. In 1921, 197 girls were enrolled in grades nine through eleven compared to 55 boys. By the end of the decade, the number of boys enrolled in grades nine through eleven had increased somewhat to a total of 139 while the number of girls registered was 226.[47] Local high-school commercial courses and evening technical education for girls were supplemented by private commercial institutions such as Miss Murphy's Business College, founded in 1918. Higher education also became possible for a few daughters of the working class. Young women in the Richmond Heights neighbourhood took advantage of new educational opportunities offering specialized training for teachers, nurses, and business girls. Although a university education was not possible for most daughters of the Hydrostone District, there were exceptions. Paul Axelrod notes that approximately 13.4 per cent of Dalhousie students in the 1930s were children of skilled or unskilled workers.[48] Young residents of Richmond Heights whose wages were not immediately needed by their families and who could live at home were poised for educational upward mobility. In 1924, Albert Kelso moved his family from the Hydrostone District to Morris Street in the South End of the city for the convenience of his eldest daughter who was enrolled at Dalhousie University. The perceived importance of education to the Kelso family outstripped their financial resources, since they were behind on their rent at the time of their move. Education, however, did not result in upward mobility for this family, because the daughter contracted tuberculosis and the family declined into poverty under the expense of unsuccessful sanatorium treatments.[49] While this unhappy example may have been exceptional, it was not unique.

New educational opportunities created their own problems. Upward mobility could alienate daughters from family, and parents who had sacrificed much to give a daughter 'a good education and "a decent start" in life' found 'Now, to our dismay, we are beginning to realise – she has made it clear in many ways – that she despises us, her home, our poverty and our ignorance. We have scraped and saved to get her lots of the good things of life, but now she has become "a cut above us."'[50] Class tensions within the family must have been one by-product of the new models of behaviour and appearance that some working-class women found it possible to adopt through education, style of dress, and new employment opportunities.

While the aspirations resulting from the expansion of lower-level white-collar work for some women could increase family conflict, women in sales could also affect household consumption. L.D. McCann's study of R.G. Dun and Company records from 1881 to 1931 demonstrated that during the economic collapse of the 1920s, branch businesses were able to survive in the midst of local businesses that were failing and thereby managed to gain a greater percentage of the market share. This change in retail structure meant that young women increasingly found themselves employed by national chains such as Eaton's, Simpson's, Woolworth's, or the Metropolitan Store. These chains were definitely expanding. The new Simpson's store and mail-order warehouse were opened at Armdale in 1919, and in May 1929, Eaton's Department Store opened in a partially reconstructed six-storey building on Barrington Street.[51]

The preference of young women for work in sales rather than at Moirs was not based on hours or wages. Branch or chain 'five and dime' stores such as Woolworth's depended on a cheap rapidly changing labour force, and poor wages were compounded by long hours. The Nova Scotia 1910 Commission on Hours of Labor reported that in the summer some Halifax stores closed early at 6:00 p.m. with a short day on Saturday, but in the winter were open eleven hours a day with extended hours on Friday and Saturday evenings. If wages and hours were comparable with existing factory work, it seems likely that the attraction to sales could be found in a notion which is more vague, the prestige of white-collar work.[52] The elevated status associated with sales work allowed young single women of slightly different class backgrounds to mix at the workplace. Admittedly, class background affected the likelihood of employment at Woolworth's or some of the city's more exclusive stores, but unlike the private home or the factory, the office and the shop held the possibility of bringing together the daughters of the middle and working classes and facilitating the exchange of class behaviours and attitudes. The mixing of classes in the office with no differentiation in responsibilities, treatment, or appearance offered some young women an experience that was unique from that available to other family members. The narrow range of employment opportunities available for women therefore tended to de-emphasize class while accentuating the 'femaleness' of specific occupations.

New opportunities in employment may have confused women's sense of class identity, but clarified their self-perception as women. Susan Porter Benson in her study of American department stores has also argued that saleswomen were particularly important to changes in consumption. Saleswomen resented any sense of subordination to the customers they might serve, since they also played the role of customer when they were not working.[53] The position of sales clerking itself often encouraged the dilution of working-class behaviour and appearance. It was necessary to blend into the middle-class or élite whom the stores hoped to attract as their clientele.[54] Clothing took on new importance, particularly for those who came in contact with customers. According to Elizabeth Ewen, 'In a consumer society, the external definitions of self take on primary importance. Dress, style, the way the self is assembled became the terms of integration ...' Once clothing was purchased rather than produced, similar styles could be reproduced at accessible prices by using cheaper material and tailoring. In stores, similar clothing eliminated the appearance of class differences between employee and customer.[55]

In these female workplaces, clothing was not the only bond. The offices and stores that employed young women also fostered a workplace culture of heterosexual romance. The young women thrown together in these female jobs developed a preoccupation with the common interests of boyfriends, clothes, evening entertainment, and the romances of their fellow workers. This fixation with boyfriends was partly rooted in the economic reality that, for low-wage women, men were necessary to provide financial access to popular entertainment.[56]

In this context, marriage not only represented the culmination of the heterosexual experience, but also brought adult status with freedom from parental control and, usually, departure from the paid labour force. The preoccupation with marriage encouraged young women to get married at an early age. The ages of brides and grooms in North End Halifax is available only for weddings performed at St Mark's, where the average age of marriage was lower for men than the national average. The average age of marriage at St Mark's in 1921 was 25.6 years for men and 25.3 years for women. This compares with national statistics of 28 years for men and 24.3 years for women.[57] While the local numbers do not reveal the large difference in ages present in national statistics, young women in Richmond Heights generally married younger than men because of their romantic expectations of marriage and the financial responsibility that men assumed. Respectable working-class men did not marry until they were in a position to support a family.[58]

The concentration of young women in specific occupations and places of employment encouraged the development of work-related marriage customs. Joy Parr has noted customs in the Canadian textile industry, but they were also present in the office.[59] Weddings, in fact, had many connections to the workplace. Showers acted as a peer recognition of the event, and were particularly important in the female workplace since marriage was usually accompanied by departure. Some showers were held in the office, the bride's 'desk artistically decorated' with pink and white wedding bells, streamers, flowers, and kewpie dolls.[60] Occasionally these decorated desks provided an opportunity to reinforce a sense of company loyalty.[61] One future bride was said to have spent her last day at work sitting under 'three mischievous Kewpies each representing one year of Miss Garvey's term of service with the company.'[61] Company welfare organizers at Moirs incorporated showers into their social program. Moirs employees held a dance and buffet luncheon shower for a three-year employee, Margaret Jackson. Twenty-five couples attended. This shower was not typical, however, since it included men and was large enough to have live music provided by the Moirs company orchestra.[62] Nevertheless, gifts were presented only to the bride even though the groom was present. All-female kitchen, grocery, or linen showers on weeknight evenings were the norm. The in-house MT&T *Monthly Bulletin* captured the atmosphere of one surprise kitchen shower as it described a group of excited young women 'engaged in an almost futile struggle to keep "hushed"' as they waited for the guest of honour. The room had been decorated with kewpie dolls, pink-shaded candles, 'festoons of pink hearts and clusters of pink blossoms.' When the future bride entered, she was presented with a 'big clothes basket filled with all conceivable kitchen articles.'[63]

The intrusion of workplace culture into wedding celebrations was not the only link between work and weddings. Although newspaper wedding announcements frequently did not describe the attire of the bride, they rarely failed to mention where the bride and groom had been employed. Custom and etiquette also seemed to dictate that the specific gift communally offered to the bride or groom from co-workers be mentioned in the announcement. Wedding gifts from fellow employees were often very generous. Generally, the skilled men at the Canadian National Railways (CNR) roundhouse received large items of furniture, such as a mahogany parlour suite or a davenette. Unskilled workmates would offer the groom less extravagant household items such as a Morris chair or a clock.[64] Although the items given to the bride were often not as large, the generosity of the bride's workmates was even more astounding in light of their lower wages. The standard gift to a bride from her co-workers was a chest of silver flatware or a silver tea service. Both gifts were genteel luxury items and certainly would have been symbols of respectability. Office, store, or factory contributions for these gifts must have been a considerable burden for young women who had very little spending money, especially in light of the frequent staff turnover. The fact that gifts were communally presented suggests the importance workmates attached to the wedding and perhaps the hope that, someday soon, they would be on the receiving end. Brides who were moving from Halifax after their wedding were likely to receive a cheque to assist with expenses in setting up a new household in a new city. The common practice was to place the cheque in a travelling bag. New consumer durables such as electric lamps and irons were also occasionally presented.[65]

Wedding gifts also revealed the persistence of paternalism in some local firms, since employers sometimes offered generous gifts that might be regarded as symbolic dowries. Gifts from employers were given only to women employees and were distinct from gifts presented by co-workers. A woman in an isolated occupation, such as a private stenographer, might receive the obligatory case of silver flatware. Some of the most vulnerable female employees in the city, engaged in domestic service or the garment industry at Clayton's, were rewarded for their loyalty with a 'substantial cheque.' The custom of employer-presented wedding gifts appear to have been associated with locally owned companies where personal contact continued between owner and employee.[66]

The workplace not only provided a source of wedding gifts, but could also play a role in the introduction of couples. Work offered many women the opportunity to meet prospective husbands. In her study of working-class youths in Hamilton, Ontario, Jane Synge concluded that 'social life and marriage chance would be seriously impaired should she have to stay home and care for an ailing mother or younger siblings.'[67] Maritime Telephone and Telegraph in the June 1923 *Monthly Bulletin* referred to one of its departments as 'the University of Intending Brides.' In an edition of the same publication a year later, the editor commented on the marriage of two employees and stated that 'Miss Gilles' intimacy with payrolls has given her an experience that will be invaluable to her as a housekeeper.' The writer continued by commenting that this experience would make it difficult for her future husband to 'pad his vouchers' when accounting for the contents of his fortnightly pay envelope.[68] While offering the suggestion that husbands sometimes hid some of their wages from their wives, this observation also reinforced the notion that pre-marriage work experience made a woman better prepared for her real, lifelong career as a housewife and mother. Since marriage changed most women's economic role and removed them from the paid public labour force into the home, it made sense that the workplace would play such a large role in the wedding. The importance of the wedding for a woman was in part a result of the identity change that was experienced as she became someone's wife.

Changing class identities or alliances did not change young women's roles. Young women almost always belonged to a household, because they could seldom afford to sever the connection. Most young, work-ing-class women went from being someone's daughter to being someone's wife. Waged labour was determined by the immediate needs of family rather than the interests of the individual concerned. Women's paid work, whether in domestic service, manufacturing, or the expand-ing areas of clerical or retail employment, was characterized by poor wages and high turnover. The growth of employment opportunities in lower-level white-collar work may have affected appearance, behaviour, aspirations, and even self-image, but it did not touch the desire to escape waged work for marriage, nor did it change young women's role within the family. Mass culture and new forms of female workplace culture combined to strengthen a universal classless ideal that was appropriate for all women. Young women, regardless of their class, generally congregated in a limited stratum of opportunities. Work-ing-class women had many things in common with their middle-class sisters. The individualism of work protest suggests that most women did not feel part of any larger community based on class. Indeed, young working women were all lumped together, and in one account emerged as a parade of high heels, silk stockings, smart coats, and chic hats flooding into the downtown each morning. The same 1930 description concluded with a statement by a Parisian who observed that women in Halifax were much better dressed than women in her own city, because in Paris it was just the wealthy who dressed well, and 'one sees them only in certain sections and they are in the minority ... But in Halifax *all* women look well and *all* are most charmingly dressed.'[69] A masculine working-class culture as it had evolved was unable to incorporate the parade of young women composed of stenographers, clerks, waitresses, and telephone operators into its mainstream. This exclusion was un-fortunate for the future of an independent class-based culture, for it was this parade of high heels and silk stockings that led the Canadian working class farther into the world of mass culture and homogeneous consumption.

Conclusion

In early 1927, a most unusual poem appeared in the Canadian Communist party's newspaper, *The Worker*. Poetry itself was not unusual; the journal often contained verse on recognized labour issues of the day. But this poem, entitled 'Romance,' was decidedly different. Firstly, it was signed only with the initials 'O.R.' – almost certainly Oscar Ryan, the then twenty-two-year-old secretary of the Young Communist League. Secondly, the poem was not the usual critique of capitalism but concerned the gender politics of the 1920s. The poem read:

> Listen, kid, I'm so blame
> tired. It's been hell
> all day, and I guess
> I need a rest.
> – Goddamit! you janes
> never leave a guy alone.
> I don't want to go to the pictures;
> I just want to fool around
> and read the paper and
> smoke my cob.
>
> Hell! – first it's the
> bloody foreman, then
> the boss, and now
> you.
> All you think of
> is to run off to those
> movie joints and cry yourself
> sick over Valentino.

But when it comes to the
fellows in the shop,
you don't fall for us.
– We don't put
axle-grease on our hair,
and we wear oil-soaked
work shirts.

Come on, kid, walk with me
in the park. There's
a shady bench.
And we can sit there
while I smoke and we
both sit together quietly. Then we can
talk of so many things ...[1]

The anger and frustration usually voiced against capitalism was in this case directed towards wives and girlfriends. The poet expressed the desire for the comforts of domesticity yet feared the possibility of rejection on the basis of mass culture. What did O.R. want to talk about in the peace away from the house? What bridges did he hope to build between men and women? What resolutions did he hope to offer? The poet offered no empathy for the frustration of women, only the realization that something was amiss between men and their 'janes' and somehow communication was necessary.

The context in which this communication and negotiation took place in Halifax in the 1920s was particularly fragile. The collapse and transformation of the Nova Scotia economy accentuated tension between those working-class men and women who stayed in the province despite the tide of outmigration. In Richmond Heights, the dramatic postwar layoffs at Halifax Shipyards and the fluctuating demands of the railways meant many male wage-earners did not possess security in their employment. This insecurity must have been particularly difficult for the households that chose to rent in the Hydrostone District, since they were consciously allocating a higher than necessary portion of limited resources to housing in exchange for superior accommodation. The desire for decent housing, at least in part, reflected the value these households placed on domestic life, comfort, and domesticity. The aspirations of these residents were also reflected in the value they placed on privacy, their attempt to participate in some aspects of consumerism, and the ways in which this consumerism was integrated into their existing definitions of respectability. The fragile economic and ideological underpinnings of this respectable working-class neighbourhood were made even more vulnerable by the awareness that the delicate negotiation between men and women took place under the watchful eye of family, neighbours, and the Halifax Relief Commission.

This book has examined the impact of gender ideals on a respectable working-class suburb in Halifax in the 1920s. It has suggested connections between the way men and women perceived masculinity and femininity and the decline of a distinct, local working-class culture in the third decade of this century. A vibrant working-class culture could encompass and foster an alternative perspective of society and criticize what was perceived to be common sense, natural, or even desirable. Alternatively, working-class culture could also reinforce and strengthen existing gender roles and power relations through patriarchy and paternalism, provide consolation for those excluded from political and economic power, and offer an essentially conservative vision of society. In Richmond Heights in the 1920s there was evidence of both, seemingly oppositional, aspects of working-class culture. Although these two extremes could differ greatly, they were shaped by and generally reflected a male world-view and proved unable to absorb new gender ideals for men and women.

Gender ideals were not universal even within the neighbourhood or individual households, nor were they unchanging, since men and women based these perceptions on age and marital status. The diversity of experience, even within the community, meant that gender ideals embodied both continuity and change. During the 1920s, the basic household gender ideals remained constant, with married men assigned to the role of breadwinner and married women responsible for household management and mothering. This rigidity appeared to conflict with an emerging mass culture that seemed to eliminate many of the extreme differences between the sexes. For many people, men and women were becoming more alike. The flapper was one example of this conjunction, as her mannish bob, boyish figure, and personal habits of swearing, drinking, and smoking encompassed what had been exclusively male characteristics.[2] Although the labour market remained segmented, women entered some previously all-male professions and occupations through expanded educational and cultural opportunities and participated in political life with the newly awarded franchise. The contradiction between domesticity and cultural change beyond the home meant that many individuals were confronted simultaneously with new, limited, and unspecified ideals around how a man or woman should act and think. As a result, the residents of Richmond Heights in the 1920s lived for the most part in a world of impossibilities. Men and women of Richmond Heights continuously had to face the impossibility of attaining the ideal of either femininity or masculinity, achieving companionate marriage, and making do on inadequate wages in a household economy that was dependent on cash.

Richmond Heights in the 1920s was rooted in the ideal of a skilled male wage sufficient to support a family. Yet this model conflicted with experience of female-headed households, new employment opportunities for young women, redundant elderly men, and technological and regional economic change that made the ideal of a male breadwinner unattainable for many working-class households.

Some Richmond Heights men through their participation in the labour movement or labour politics may have claimed to desire a new vision of the world, but this vision was essentially one in which they remained economically, politically, and socially privileged over their mothers, wives, sisters, daughters, and girlfriends. Regional deindustrialization and the introduction of new workplace technology fostered a local crisis of masculinity, and many working-class men found comfort in their role of breadwinner and a sense of albeit limited power in their ability to support a household. In promoting themselves as breadwinners, men reinforced the ideal of their wives and mothers as domestic-based consumers, excluding them from a class-based movement. Furthermore, working-class daughters, who traditionally composed the most important group of wage-earning women, were also alienated as they entered new female job ghettoes in retail and clerical work where sex seemed to be more important than class. This is not to claim that women were less class-conscious than men – rather, working-class culture continued to be defined in male terms.

Women may have formed the core of working-class culture in communities where the ideal of the male wage did not hold such power, but in Richmond Heights in the 1920s, the most obvious examples of a distinct working-class culture remained exclusively male and removed from the home.[3] Trade unions, political activism, and sports continued to succeed in combining masculinity and working-class culture, but seldom did they breach the threshold of the private home. This spatial separation was perpetuated despite the increased importance of home and family and changing leisure patterns where men and women were likely to spend more time together. The exclusion of women from mainstream working-class culture along the lines of skill and gender, or by the sheer weight of custom, weakened the entire class.

Given that working-class identity remained largely synonymous with being a man, it was impossible for an all-encompassing class identity that included both men and women to emerge. The home, dominated by women and removed from institutional working-class culture, partially aligned itself with the mass culture, and this had important implications for the next generation of working-class Haligonians. A distinct local working-class culture continued to survive, but often in subtle forms that could exist and reproduce themselves comfortably within the new context of the household. These changes were happening across North America, but they had particular significance in a region with increasingly limited industrial opportunities for women and where the labour movement was so closely identified with one of the most masculine of occupations, coal mining.

The increased emphasis placed on home life in twentieth-century Canada has camouflaged much class conflict. Class and gender conflict was partially relocated in the household and manifested itself in the friction between men and women or the generational differences between mothers and daughters. The poet who raged against his 'jane's' attraction to Rudolph Valentino was not simply jealous, but rather angry that he and 'the fellows in the shop' with clean hair but dirty shirts had been excluded from a new ideal of masculinity and were not perceived as desirable. Class conflict could also erupt in a generational context. One need only think of the tension-ridden relationships of fictional working-class couples portrayed in the entertainment media, from Maggie and Jiggs in the early 1920s comic strip *Bringing up Father* through the television incarnations of Edith and Archie Bunker and Roseanne and Dan Connors. It is surely not a coincidence that in each of these fictitious working-class families, marriages were stormy and intergenerational conflict was represented through daughters.

The home and the workplace are interconnected in innumerable ways, not the least of which is the way that tensions emerging in one arena also appear in the other. In 1929, an advertisement for wax paper promised consumers its use would bring 'A Revolution in the Kitchen.'[4] After the period of dramatic political and labour upheaval that took place in Canada following the First World War, the word 'revolution' rarely appeared. It is significant that it was used in this context. It is conceivable that the legacy of the post-First World War labour revolt was connected to new aspirations surrounding domestic consumption and did occur in the kitchen, in as much as the kitchen symbolized domestic life and its crucial role in shaping class experience. The poet's image of a workingman smoking and a woman patiently waiting for him remains haunting. Perhaps on warm summer evenings men and women from Richmond Heights climbed the crest of Fort Needham to view the harbour or walked north to watch the sun set over the Bedford Basin; and as they wandered they spoke of their day and their dreams. Perhaps it was possible only for a poet to grasp the revolutionary potential of men and women's sitting and talking together.

Appendix

TABLE A
Occupations of Richmond Heights men, 1920–1929 (as listed in *City Directory*)

	1920	1921	1922	1923	1924	1925	1926	1927	1928	1929
alderman	–	–	–	–	–	1	–	–	–	–
barrister	–	–	–	–	–	1	1	2	1	1
chiropodist	–	–	–	–	–	–	–	1	1	–
editor	–	–	–	–	–	–	–	1	–	–
druggist	1	1	1	–	–	–	–	–	–	1
manager	–	1	3	2	1	5	3	1	5	8
self – retail	9	12	10	8	8	6	7	6	5	5
self – builder	6	7	2	2	1	1	3	–	1	2
teacher	2	–	–	1	–	1	1	1	1	1
	18	**21**	**16**	**13**	**10**	**15**	**15**	**12**	**14**	**18**
agent	5	1	2	2	2	1	3	3	3	2
bookkeeper	3	4	7	1	1	–	2	3	5	2
clerk	22	29	20	20	36	18	22	28	25	41
draftsman	1	1	1	1	–	–	–	–	–	2
sales	10	6	8	11	6	10	9	10	15	13
	41	**41**	**38**	**35**	**45**	**29**	**36**	**44**	**48**	**60**
baker	6	2	–	2	1	3	2	–	2	2
barber	3	3	4	3	4	4	4	6	4	9
blacksmith	10	12	8	7	3	3	3	3	3	3
boilermaker	2	2	5	1	1	–	–	3	5	5
bricklayer	5	4	3	3	3	1	1	2	1	3

	1920	1921	1922	1923	1924	1925	1926	1927	1928	1929
butcher	–	–	2	1	1	–	1	–	–	1
carpenter	59	52	42	31	25	21	24	27	24	23
chauffeur	35	43	40	36	26	40	43	21	31	32
checker	4	4	6	6	4	2	3	2	2	3
cook	6	5	5	3	1	2	2	6	7	8
cooper	3	3	2	2	1	–	–	1	1	–
craneman	1	1	2	2	1	4	1	3	3	2
dry cleaner	–	–	1	–	–	–	–	–	–	–
electrician	6	7	6	2	1	2	2	3	3	1
el. worker	10	10	9	9	6	9	9	9	8	10
elevator	1	–	–	–	1	–	–	–	–	–
fireman	2	1	1	–	–	1	–	1	–	–
fisherman	–	–	1	–	–	–	–	–	–	1
foreman	10	11	13	10	9	5	8	3	7	10
harness mkr	1	1	–	–	–	–	–	–	–	–
Hfx Fireman	1	2	1	2	1	6	2	4	4	5
gardener	1	1	1	–	–	–	–	–	–	–
glazier	1	1	2	–	–	–	–	–	1	1
ironworker	7	8	4	1	2	2	–	5	5	10
janitor	–	–	1	3	2	3	3	3	2	2
labourer	36	36	40	23	17	14	16	27	46	40
machinist	23	16	20	12	13	7	12	14	16	18
mail	–	–	3	2	3	4	6	3	2	3
mechanic	3	3	4	1	–	1	2	3	8	10
messenger	4	3	5	4	2	3	2	2	3	2
military	18	12	9	17	7	11	10	11	15	12
motorman	4	7	8	12	8	13	16	15	16	15
moulder	–	3	4	2	1	1	2	1	2	3
musician	2	–	–	–	–	–	–	–	1	1
orderly	1	1	1	1	1	2	2	2	2	4
painter	16	12	6	12	8	4	5	5	4	8
patternmkr	2	1	1	–	–	–	–	–	–	–
plasterer	–	1	1	1	–	–	–	–	–	1
plumber	15	12	8	7	5	4	5	2	4	5
police	1	3	7	7	6	11	18	17	23	21

	1920	1921	1922	1923	1924	1925	1926	1927	1928	1929
porter	3	6	4	4	3	3	4	3	5	7
print	2	5	3	1	2	10	9	9	11	8
projectionist	–	1	1	1	–	–	–	–	1	1
railway emp.	30	35	23	22	23	33	34	32	26	22
railway										
brakeman	11	6	7	5	5	3	4	4	6	5
fireman	12	4	5	2	3	2	4	6	7	6
engineer	8	7	6	9	9	5	3	3	5	8
conductor	1	–	–	1	–	–	–	–	–	–
repairs	1	–	–	–	–	–	–	1	1	3
rigger	4	4	1	1	2	3	–	3	4	3
roofer	–	–	–	–	–	–	–	1	–	–
sailor	18	13	21	21	19	28	34	15	14	30
shipper	6	5	5	3	–	3	4	3	5	12
shipyard	98	99	15	12	4	5	17	11	8	9
shoe repair	3	4	4	2	2	2	2	–	–	2
stevedore	10	4	8	4	1	2	–	–	1	5
tailor	6	4	4	5	1	4	1	2	1	1
tinsmith	1	1	2	2	1	–	–	–	4	5
usher/waiter	2	2	–	–	2	2	1	1	5	8
warehouse	7	9	7	5	6	5	1	6	10	12
watchman	6	7	5	6	4	1	1	–	–	–
welder	6	23	4	4	1	–	1	1	2	2
	534	**522**	**401**	**335**	**252**	**294**	**324**	**305**	**371**	**423**
employee										
unspecified	50	56	49	39	38	36	46	55	41	40
Total	**643**	**640**	**504**	**422**	**345**	**374**	**421**	**416**	**474**	**541**

TABLE B

Occupations of Richmond Heights women, 1920–1929 (as listed in *City Directory*)

	1920	1921	1922	1923	1924	1925	1926	1927	1928	1929
asst librarian	–	–	–	–	–	–	–	–	–	1
doctor	1	1	–	–	–	–	–	–	–	–
teacher	3	–	1	1	2	1	2	1	–	1
nurse	3	1	1	1	2	2	1	3	4	2
self – retail	2	1	–	–	3	2	1	–	2	3
	9	**3**	**2**	**2**	**7**	**5**	**4**	**4**	**6**	**7**
bookkeeper	2	2	1	–	–	1	–	2	5	1
clerk	14	22	9	8	5	12	17	15	22	23
operator	6	4	6	4	4	5	7	9	9	13
stenographer	10	7	6	5	6	10	6	4	5	5
sales	7	9	1	1	1	1	1	4	5	9
	39	**44**	**23**	**18**	**16**	**29**	**31**	**34**	**46**	**51**
domestic	1	1	1	1	–	4	2	1	–	4
forelady	–	1	–	–	–	1	–	–	–	–
messenger	1	–	–	–	–	–	–	–	–	–
Moirs	19	18	24	17	13	14	6	13	7	14
packer	2	1	–	–	–	–	–	1	2	1
print shop	2	1	–	3	–	2	2	3	3	1
seamstress	1	3	2	1	–	2	–	–	–	2
waitress	–	3	–	1	–	–	1	–	–	1
	26	**28**	**27**	**23**	**13**	**23**	**11**	**18**	**12**	**23**
employee unspecified	12	17	18	12	8	9	2	6	3	12
Total	**86**	**92**	**70**	**55**	**44**	**66**	**48**	**62**	**67**	**93**

Notes

ABBREVIATIONS

DUA   Dalhousie University Archives
HRC   Halifax Relief Commission
JHA   *Journal of the House of Assembly*
NAC   National Archives of Canada
PANS Public Archives of Nova Scotia

Introduction

1 *Evening Mail* (Halifax), 11 Sept. 1923 All neighbourhood residents in this study have been given fictitious surnames, with the exception of Florence Murray, who created a public identity for herself with the publication of her autobiography, and Robert Daw, Ward 6 alderman and labour politician. The actual surnames of individuals who did not live in the neighbourhood and whose activities in such fields as politics, law, or religion are a matter of public record are left unchanged.
2 *Evening Mail*, 14 May 1928
3 Janet Guildford and Suzanne Morton, eds, 'Introduction,' *Separate Spheres: Women's World in the 19th Century Maritimes* (Fredericton 1994)
4 Important Canadian sociological studies include Herbert B. Ames, *The City below the Hill* (1897), the work of the McGill Social Research Series in the 1930s, and John Seeley, et al., *Crestwood Heights* (1956). The finest example of the Annales school in Canada remains Louise Dechêne, *Habitants et marchands de Montréal au XVIIe siècle* (Paris 1974; trans. Montreal 1992). For examples of anthropology and geography, see Kay Anderson, *Vancouver's Chinatown: Racial Discourse in Canada, 1875–1980* (Montreal 1991), and

Gerald Sider, *Culture and Class in Anthropology and History: A Newfoundland Illustration* (Cambridge 1986). Rural community studies include David Gagan, *Hopeful Travellers: Families, Land and Social Change in Mid-Victorian Peel County, Canada West* (Toronto 1981), and Paul Voisey, *Vulcan: The Making of a Prairie Community* (Toronto 1988). Urban and working-class studies based on community studies include Terry Copp, *The Anatomy of Poverty: The Condition of the Working Class in Montreal, 1897–1929* (Toronto 1974); Michael Katz, *The People of Hamilton, Canada West: Family and Class in a Mid-Nineteenth Century City* (Cambridge 1975); Michael Piva, *The Condition of the Working Class in Toronto, 1900–1921* (Ottawa 1979); Bryan Palmer, *A Culture in Conflict: Skilled Workers and Industrial Capitalism in Hamilton, Ontario, 1860–1914* (Montreal 1979); and Gregory S. Kealey, *Toronto Workers Respond to Industrial Capitalism, 1867–1892* (Toronto 1980). Immigrant populations are studied in the context of community studies in John Zucchi, *Italians in Toronto: Development of a National Identity, 1875–1935* (Montreal 1988), and Franca Iacovetta, *Such Hardworking People: Italian Immigrants in Postwar Toronto* (Montreal 1992). Community studies have played a greater role in U.S. women's and family history; but see Joy Parr, *The Gender of Breadwinners: Women, Men and Change in Two Industrial Towns, 1880–1950* (Toronto 1990), and Bettina Bradbury, *Working Families: Age, Gender and Daily Survival in Industrializing Montreal* (Toronto 1993).

5 Edward Anthony Rotundo, 'Manhood in America: The Northern Middle Class, 1770–1920' (PhD diss., Brandeis University 1982), 8. The use of the ideal corresponds with the work of Jill Matthews who stresses the impossibility of complying with all gender ideals and the inevitability of failure: Jill Julius Matthews, *Good and Mad Women: The Historical Construction of Femininity in Twentieth Century Australia* (Sydney 1984).

6 R.W. Connell, *Gender and Power: Society, the Person and Sexual Politics* (Stanford 1987), 156; Mark Rosenfeld, '"It Was a Hard Life": Class and Gender in the Work and Family Rhythms of a Railway Town, 1920–1950,' *Historical Papers* (Ottawa 1988), 237–79. See also, Maurine Weiner Greenwald, 'Working-Class Feminism and the Family Wage Ideal: The Seattle Debate on Married Women's Right to Work, 1914–1920,' *Journal of American History* 76, no. 1 (June 1989): 118–49; Martha May, 'The Historical Problem of the Family Wage: The Ford Motor Co. and the Five Dollar Day,' *Feminist Studies* 8 (Summer 1982): 399–424; and her 'Bread before Roses: American Workingmen, Labor Unions and the Family Wage,' in Ruth Milkman, ed., *Women, Work and Protest: A Century of U.S. Women's Labor History* (Boston 1985), 1–21.

7 Lizabeth Cohen, *Making a New Deal: Industrial Workers in Chicago, 1919–1939* (Cambridge 1990); David Montgomery, 'Trends in Working-Class History,'

Labour / Le Travail 19 (Spring 1987): 18; David Montgomery, 'Thinking about American Workers in the 1920s,' *International Labor and Working-Class History* 32 (Fall 1987): 4–24; David Brody, *Workers in Industrial America: Essays on the Twentieth Century Struggle* (New York 1980); Sanford M. Jacoby, *Employing Bureaucracy: Managers, Unions and the Transformation of Work in American Industry, 1900–1945* (New York 1985)

8 Robert S. Lynd and Helen Merrel Lynd, *Middletown: A Study of Contemporary American Culture* (New York 1928)

9 Susan Porter Benson, 'The 1920s through the Looking Glass of Gender: A Response to David Montgomery,' *International Labor and Working-Class History* 32 (Fall 1987), 31–8

10 Parr, *Gender of Breadwinners; Elizabeth Faue, Community of Suffering and Struggle: Women, Men and the Labor Movement in Minneapolis, 1915–1945* (Chapel Hill 1991)

11 The term 'North End Halifax' can be confusing, as there were two distinct 'North Ends' in the city. Richmond Heights was located in the far North End – a location quite separate from the Ward Five 'North End' associated with the area between the Citadel and North Street. The Ward Five North End contained some of the city's worst housing and poorest neighbourhoods. Part of the confusion around the two North Ends lay in the almost complete isolation of both areas from the generally more prosperous South End. The North Street passenger train station and the old train route along the harbour had been the only exposure of most South End residents to the district, and with the destruction of the terminus and the permanent redirection of all passenger traffic through the new southwest route, even this very limited contact ended. Nova Scotia, Department of Lands and Forests, *Map*, 5N11. 86 SE (Halifax 1969). The actual street boundaries of Richmond Heights were West Young Street to the south, Gottingen Street to the east, Duffus Street to the north, and Robie Street to the west. For the purposes of this study, the houses were all on the east-west streets with the exception of the twelve apartments above the shops and offices on West Young Street, as this thoroughfare was too populous to isolate only the Hydrostone block. PANS, MG 20, vol. 526, 2, HRC Minutes, 9 Mar. 1921

12 See James Morrison, 'Soldiers, Storms and Seasons: Weather Watching in Nineteenth Century Halifax,' *Nova Scotia Historical Quarterly* 10, nos 3, 4 (Sept./Dec. 1980): 221–41; Canada, Department of Transport, Meteorological Division, *Climatic Summaries for Selected Meteorological Stations in the Dominion of Canada*, vol. 1 (Toronto 1947), 28, 36, 54–5, 58–9, 61, 63.

13 *Evening Mail*, 22 Sept. 1923

14 See Claude Darrach, *Race to Fame: The Inside Story of the Bluenose* (Hantsport

1985); John Herd Thompson with Allen Seager, *Canada 1922–1939: Decades of Discord* (Toronto 1985), 186–90.

15 *Evening Mail*, 10 Jan. 1924

16 Canada, *Census*, 1931, vol. 2, 31; PANS, RG 35, vol. 102, City of Halifax, ser. 34, H.7, Housing Report 1932, A.G. Dalzell, A.C. Pettipas, S.H. Prince. Requested by the Citizen's Housing Committee, Spring/Summer 1931 under Board of Health, 1

17 S.A. Saunders, *The Economic History of the Maritime Provinces* (Fredericton 1984 [1939]); L.D. McCann, 'Metropolitanism and Branch Businesses in the Maritimes, 1881–1931,' *Acadiensis* 13, no. 1 (Autumn 1983): 112–25

18 The deindustrialization experience in the Maritimes was not unique in the North American context. Old industries in New England were also closing and relocating, and parallels between the two regions remain uninvestigated. For a discussion of deindustrialization in the Maritimes see Nolan Reilly, 'The Emergence of Class Consciousness in Industrial Nova Scotia: A Study of Amherst, 1891–1925' (PhD diss., Dalhousie University 1983). For the New England experience see Judith Smith, *Family Connections: A History of Italian and Jewish Immigrants in Providence, Rhode Island, 1900–1940* (Albany, N.Y. 1985).

19 Canada, *Census*, 1921, vol. 2, 347; PANS, MG 1, vol. 2898, Robert McConnell Hattie Papers, 43, 'A Report Indicating the Need of a Social Survey' (1912), 1

20 *Mail-Star* (Halifax), 17 Mar., 2 Sept. 1943, 15 Mar. 1944, 27 Apr. 1956, 3 Oct. 1963; *Evening Mail*, 23 Dec. 1929; PANS, MG 36, HRC, R.846, R.1405, R.1870

21 Graham Metson, ed., *The Halifax Explosion, December 6, 1917* (Toronto 1978), 119. Casualty totals from the explosion note the death of only ten 'Africans.'

22 *Daily Star* (Halifax), 19 Apr. 1928; *Evening Mail*, 1 Jan. 1929; PANS, MG 36, HRC, R.851, 22 Kane Place, 5 Apr. 1926. Emphasis in original

23 I have not corrected the spelling or grammar, nor have I adopted the use of [*sic*] in these notes. Additional information necessary for comprehension has been included in brackets.

24 In 1927 the *Might Directory* published the names of married women.

25 Linda Gordon, *Heroes in Their Own Life: The Politics and History of Family Violence, Boston, 1880–1960* (New York 1988), v

26 This was also the approach employed by Veronica Strong-Boag, in *The New Day Recalled: The Lives of Girls and Women in English Canada, 1919–1939* (Toronto 1988).

CHAPTER 1 Richmond Heights

1 Janet Kitz, *Shattered City: The Halifax Explosion and the Road to Recovery* (Halifax 1989); *The Halifax Catastrophe: Forty Views on the Halifax Disaster*

(Halifax nd); Samuel Henry Prince, *Catastrophe and Social Change: Based upon a Sociological Study of the Halifax Disaster* (New York 1920); Graham Metson, ed., *The Halifax Explosion, December 6, 1917* (Toronto 1978); John Weaver, 'Reconstruction of Richmond District of Halifax: A Canadian Episode in Public Housing and Town Planning, 1918–1921,' *Plan Canada* 6, no. 1 (Mar. 1976): 36–47. In 'Exploding Myths: The Halifax Harbour Explosion in Historical Context,' in Alan Ruffman and Colin Howell, eds, *Ground Zero* (Halifax forthcoming), Jay White lists five other non-atomic explosions that compare in size to the 1917 Halifax disaster.

2 Bishop Leonard F. Hatfield, 'Professor S.H. Prince – Social Pioneer,' paper read to History of Dalhousie University Seminar Series, 14 Feb. 1985

3 Canada, House of Commons, *Sessional Papers* 56, no. 7 (1920): 16; Suzanne Morton, 'Labourism and Economic Action: The Halifax Shipyards Strike of 1920,' *Labour / Le Travail* 22 (Fall 1988): 84

4 Suzanne Morton, 'The Halifax Relief Commission and Labour Relations during the Reconstruction of Halifax, 1917–1919,' in Michael Earle, ed., *Workers and the State in Twentieth Century Nova Scotia* (Fredericton 1989). A parallel relief agency, the Massachusetts-Halifax Relief Commission (after the summer of 1918 the Massachusetts-Halifax Health Commission), was established after the explosion to administer donations made by the people of Massachusetts.

5 NAC, Privy Council Minutes, PC 112, 22 Jan. 1918; Nova Scotia, 'An Act to Incorporate the HRC,' *Statutes of Nova Scotia*, 1918, 8–0 Geo. V, ch. 61

6 Canada, Commission of Conservation, *Report of the Ninth Annual Meeting*, Ottawa, 27–8 Nov. 1917, 195

7 PANS, MG 36, HRC, R.1715.8, Town Planning Scheme for Devastated Area; *Evening Mail*, 27 Sept. 1918; PANS, MG 20, vol. 526, 1, HRC Minutes, 21 June 1918, 346

8 PANS, MG 36, HRC, R.1715.10, The Plans and Policy of the Halifax Relief Commission for the Rebuilding of the Devastated Area on Modern Lines, 4

9 Extensive development of the slope would wait until the Second World War. PANS, MG 36, HRC, R.1723, Progress Report Halifax Rehousing, Oct. 1918

10 Hugh MacLennan, *Barometer Rising* (Toronto 1963), 88–9

11 William Ashworth, *The Genesis of Modern British Town Planning: A Study in Economic and Social History of the Nineteenth and Twentieth Centuries* (London 1954), 48; PANS, MG 1, vol. 2898, Robert McConnell Hattie Papers, 45

12 Kevin David Kane and Thomas Bell, 'Suburbs for a Labor Elite,' *The Geographic Review* 75, no. 3 (July 1985): 319–34; Donna McCririck and Graeme Wynn, '"Self-Respect and Hopefulness": The Development of Blue-Collar Suburbs in Early Vancouver,' in Graeme Wynn, ed., *People,*

Places, Patterns, Processes: Geographical Perspectives on the Canadian Past
(Toronto 1990), 267–84; Madeleine McKenna, 'The Suburbanization of the
Working-Class Population of Liverpool between the Wars,' *Social History*
16, no. 2 (May 1991): 173–89; Anthony Sutcliffe, *Towards the Planned City:
Germany, Britain, the United States and France* (New York 1981), 68
13 Sutcliffe, *Towards the Planned City*, 57
14 Ashworth, *Genesis of Modern British Town Planning*, 138, 142; M.J. Daunton,
   'Urban Britain,' in T.R. Gourvish, ed., *Later Victorian Britain, 1867–1900*
   (London 1988)
15 Ashworth, *Towards the Planned City*, 160; Shirley Spragge, 'The Provision of
   Workingmen's Housing, Attempts in Toronto, 1904–1920' (MA thesis,
   Queen's University 1974); Robert Sean Purdy, 'The Political Economy of
   Housing Reform in Toronto, 1900–21' (MA thesis, Queen's University 1991)
16 Sutcliffe, *Towards the Planned City*, 66, 175; Alan H. Armstrong, 'Thomas
   Adams and the Commission of Conservation,' in L.O. Gertler, ed., *Planning
   the Canadian Environment* (Montreal 1968); Martin Hawtree, 'The Emergence
   of the Town Planning Professional,' in Anthony Sutcliffe, ed., *British Town
   Planning: The Formative Years* (New York 1981); Jill Delaney, 'The Garden
   Suburb of Lindenlea, Ottawa: A Model Project for the First Federal Housing Policy, 1918–24,' *Urban History Review / Revue d'histoire urbaine* 19, no. 3
   (Feb 1991): 151–65
17 John Bacher, '"Keeping to the Private Market": The Evolution of Canadian
   Housing Policy: The Role of the Canadian Federal Government in Housing,
   1919–1968' (PhD diss., McMaster University 1985), 71, 75
18 Thomas Adams, 'Town Planning and Better Housing, as an Aid to the
   Development of Natural Resources in Nova Scotia,' *Proceedings of the
   Fifteenth Annual Convention of the Union of Nova Scotia Municipalities*,
   Windsor, 25–7 Aug. 1920, 52
19 PANS, MG 20, vol. 526, 1, 8 June 1918; PANS, MG 36, HRC, R.1715,
   Statement of Chairman Rogers, 10 Sept. 1918
20 George Ross may have been the most adaptable and important architect
   working in Canada during the interwar period. His Montreal firm was
   responsible for such prominent buildings as the downtown Eaton's store,
   the Dominion Square Building, and the Holt Renfrew store in Montreal,
   and Eaton's College Street, Maple Leaf Gardens, and Union Station in
   Toronto. The similarity between the houses of Unwin and Parker and
   George Ross was understated as 'resemblance' in Stanley H. Pickett's,
   'Hydrostone,' *Community Planning Review* 10, no. 1/2 (1960): 29–32.
21 S. Martin Gaskell, 'The Suburbs Salubrious: Town Planning in Practice,'

and Michael G. Day, 'The Contribution of Sir Raymond Unwin (1863–1940) and R. Barry Parker (1867–1947) to the Development of Site Planning Theory and Practice c. 1890–1918,' in Sutcliffe, ed., *British Town Planning*, 172

22 By 1930 furnaces had been installed in 168 of the homes. PANS, MG 36, HRC, R.1733, Reconstruction: Chimneys and Furnaces; M.J. Daunton, *House and Home in the Victorian City: Working-Class Housing, 1850–1914* (London 1983), 238

23 PANS, MG 36, HRC, R.1717, 29; George Ross, 'The Halifax Disaster and the Rehousing,' *Construction* 12, no. 10 (Oct. 1919): 300

24 Paul Erikson, *Halifax's North End* (Hantsport, N.S. 1986), 50

25 PANS, MG 20, vol. 526, 1, HRC Minutes, 21 June 1919; PANS, MG 36, HRC, R.1715, Reconstruction, General Description

26 NAC, RG 24, Department of National Defence, vol. 4273, f. 22.1.245, 13 Jan. 1918

27 The ratings of poor, fair, and good appeared to be at the discretion of the assessor, to be used in estimating the value of the property in question. There were no set criteria in the municipal statutes and not all houses were given a rating.

28 PANS, RG 35, vol. 102, City of Halifax, 19, H 9–12, Ward Six Assessment Field Cards

29 Ibid., City of Halifax, 34, H.7, Housing Report 1932, A.G. Dalzell, A.C. Pettipas, and S.H. Prince Requested by Citizen's Housing Committee, Spring/Summer 1931 under the Board of Health, 4–5

30 *Acadian Recorder* (Halifax), 23 Jan. 1919; *Evening Mail*, 11 Feb. 1919

31 *Daily Echo* (Halifax), 1 May 1919; *Evening Mail*, 4 Aug. 1920

32 *Acadian Recorder*, 23 Jan. 1919; *Daily Echo*, 23 Jan. 1919

33 PANS, MG 36, HRC, R.1446, 12 Stanley Place, 27 Nov. 1929

34 PANS, MG 36, HRC, R.1462, 28 Stanley Place, 12 Dec. no year

35 Richard Harris, 'Working-Class Home Ownership and Housing Affordability across Canada in 1931,' *Histoire sociale / Social History* 14, (May 1986): 121–38, 136; Richard Dennis, 'Landlords and Rented Housing in Toronto, 1885–1914,' Centre for Urban Community Studies, no. 162 (Toronto 1987), 5

36 *Halifax City Directory*, 1910–30; *Evening Mail*, 3 Jan. 1920

37 Janet Kitz, private correspondence with author. L.D. McCann, 'Dimensions of Corporatism: Railway Workers and Residential Segregation in Halifax, 1878–1926,' paper presented to the Atlantic Canada Studies Conference, Memorial University, St John's, Newfoundland, May 1992, 10–1, 30

38 NAC, MG 26, Borden Papers, H 90, OCA 109, no. 74803, Edward

McCarthy, H 141, OCA 109, no. 74815, A.R. Mosher, 3 Jan. 1918

39 Suzanne Morton, 'Labourism and Independent Labor Politics in Halifax, 1919–1926' (MA thesis, Dalhousie University 1986), Appendix 1, 195, Appendix 3, 203–7

40 Erikson, *Halifax's North End; The Novascotian* (Halifax), 16 Apr. 1881

41 Halifax Board of Trade, *The City of Halifax: The Capital of Nova Scotia, Canada* (Halifax 1909), 78–9

42 Robert Inglis, *United Memorial Church, Kaye Street, Halifax, 1918–1975* (Halifax 1975), 2, 4. I am indebted to George Rawlyk for this point.

43 Ward 6 included the area north of North Street to the Bedford Basin, and from the harbour west to the city limits at Dutch Village Road. *Chronicle-Herald* (Halifax), 2 July, 4 Dec. 1965; *Mail-Star*, 18 Feb. 1952

44 Nolan Reilly, 'The Emergence of Class Consciousness in Industrial Nova Scotia: A Study of Amherst, 1891–1925' (PhD diss., Dalhousie University 1983); S.A. Saunders, *The Economic History of the Maritime Provinces* (Fredericton 1984 [1939]); T.W. Acheson, 'The National Policy and the Industrialization of the Maritimes, 1880–1910,' *Acadiensis* 1 (1972): 3–28; L.D. McCann, 'Metropolitanism and Branch Businesses in the Maritimes, 1881–1931,' *Acadiensis* 13, no. 1 (Autum 1983): 112–25, and David Alexander, 'Economic Growth in the Atlantic Region, 1880 to 1940,' *Acadiensis* 8, no. 1 (Autumn 1978): 47–76

45 *Citizen* (Halifax), 5 Feb. 1926

46 E.R. Forbes, *The Maritime Rights Movement, 1919–1927: A Study in Canadian Regionalism* (Montreal 1979)

47 Canada, Department of Labour, *Labour Gazette*, Feb. 1921, 181; *Evening Mail*, 1 Jan., 25 Mar., 4 June 1922; 1 Feb., 1, 22 Mar., 3 May, 12 July, 9 Aug., 6 Sept., 1 Nov., 29 Dec. 1923; 14 Aug. 1924; 12 Feb. 1925; 21, 30 Dec. 1926; 6, 13, 20 Jan., 3, 10, 17 Feb., 10, 25 Mar., 26 May, 4 Aug., 29 Sept., 13, 20 Oct., 17 Nov., 1, 15, Dec. 1927; 19, 26 Jan., 9, 23 Feb., 1, 23 Mar. 1928

48 George Meredith Rountree, *The Railway Worker: A Study of the Employment and Unemployment Problems of the Canadian Railways* (Montreal 1936), 75

49 Ibid., 67–70, 312

50 PANS, MG 36, HRC, C.40.13, Community Chest, Halifax, 1927–1942, clipping 'no military tenants,' nd

51 PANS, MG 20, vol. 526, 2, HRC Minutes, 9 Sept. 1923

52 *Evening Mail*, 3 Oct. 1929

53 PANS, MG 20, vol. 526, 2, HRC Minutes, 20 Apr. 1925; *Evening Mail*, 20 Apr. 1925

54 Elizabeth Ewen, *Immigrant Women in the Land of Dollars: Life and Culture on*

the Lower East Side, 1890–1925 (New York 1985), 154; Morning Chronicle (Halifax), 29 Apr. 1920; In 'A Winter's Tale: The Seasonal Contours of Pre-industrial Poverty in British North America, 1815–1860,' *Historical Papers* (1974), Judith Fingard notes that May Day was the main moving day for Saint John tenants in 1842.

55 For example, see PANS, MG 36, HRC, R.224, R.229, R.252, R.254, R.256, R.260, R.264, and R.276.

56 Kitz, *Shattered City*, 12

57 PANS, RG 35, vol. 102, City of Halifax, 39, I, City Engineer Building Permits

58 For a discussion of keeping animals in an urban setting in Crowland, Ontario, during the same period see Carmela Patrias, *Relief Strike: Immigrant Workers and the Great Depression in Crowland, Ontario, 1930–1935* (Toronto 1990), 17. *Evening Mail*, 7 June 1927; 8 May 1922; 20 May 1926; 1 Nov. 1922

59 Daunton, *House and Home*, 268; *Evening Mail*, 5 June 1925; 26 Oct. 1922

60 *Evening Mail*, 28 Apr. 1927; 23 July 1920; 8 June, 25 Aug. 1921; 4 Aug. 1922

61 Margaret Giles, '"Something That Bit Better": Working-Class Women, Domesticity and Respectability, 1919–1939' (PhD diss., University of York 1989), 19

CHAPTER 2 Values and Daily Life

1 PANS, MG 20, vol. 200, Massachusetts-Halifax Relief Committee Minute Book

2 These images come from photos of the living-rooms of three temporary homes that housed the displaced residents of Richmond before the construction of the Hydrostone. Two of these three households later took up residence in Richmond Heights. PANS, MG 20, vol. 200, Massachusetts-Halifax Relief Committee, 1 and 29 Massachusetts Ave., 90 North Park Street. Lizabeth Cohen describes similar taste and detail in 'Embellishing a Life of Labor: An Interpretation of the Material Culture of American Working-Class Homes, 1885–1915,' in Thomas J. Schlereth, ed., *Material Culture Studies in America* (Nashville, TN 1982), 289–305.

3 PANS, RG 42, A 9, 1927, unsorted Halifax Magistrate's Court, Civil Case 76, marriages; Suzanne Morton, 'The June Bride as the Working-Class Bride: Getting Married in a Halifax Working-Class Neighbourhood in the 1920s,' in Bettina Bradbury, ed., *Canadian Family History: Selected Readings* (Toronto 1992)

4 Brian Harrison, 'Traditions of Respectability in British Labour History,' in his *Peaceable Kingdom: Stability and Change in Modern Britain* (Oxford 1982), 157–216

5 Lizabeth Cohen, *Making a New Deal: Industrial Workers in Chicago, 1919–1939* (Cambridge 1990), 52

6 *Evening Mail*, 12 Oct., 29 Dec. 1922; Janet Kitz, *Shattered City: The Halifax Explosion and the Road to Recovery* (Halifax 1989), 191

7 *Evening Mail*, 18 June 1921

8 Archibald MacMechan, 'The Halifax Disaster,' in Graham Metson, ed., *The Halifax Explosion, December 6, 1917* (Toronto 1978), 18

9 Elizabeth Roberts, *A Woman's Place: An Oral History of Working-Class Women, 1890–1940* (Oxford 1984), 4–5

10 PANS, MG 20, vol. 200, Massachusetts-Halifax Relief Committee, interior photos; PANS, MG 27, vol. 1, 285, 'Some Details That May Assist in the Identification of the Hundreds of Unclaimed Bodies Which Have Been Interned,' 1917–8; Hugh McLeod, *Class and Religion in the Late Victorian City* (London 1974), 29; Theodore Caplow, *All Faithful People: Change and Continuity in Middletown's Religion* (Minneapolis 1983), 40

11 Mark Rosenfeld, '"She Was a Hard Life": Work, Family, Politics and Ideology in the Railway Ward of a Central Ontario Town, 1900–1960' (PhD diss., York University 1990), 126

12 *Evening Mail*, 6 June 1921

13 PANS, MG 20, vol. 200, Massachusetts-Halifax Relief Committee. For example, see Cases 40, 99, 158, 453, 1716.

14 PANS, MG 36, HRC, Correspondence, A.163; *Evening Mail*, 14 July 1926

15 *Daily Star*, 9 Apr. 1928; *Evening Mail*, 4 June 1929

16 See Janet Guildford and Suzanne Morton, eds, 'Introduction,' *Separate Spheres: Women's Worlds in the 19th Century Maritimes* (Fredericton 1994).

17 Peter Stearns, *Be a Man! Males in Modern Society* (New York 1979), 72

18 *Evening Mail*, 28 Dec. 1923, 10 Nov., 12 Dec. 1928, 18 May 1929; *Citizen*, 19 Feb. 1926

19 *Evening Mail*, 9 Mar. 1928

20 PANS, Micro: Churches, Halifax, United Memorial Session Minutes, 1 Nov. 1928

21 Stan Gray, 'Sharing the Shop Floor,' in Michael Kaufman, ed., *Beyond Patriarchy: Essays by Men on Pleasure, Power and Change* (Toronto 1987), 227

22 Joy Parr, *The Gender of Breadwinners: Women, Men and Change in Two Industrial Towns, 1880–1950* (Toronto 1990), 188

23 Bettina Bradbury, 'Pigs, Cows and Boarders: Non-Wage Forms of Family Strategy among Montreal Families, 1861–1891,' *Labour / Le Travailleur* 14

(Fall 1984): 9–46; Ellen Ross, 'Not the Sort That Would Sit on the Doorstep:
Respectability in Pre World War 1 London Neighborhoods,' *International
Labor and Working Class History* 27 (Spring 1985): 39–59; Ross, 'Survival
Networks: Women's Neighbourhood Sharing in London before World War
One,' *History Workshop* 24 (Autumn 1987): 4–27; Ross, 'Labour and Love:
Rediscovering London's Working-Class Mothers, 1870–1918,' in Jane Lewis,
ed., *Labour and Love: Women's Experience of Home and Family, 1850–1940*
(Oxford 1985); Neville Kirk, *The Growth of Working-Class Reformism in Mid-
Victorian England* (Urbana, Ill. 1985), 176

24 Ross, 'Not the Sort That Would Sit on the Doorstep,' 39
25 Ross, 'Labour and Love,' 51
26 Denyse Baillargeon notes the importance of privacy in her study of
Montreal working-class women in the 1930s. *Ménagères au Temps de la Crise*
(Montreal 1991), 222–3; Diane Duke, 'An Analysis of the Pension System
for the Victims of the Halifax Explosion, 1917,' essay prepared for Legal
History Course, Dalhousie Law School, 1988, 27; and PANS, MG 36, HRC,
R.1358, 22 Sebastian Place
27 *Daily Echo*, 1 May 1919; *Evening Mail*, 4 Aug. 1920
28 PANS, MG 36, HRC, R.276, 34 Cabot Place, 26 July 1930
29 PANS, MG 36, HRC, R.1358, 22 Sebastian Place, 19 Aug. 1927
30 PANS, MG 36, HRC, R. 1854, Vacated Balances, Rent Ledger; R.276,
24 Cabot Place
31 *Evening Mail*, 6 July 1921
32 *Evening Mail*, 7 Sept. 1920
33 PANS, MG 36, HRC, R.1075, 4 Merkel Place, HRC to George MacInnis,
Nova Scotia Light and Power, 24 Aug. 1929. The HRC was particularly
concerned about relations between neighbours, as disputes could cause
respectable tenants to leave. See PANS, MG 36, HRC, R.763, 13 Hennessey
Place, 27 June 1928.
34 My mother and your mother
Were hanging out the clothes.
My mother gave your mother
A punch in the nose.
What colour was the blood?
Blue!
B- L- U- E- spells blue, and out you must go
As fast as your little slippers will carry you.
(Edith Fowke, *Sally Go Round the Sun* [Toronto 1969], 57)
35 PANS, MG 36, HRC, R.765, 15 Hennessey Place
36 PANS, MG 36, R.828, 2 Kane Place

37 In Kareen Reiger's study of the Australian Minimum Wage Commission of 1920, she quotes a woman's testimony on her respectable working-class neighbourhood ('not "common people" at all. Most of them have pianos'): 'Perhaps I am a little more sensitive ... but ... if I went to the back door I saw nothing but chimneys and galvanized iron fences, while if I went to the front veranda, if other people's front doors were open, I saw their private life, and if the doors were shut it was a pleasant relief.' Kareen Reiger, '"Clean and Comfortable and Respectable:" Working-Class Aspirations and the Australian 1920 Royal Commission on the Basic Wage,' *History Workshop Journal* 27 (Spring 1989): 94

38 PANS, MG 36, HRC, R.851, 22 Kane Place, 5 Apr. 1926. Emphasis in original

39 PANS, MG 36, HRC, R.1462, 28 Stanley Place

40 PANS, MG 36, HRC, R.851, 22 Kane Place, Apr. 1926

41 Elizabeth Ewen, *Immigrant Women in the Land of Dollars: Life and Culture on the Lower East Side, 1890–1925* (New York 1985), 52, 159–60

42 PANS, MG 36, HRC, R.276, 34 Cabot Place, 3 May 1926

43 For example PANS, MG 36, R.244, 3 Cabot Place; R.276, 34 Cabot Place. According to Stella Shore, 'everybody had lovely white lace curtains in the window – very clean ... people didn't seem to be dirty.' Telephone interview, Halifax, July 1989

44 PANS, MG 20, vol. 526, 2, HRC Minutes, 9 Sept. 1923

45 PANS, MG 36, HRC, R.843, 14 Kane Place, 14 May 1924, not sent

46 PANS, MG 36, HRC, R.861, 32 Kane Place, J.M. Hire to HRC, 15 May 1924, sent Hogan letter

47 PANS, MG 36, R.1004, 18 Livingstone Place, clipping 19 Apr. 1932

48 PANS, MG 36, HRC, R.1004, 18 Livingstone Place, 19 Apr. 1927

49 PANS, MG 20, vol. 526, 2, HRC Minutes, 16 Nov. 1927

50 PANS, MG 36, HRC, R.780, 30 Hennessey Place, 15 July 1927

51 PANS, MG 36, HRC, R.242, 2 Cabot Place

52 PANS, MG 36, HRC, R.1462, 28 Stanley Place

53 PANS, MG 36, HRC, R.1437, 3 Stanley Place

54 Cynthia Jane Wright, '"The Most Prominent Rendezvous of the Feminine Toronto": Eaton's College Street and the Organization of Shopping in Toronto, 1920–1950' (PhD diss., University of Toronto 1992), 15

55 Winnifred Bolin Wandersee, *Women's Work and Family Values, 1920–1940* (Cambridge, Mass. 1981), 19; *Evening Mail*, 2 Oct. 1925; 12 Nov. 1929

56 Stella Shore, telephone interview, Halifax, July 1989. Some suggestion of the importance of the piano was indicated in the debate around compensation after the explosion. *Evening Mail*, 19 Feb. 1918

57 *Halifax City Directory*

58 In 1941, 73.3 per cent of Halifax households had a telephone installed. In cities over 30,000, only Outremont (91.5 per cent) and Ottawa (74.0 per cent) could boast a greater percentage of households with telephones. *Halifax City Directory*, 1921–9; Canada, *Census*, 1941, vol. 4, T. 18, 81–2

59 Sometime in mid-1928, the HRC in an attempt to collect back rent made new tenants list any items in their possession that were not paid for in full. Examples of these items appear in PANS, MG 36, HRC, R.248, R.252, R.507, R.759, R.845, R.846, R.989, R.1013, R.1017, R.1078, R.1097, R.1356, R.1870.

60 PANS, MG 36, HRC, R.507, 4 Duffus Street

61 PANS, MG 36, HRC, R.1879, Mortgage and Rental Records

62 PANS, RG 42, A 9, 1927, unsorted Halifax Magistrate's Court – Civil, Oct. 1928, Maritime Telephone and Telegraph, $12.70; Oct. 1927, goods sold and delivered, $63.36; no. 32, Maritime Telephone and Telegraph, $13.08; no. 58, Merchants Guarantee Assoc. $9.00; Healy and Co. (coal), $23; no. 95, Nova Scotia Furnishings, $20; and no. 102, O'Malley's Bakers, $42.65

63 PANS, MG 20, vol. 200, Minutes, Massachusetts-Halifax Relief Committee, Thank-you note from P.J. Wylie noted that he lost $165 in the disaster; MG 36, HRC, R.1730, Reconstruction Projects; RG 42, A 9, 1927, unsorted Halifax Magistrate's Court – Civil, no. 76, Promissory note, $75 to street railway conductor

64 Paul Johnson, 'Credit and Thrift in the British Working Class, 1870–1939,' in Jay Winter, ed., *The Working Class in Modern British History* (Cambridge 1983), 153

65 *Evening Mail*, 5 Jan., 18 June, 25 Oct., 14 Dec. 1920

66 *Evening Mail*, 24 Oct. 1919. Another appeared on the same day requesting 'sober' boarders on nearby Agricola Street.

67 Nova Scotia, *JHA*, 1921, App. 34, 'Report of the Commission on Mothers Allowances,' 11. See Tamara Hareven and John Modell, 'Urbanization and the Malleable Household: An Examination of Boarding and Lodging in American Families,' *Journal of Marriage and the Family* 35 (1973): 467–79.

68 Leonore Davidoff, 'Landladies and Lodgers in Nineteenth- and Twentieth-Century England,' in Susan Barman, ed., *Fit Work for Women* (New York 1979), 92

69 *Evening Mail*, 26 Mar., 17 May 1920, 13 Apr. 1921, 4 Oct., 10 and 18 Nov. 1922

70 *Evening Mail*, 20 July 1920; 9 May and 1 Sept. 1921

71 PANS, MG 36, HRC, R.1855, Vacated Balances, 1919–29

72 PANS, MG 36, HRC, R.1462, 28 Stanley Place

73 PANS, MG 36, HRC, R.1854, Vacated Balances, Rent Ledger, 1919–25

74 PANS, MG 36, HRC, R.1854, Vacated Balances, Rent Ledger, 1919–25
75 PANS, MG 36, HRC, R.760, 4 July 1923, 10 Hennessey Place
76 *Evening Mail*, 21 Feb. 1922
77 *Evening Mail*, 28 June 1922
78 PANS, MG 36, HRC, R.789, 8 Hennessey Street; MG 36, HRC, R.1879, Mortgage and Rental Records
79 *Citizen*, 4 July 1930
80 PANS, RG 39, 'D,' Supreme Court, Halifax Divorce Court, vol. 31, 1924, Case 389

CHAPTER 3 Elderly Men and Women

1 Canada, *Census*, 1881, vol. 1, T. 1, 9; 1921, vol. 1, T. 16, 254
2 James Seth, 'Halifax Revisited,' *Dalhousie Review* 1, no. 4 (Jan. 1922): 338–9
3 Jackson Lears, *No Place of Grace: Antimodernism and the Transformation of American Culture, 1880–1920* (New York 1981)
4 M.C. MacLean, 'The Age Distribution of the Canadian People,' *Census*, 1931, vol. 12, 768
5 Canada, *Census*, 1921, vol. 4, T. 40, 200–3
6 Peter N. Stearns, 'Old Women: Some Historical Observations,' *Journal of Family History* 5 (Spring 1980): 44–5. In *The New Day Recalled: The Lives of Girls and Women in English Canada, 1919–1939* (Toronto 1988), Veronica Strong-Boag uses the age of forty to mark the final life stage. For a critique of the history of older women, see Marjorie Chary Feinson, 'Where Are the Women in the History of Aging?' *Social Science History* 9, no. 4 (Fall 1985): 429–52.
7 DUA, MS 4, 180, H 301, Maritime Telephone and Telegraph Personnel Benefits; Stearns, 'Old Women,' 45
8 Tamara Hareven, *Family Time, Industrial Time: The Relationship between the Family and Work in a New England Industrial Community* (Cambridge 1982), 173; Howard Chudacoff and Tamara K. Hareven, 'From the Empty Nest to Family Dissolution,' *Journal of Family History* 4, no. 1 (Spring 1979): 59–63
9 Chris Gordon, 'Familial Support for the Elderly in the Past: The Case of London's Working Class in the Early 1930s,' *Ageing and Society* 8 (1988): 309
10 James Struthers, 'Regulating the Elderly: Old Age Pensions and the Formation of a Pension Bureaucracy in Ontario, 1919–1945,' *Journal of the Canadian Historical Association*, New Series, 3 (Charlottetown 1993): 237. Struthers carefully notes that, although the program's intent was inclusive, 'gender played an important role in limiting and constraining the entitlement of women to state support in their old age.'

11 For examples of birthdays and anniversaries see *Evening Mail*, 24 Nov. 1921, 13 Sept. 1923, 26 Sept. 1929; Hareven, *Family Time*, 180.

12 See W. Andrew Achenbaum, *Old Age in the New Land: The American Experience* (Baltimore 1978), ch. 6, 'Old Age Becomes a National Problem,' and David Hackett Fischer, *Growing Old in America* (Oxford 1978), ch. 4, 'Old Age Becomes a Social Problem.' Also Carol Haber, *Beyond 65: The Dilemma of Old Age in America's Past* (Cambridge 1983); Brian Gratton, *Urban Elders: Family, Work and Welfare among Boston's Aged, 1890–1950* (New York 1986), and 'The Labor Force Participation of Older Men, 1890–1950,' *Journal of Social History* 20, no. 4 (Summer 1987): 689–710; N. Sue Weiler, 'Industrial Scrap Heap: Employment Patterns and Change for the Aged in the 1920s,' *Social Science History* 13, no. 1 (Spring 1989): 65–88, and 'Family Security or Social Security? The Family and the Elderly in New York State during the 1920s,' *Journal of Family History* 11, no. 1 (1986): 77–95

13 E.R. Forbes, 'Prohibition and the Social Gospel in Nova Scotia,' *Challenging the Regional Stereotype: Essays on the Twentieth-Century Maritimes* (Fredericton 1989), 36–7; *Citizen*, 17 Jan. 1920, 29 June 1923, 19 June 1925

14 *Citizen*, 19 June 1925; PANS, MG 20, vol. 517, no. 1, Minutes of the Society for the Prevention of Cruelty, President's Report, 31 Mar. 1921

15 Nova Scotia, *JHA*, 1930, App. 29, 'Report of Commission on Old Age Pensions,' 6. The Halifax statistics found that 41.7 per cent had incomes over $400, 3.9 per cent $300 to $399, 4.3 per cent $200 to $299; 7.3 per cent $100 to $199; 8.5 per cent less than $100, and 34.6 per cent no income at all. The elderly in Halifax had a greater opportunity to accumulate wealth in the city than in the rural counties (4, 7). Achenbaum, *Old Age*, 115; Gratton, 'Labor Force Participation,' 689, 703; Brian Gratton, 'The New History of the Aged: A Critique,' in David Van Tassel and Peter N. Stearns, eds, *Old Age in a Bureaucratic Society: The Elderly, the Experts, and the State in American History* (New York 1986)

16 Howard P. Chudacoff, 'The Life Course of Women, Age, and Age Consciousness, 1865–1915,' *Journal of Family History* 5, no. 3 (Fall 1980): 290; Canada, *Census*, 1921, vol. 4, T. 5, 382–99; Canada, *Census*, 1931, vol. 3, T. 15, 134–5, and vol. 7, T. 5, 7

17 DUA, MS 10, 2, A.1, Correspondence: Fred W. Thompson to J. Bell, 9 Aug. 1976, 8–9

18 *Evening Mail*, 13 June 1924; *Monthly Bulletin* (Halifax, Maritime Telephone and Telegraph), June 1924; PANS, MG 36, HRC, R.1361, 25 Sebastian Place, and A.79, Correspondence re: claims, John and Barbara Green, property; *Evening Mail*, 27 Feb. 1924; Halifax City Directory, 1904–14; 1920–9; PANS,

RG 35, vol. 102, City of Halifax, 8A, 1920s. The voters' list included a total of 448 men.

19 *Evening Mail*, 26 Sept. 1929

20 NAC, RG 43, Department of Railways, vol. 291, 3871

21 DUA, MS 4, 180, Maritime Telephone and Telegraph, H 302, Employee Benefits. See also James Stafford, 'The Class Struggle and the Rise of Private Pensions, 1900–1950,' *Labour / Le Travail* 20 (Fall 1987): 147–71.

22 Craig Heron, *Working in Steel: The Early Years in Canada, 1883–1935* (Toronto 1988), 102; Joy Parr, *The Gender of Breadwinners: Women, Men and Change in Two Industrial Towns, 1880–1950* (Toronto 1990), 48

23 Canada, Department of Labour, *Labour Gazette*, July 1923, 704; Feb. 1929, 170; Oct. 1929, 1123

24 *Daily Star*, 9 Mar. 1927

25 Joanne J. Meyerowitz, *Women Adrift: Independent Wage Earners in Chicago, 1880–1930* (Chicago 1988), 37, and Strong-Boag, *New Day Recalled*, 182

26 Canada, *Census*, 1921, vol. 4, T. 5, 382–99

27 Nova Scotia, *JHA*, 1930, App. 29, 'Report of Commission on Old Age Pensions,' 14

28 Ibid. The report was based on research in Halifax city and the counties of Cape Breton, Richmond, and Shelburne.

29 *Evening Mail*, 16 June 1922

30 See, for example: Haber, *Beyond 65*, as cited in Feinson, 'Where Are the Women?' 433; The 1931 census listed 126 men and 165 women over the age of sixty in Nova Scotia who resided in charitable or benevolent institutions. Although women outnumbered men in the province's institutions, the circumstances of their residence were remarkably different. In 23.8 per cent of the cases for men and 51.4 per cent of the cases for women, someone was paying the full or partial cost of their maintenance. Canada, *Census*, 1931, vol. 9, T. 14, 286–7

31 Struthers, 'Regulating the Elderly,' 238

32 PANS, RG 35, vol. 102, City of Halifax, 33, 31.A, City Home, Inmates Admitted and Discharged, May 1919 – May 1929; 36, City Home, City Inmates, 1919–29

33 Michael Katz, 'Poorhouses and the Origins of the Public Old Age Home,' *Milbank Memorial Fund Quarterly* 62, no. 1 (1984): 134

34 PANS, MG 1, vol. 315, no. 2, Diary of George Morton; Sister Maura, *The Sisters of Charity of Halifax* (Toronto 1956), 32; Bettina Bradbury, 'Mourir chrétiennement: La vie et la mort dans les éstablissements catholiques pour personnes âgées à Montréal au XIXe siècle,' *Revue d'histoire de l'Amérique française* 46, no. 1 (Summer 1992): 143–75

35 *Daily Star*, 14 Feb. 1927

36 Nova Scotia, *JHA*, 1930, App. 29, 'Report of Commission on Old Age Pensions,' 12. It is interesting to note that the Canadian census did not differentiate between elderly parents and other dependents within a household, despite the fact that this specific group were supposedly regarded as a social problem.

37 PANS, MG 36, HRC, R.748, 2 Hennessey Place; R.1854, Vacated Balances, Rent Ledger, 1919–25

38 *Daily Star*, 26 Jan. 1927, *Acadian Recorder*, 29 Dec. 1919; *Daily Echo*, 14 May 1920; *Evening Mail*, 28 Jan. 1925

39 PANS, MG 36, HRC, R.1854, Vacated Balances, Rent Ledger, 1919–25

40 Gratton, *Urban Elders*, 177

41 Daniel Scott Smith, 'Life Course, Norms, and the Family System of Older Americans in 1900,' *Journal of Family History* 4, no. 3 (Fall 1979), 285–98

42 Overall in Canada, 208.7 per 10,000 over the age of seventy were institutionalized compared to 91.5 in Nova Scotia, 199.7 in New Brunswick, 378.5 in Quebec, and 193.3 in Ontario. Canada, *Census*, 1931, vol. 9 , T. 9, 280–1

43 L.M. Montgomery, *The Tangled Web* (Toronto 1931 [1972]), 3

44 Nova Scotia, *JHA*, 1930, App. 29, 'Report of Commission on Old Age Pensions,' 10

45 PANS, MG 36, HRC, R.1411, 30 Stairs Place

46 PANS, MG 36, R.1365, 29 Sebastian Place

47 Nova Scotia, *JHA*, 1935, App. 32, Old Age Pensions, 7–8

48 *Evening Mail*, 21 Nov. 1928; *Citizen*, 17 Nov. 1922; Jessie L. Ross, 'Attacking Infant and Maternal Mortality. A Group of Papers Read before the Canadian Council of Child Welfare, Toronto, Ontario, Sept., 1922. 1. In a City. The Halifax Experiment,' *The Public Health Nurse* (Mar. 1923): 126

49 Michael Roper and John Tosh, 'Introduction,' *Manful Assertions: Masculinities in Britain since 1800* (London 1991), 17

50 Gratton, *Urban Elders*, 76, 96

51 Stearns, 'Old Age,' 48

52 PANS, MG 27, vol. 1, 285, 'Some Details That May Assist in the Identification of the Hundreds of Unclaimed Bodies Which Have Been interned,' 1917–18, 114, 183

53 *Evening Mail*, 12 May 1928

CHAPTER 4 Domestic Responsibilities

1 *Evening Mail*, 2 Apr. 1927

2 PANS, MG 36, HRC, R.401, 10 Columbus Place

3 DUA, MS 2, 240, Halifax Visiting Dispensary, Record of Patients, 1924–37
4 Jean Barman, '"Knowledge Is Essential for Universal Progress but Fatal to Class Privilege": Working People and the Schools in Vancouver during the 1920s,' *Labour / Le Travail* 22 (Fall 1988): 52
5 Kareen Reiger, *The Disenchantment of the Home: Modernizing the Australian Family* (Melbourne 1985), 39
6 Domestic values were by no means new to working-class Canadians in the 1920s. The struggle for a 'family wage' and labour's critique of prostitution were imbued with domestic ideals; however, there appear to have been discrepancies among rhetoric, aspirations, and practices. Janice Newton, 'From Wage Slave to White Slave: The Prostitution Controversy and the Early Canadian Left,' in Linda Kealey and Joan Sangster, eds, *Beyond the Vote: Canadian Women and Politics* (Toronto 1989); Lynne Marks, in her study of religion in late-nineteenth-century small-town Ontario, has noted that working-class households were less likely to attend church together than their middle-class counterparts and stressed the importance of same-sex leisure. Lynne Sorrel Marks, 'Ladies, Loafers, Knights and "Lasses": The Social Dimensions of Religion and Leisure in Late Nineteenth Century Small Town Ontario' (PhD diss., York University 1992), 76
7 PANS, MG 20, vol. 20, Massachusetts-Halifax Relief Committee, Case 67
8 Canada, *Census*, 1921, vol. 5, T. 5, 382–3; 1931, vol. 2, T. 25, 272–3. In addition, see Patricia Thornton, 'The Problem of Outmigration from Atlantic Canada, 1871–1921: A New Look,' *Acadiensis* 15, no. 1 (Autumn 1985): 3–34; Alan A. Brookes, 'Outmigration from the Maritimes, 1860–1900,' *Acadiensis* 5, no. 2 (Spring 1976): 25–55.
9 PANS, Cemeteries: Halifax: Mount Olivet, Burial Records; Cemeteries: Halifax: St John's (Fairview); Churches: Halifax: St Joseph's Roman Catholic Church, Marriages and Baptisms 1869–1909; Churches: Halifax: United Memorial United Church, Marriages and Baptisms; *Halifax City Directory*; Noble Tinsdall, interview, Halifax, Nov. 1988; Glady McTier, interview, Ottawa, July 1988
10 *Evening Mail*, 5 Oct. 1922, 11 Dec. 1924, 7 Jan. 1926; *Citizen*, 4 Nov. 1927
11 *Citizen*, 13 May 1927
12 *Evening Mail*, 25 Oct. 1928
13 *Citizen*, 20 Apr. 1921
14 Canada, Department of Health, *The Canadian Mother: Taking Care of Father and the Family*, 'Little Blue Book Series' 6 (Ottawa 1923), 5–6
15 John Demos, 'The Changing Faces of Fatherhood,' in his *Past, Present and Personal: The Family and Life Course in American History* (Oxford 1986), 62.

The timing of such shifts is difficult, as it is not uniform and is largely a matter of degree. This is not the middle-class, child-centred family of the 1950s described by Elaine Tyler May in *Homeward Bound: American Families in the Cold War Era* (New York 1988).

16 PANS, MG 20, Halifax Rotary Club, vol. 1979, Charles Butcher to Professor McKay, 3 Apr. 1918

17 Stella Shore, telephone interview, Halifax, July 1989; Glady McTier, interview, Ottawa, July 1988

18 *Morning Chronicle*, 30 Sept. 1920; *Evening Mail*, 1 Nov., 27 Dec. 1928

19 PANS, MG 36, HRC, R.1079, 13 Merkel Place

20 PANS, MG 36, HRC, R.983, 1 Livingstone Place

21 Neil Sutherland, *Children in English-Canadian Society: Framing the Twentieth Century Consensus* (Toronto 1976), 92. For employment of working-class children see Neil Sutherland, '"We Always Had Things to Do": The Paid and Unpaid Work of Anglophone Children between the 1920s and the 1960s,' *Labour / Le Travail* 25 (Spring 1990): 105–41.

22 Winnifred Bolin Wandersee, *Women's Work and Family Values, 1920–1940* (Cambridge, Mass. 1981), 4; Katherine Arnup, 'Education for Motherhood: Women and the Family in Twentieth Century English Canada' (PhD diss., University of Toronto 1991)

23 PANS, MG 36, HRC, R.1855, Vacated Balances, 1919–29, 17 Jan. 1923

24 PANS, MG 36, HRC, R.851, 22 Kane Place, 30 Mar. 1926

25 PANS, MG 36, HRC, R.242 (2 files), 33 Columbus Place, 27 July 1928; R.404, 13 Columbus Place

26 For a discussion of health concerns see Cynthia R. Comacchio, *Nations Are Built of Babies: Saving Ontario's Mothers and Children, 1900–1940* (Montreal 1993). PANS, MG 36, HRC, R.837, 8 Kane Place, 12 Mar. 1928

27 Jill Julius Matthews, *Good and Mad Women: The Historical Construction of Femininity in Twentieth Century Australia* (Sydney 1984), 87

28 Ellen Ross, 'Labour and Love: Rediscovering London's Working-Class Mothers, 1870–1918,' in Jane Lewis, ed., *Labour and Love: Women's Experience of Home and Family, 1850–1940* (Oxford 1985), 73

29 Nova Scotia, *JHA*, 1920, App. 28, 'Report of the Superintendent of Neglected and Delinquent Children,' 15

30 *Evening Mail*, 27 Nov., 14 Jan. 1926

31 PANS, MG 20, vol. 755, 86, Victorian Order of Nurses (VON), 'Report of Board of Governors, 1919,' 119–20; vol. 761, 'Report of the Board of Management of VON 1921'; Mrs E.M. Murray, 'Saving Babies in Halifax,' *The Canadian Nurse* 15, no. 12 (Dec. 1919): 2171–4; *Evening Mail*, 25 Mar.

1919, 28 Apr. 1927; Veronica Strong-Boag, 'Intruders in the Nursery: Childcare Professionals Reshape the Years One to Five, 1920–1940,' in Joy Parr, ed., *Childhood and Family in Canadian History* (Toronto 1982)

32 *Evening Mail*, 21 Aug. 1924; Jessie L. Ross, 'Attacking Infant and Maternal Mortality. A Group of Papers Read before the Canadian Council of Child Welfare, Toronto, Ontario, September, 1922. 1. In a City. The Halifax Experiment,' *The Public Health Nurse* (Mar. 1923): 125–7

33 Ellen Gee, 'Fertility and Marriage Patterns in Canada: 1851–1971' (PhD diss., University of British Columbia 1978), 83

34 PANS, MG 36, HRC, R.1879, Mortgage and Rental Records, and R.873, 17 Kane Street, 16 Mar. 1931; R.460, 56 North Creighton, 20 June 1935; R.1854, Vacated Balances, Rent Ledger, 1919–25

35 *Canada Yearbook*, 1932 (Ottawa 1932), 138, 143; Terry Copp, *The Anatomy of Poverty: The Condition of the Working Class in Montreal, 1897–1929* (Toronto 1974); PANS, Cemeteries: Halifax: St John's [Fairview], Burial Records; PANS, RG 35, vol. 102, City of Halifax, 28, D.3, 'Infectious Diseases Cases'; Kathleen Ann Pickard, 'Choosing Hospitalised Childbirth: The Ottawa Maternity Hospital, 1895–1924' (MA thesis, Queen's University 1986), 12; *Mail-Star*, 17 Mar. 1962

36 *Evening Mail*, 8 Mar. 1928

37 PANS, MG 36, HRC, R.1854, Vacated Balances, Rent Ledger, 1919–25

38 Christine Stansell, *City of Women: Sex and Class in New York, 1789–1860* (New York 1986), 52

39 *Evening Mail*, 11 Jul. 1928

40 *Morning Chronicle*, 15 Apr. 1920; *Evening Mail*, 18 May 1921, 3 Jan. 1923, 11 July 1928; NAC, RG 43, Railways and Canals, vol. 5616, Theft of Coal at Halifax. See also Sutherland, '"We Always Had Things to Do."'

41 *Evening Mail*, 22 Dec. 1921; PANS, MG 36, HRC, R.1854, Vacated Balances, Rent Ledger; MG 20, vol. 526, 2, HRC Minutes, 7 Oct. 1926

42 Canada, *Census*, 1931, vol. 5, 1092–3, 1070–1

43 PANS, MG 36, HRC, R.276, 34 Cabot Place

44 *Evening Mail*, 5 Apr. 1920, 13 Feb. 1922

45 PANS, MG 36, HRC, R.851, 22 Kane Place, 5 Apr. 1926

46 PANS, RG 39, 'B,' vol. 21, Case 458, 1928 Supreme Court of Nova Scotia, Bankruptcy, Annie Thomas, married woman debtor

47 PANS, RG 35, vol. 102, City of Halifax, 39, I, City Engineer Building Permits, 64 Stairs Street

48 *Citizen*, 6 May 1927

49 Bettina Bradbury, 'Women's History and Working-Class History,' *Labour / Le Travail* 19 (Spring 1987): 35

50 PANS, MG 36, HRC, R.1382, 3 Stairs Place, R.273, 32 Cabot Place

51 PANS, MG 36, HRC, R.424, 33 Columbus Place, 12 May no year

52 PANS, MG 36, HRC, R.1398, 18 Stairs Place, 26 June 1926

53 PANS, MG 36, HRC, R.1340, 4 Sebastian Place, 17 June 1926

54 Rosenfeld, '"It Was a Hard Life,"' 257

55 PANS, MG 36, HRC, R.276, 34 Cabot Place, 26 July 1930

56 *Evening Mail*, 12 Sept. 1928

57 PANS, MG 36, HRC, R.1341, 28 Duffus Street, 3 Mar. 1924

58 PANS, MG 36, HRC, R.1854, Vacated Balances, Rent Ledger, 1919–24

59 PANS, MG 36, HRC, R.834, 6 Kane Place, 6 Nov. 1924

60 *Evening Mail*, 9 Dec. 1920

61 PANS, MG 36, HRC, R.1854, Vacated Balances, Rent Ledger, 1919–25

62 *Halifax City Directory* 1925, 1926, 1927, 1928

63 PANS, MG 36, HRC, R.1437, 3 Stanley Place, MG 26, HRC, R.1854, Vacated Balances, Rent Ledger, 1919–25

64 Judith Fingard, 'The Nova Scotian Anti-Cruelty Movement, Marriage Breakdown and the Rights of Wives, 1880–1900,' in Janet Guildford and Suzanne Morton, ed, *Separate Sphere's: Women's Worlds in the 19th Century Maritimes* (Fredericton 1994)

65 James Snell, 'Marital Cruelty: Women and the Nova Scotia Divorce Court, 1900–1939,' *Acadiensis* 18, no. 1 (Autumn 1988): 6

66 Elaine Tyler May, *Great Expectations: Marriage and Divorce in Post-Victorian America* (Chicago 1980), 62; Robert S. Lynd and Helen Merrel Lynd, *Middletown: A Study of Contemporary American Culture* (New York 1928), 114–15

67 *Evening Mail*, 21 Mar. 1922, 29 June 1919; PANS, RG 48, 366, vol. 16, Halifax County Wills, 1919–25, 9704, 367; vol. 17, 11251, Halifax County Wills, 1925–9. A total of thirteen wills was found, 1919–31, by residents of Richmond Heights. May, *Great Expectations*, 71, 90

68 See Meg Luxton, *More Than a Labour of Love* (Toronto 1980); Veronica Strong-Boag, 'Keeping House in God's Country: Canadian Women at Work in the Home,' in Craig Heron and Robert Storey, eds, *On the Job: Confronting the Labour Process in Canada* (Montreal 1986); Ellen Ross, '"Fierce Questions and Taunts": Married Life in Working-Class London, 1870–1914,' *Feminist Studies* 8, no. 3 (Fall 1982): 575–602; Elizabeth Roberts, *A Woman's Place: An Oral History of Working-Class Women, 1890–1940* (Oxford 1984)

69 Mary Ann Clawson, *Constructing Brotherhood: Class, Gender and Fraternalism* (Princeton 1989), 263

70 *Evening Mail*, 9 Jan. 1928; 2 Nov. 1927; 17 Apr. 1928; 26 Sept. 1929

71 Sylvie Murray, 'Quand les ménagères se font militantes: La lige auxiliarie de l'Association internationale des machinistes, 1905–1980,' *Labour | Le Travail* 29 (Spring 1992): 157–86; *Morning Chronicle*, 30 Sept. 1920; *Evening Mail*, 8 Nov. 1928, 19 Oct. 1929

72 *Evening Mail*, 29 Oct. 1925; 21, 25 Jan., 26 May 1921, 12 Oct., 12 Dec. 1922, 12 Jan., 24 Feb., 27 Nov. 1924

73 *Citizen*, 1 Mar. 1929

CHAPTER 5 Single Mothers and Female Household Heads

1 PANS, Micro: Churches, Halifax, St Joseph's Roman Catholic Church, Baptismal Register; *Mail-Star*, 1 June 1972; Halifax, Nova Scotia, Probate Court, 9537; PANS, MG 36, HRC, R.1864, 'City Assessments, 1917/1920'; PANS, RG 35, vol. 102, City of Halifax, 19, H 9-12, Ward Six Assessment Field Cards

2 *Evening Mail*, 26 June, 2, 5, 29 July, 9 Oct., 3 Nov. 1920, 5 Apr., 15 Aug., 19 Nov. 1921; 27 Jan., 23 May 1922

3 PANS, MG 36, HRC, C.32.59.5f, Children's Department, Alphabetical List of Children at Convent of the Sacred Heart and C.32.5i, St Joseph's Orphanage; Nova Scotia, *JHA*, 1920, App. 28, 'Report of the Superintendent of Neglected and Delinquent Children,' 80

4 *Halifax City Directory*, 1925, 1927

5 *Evening Mail*, 23 May 1932. For a discussion of school-leaving stories, see Ellen Ross, 'Labour and Love: Rediscovering London's Working-Class Mothers, 1870–1918,' in Jane Lewis, ed., *Labour and Love: Women's Experience of Home and Family, 1850–1940* (Oxford 1985).

6 *Evening Mail*, 22 Feb., 18 Mar. 1922

7 PANS, Cemeteries: Halifax: Mount Olivet, Burials 1843–1955, 6 Dec. 1919

8 *Evening Mail*, 23 May 1932; *Mail-Star*, 1 June 1972

9 Bettina Bradbury, 'Surviving as a Widow in 19th-Century Montreal,' *Urban History Review* 17, no. 3 (Feb. 1989): 148–60, and 'The Fragmented Family: Family Strategies in the Face of Death, Illness, and Poverty, Montreal, 1860–1885,' in Joy Parr, ed., *Childhood and Family in Canadian History* (Toronto 1982); Arlene Scadron, ed., *On Their Own: Widows and Widowhood in the American Southwest, 1848–1939* (Chicago 1988); Veronica Strong-Boag, 'Wages for Housework: Mothers' Allowances and the Beginnings of Social Security in Canada,' *Journal of Canadian Studies* 14, no. 1 (Spring 1979): 24–34. Recent work by Margaret Little on single mothers and the welfare state provides insight into the actual female recipients as well as state policy. Margaret Hillyard Little, '"No Car, No Radio, No Liquor Permit": The Moral Regulation of Single Mothers in Ontario, 1920–1993' (PhD diss.,

York University 1994); Tamara Hareven, *Family Time, Industrial Time: The Relationship between the Family and Work in a New England Industrial Community* (Cambridge 1982); Susan J. Kleinburg, *The Shadow of the Mills: Working-Class Families in Pittsburgh, 1870–1907* (Pittsburgh 1989). Women-led households in the early nineteenth century are well integrated into Christine Stansell's *City of Women: Sex and Class in New York, 1789–1860* (New York 1986).

10 Canada, *Census*, 1931, vol. 5, 1188–9; 1921, vol. 3, T. 26, 88–9

11 PANS, MG 20, Halifax Rotary Club, vol. 1979, 35, Ernest H. Blois to Professor McKay, 1 Feb. 1918; Case 3237

12 PANS, RG 35, vol. 102, City of Halifax, 8, A.6, Card Index File of Voters, Ward 6, 1920s–30s

13 Seven per cent of all women in Halifax, Hamilton, Moncton, and Ottawa were widows. Canada, *Census*, 1921, vol. 2, 45–64, 224. In 1931 the percentage of widows in the female population remained at 7 per cent. *Census*, 1931, vol. 2, T.30, 290

14 Canada, *Census*, 1931, vol. 1, T. 17b, 444–7

15 Nova Scotia, *JHA*, 1927, App. 10, 'Report of the Workmen's Compensation Board,' 23

16 *Evening Mail*, 4 Feb. 1928; PANS, MG 36, HRC, R.1855, Vacated Balances, 1919–29

17 PANS, MG 36, HRC, R.1855, Vacated Balances, 1919–29

18 Elizabeth Ewen, *Immigrant Women in the Land of Dollars: Life and Culture on the Lower East Side, 1890–1925* (New York 1985), 113–15

19 Cases 41, 42, and 52 in Mary Richmond and Fred S. Hall, *A Study of Nine Hundred and Eighty-Five Widows Known to Certain Charity Organization Societies in 1910* (New York 1913 [1974]), 53–5

20 PANS, MG 36, HRC, R.276, 34 Cabot Place

21 PANS, MG 36, HRC, R.1854, 21 Cabot Place

22 Nova Scotia, *JHA*, 1921, App. 34, 'Report of the Commission on Mothers' Allowances,' 10

23 Ibid.

24 PANS, MG 36, HRC, R.1869, Rental Accounts by street with section on wooden houses, 1919–27

25 Bradbury, 'Fragmented Family,' 119; Christina Simmons, '"Helping the Poorer Sisters": The Women of the Jost Mission, Halifax, 1905–1945,' in Veronica Strong-Boag and Anita Clair Fellman, eds, *Rethinking Canada: The Promise of Women's History* (Toronto 1986)

26 Nova Scotia, *JHA*, 1927, App. 28, 'Report of the Superintendent of Neglected and Delinquent Children,' 24

27 *Evening Mail*, 19 June 1924, 3 Feb. 1920, 15 May 1922

28 *Evening Mail*, 16 Sept. 1920
29 *Evening Mail*, 23 June 1922
30 *Evening Mail*, 26 June 1920, 11 Nov. 1921. Children could be boarded at the city's orphanages or in private homes for approximately $3 a week.
31 *Evening Mail*, 8 Jan. 1927
32 Joanne J. Meyerowitz, *Women Adrift: Independent Wage Earners in Chicago, 1880–1930* (Chicago 1988), 37
33 PANS, MG 36, HRC, R.1854, Vacated Balances, Rent Ledger, 1919–25, R.791, 10 Hennessey Street
34 *Evening Mail*, 1 Mar. 1926
35 Nova Scotia, *JHA*, 1921, App. 34, 'Report of the Commission on Mothers' Allowances,' 11. See Tamara Hareven and John Modell, 'Urbanization and the Malleable Household: An Examination of Boarding and Lodging in American Families,' *Journal of Marriage and the Family* 35 (1973): 467–79.
36 Nova Scotia, *JHA*, 1921, App. 34, 'Report of the Commission on Mothers' Allowances,' 11
37 *Evening Mail*, 1 Mar. 1926
38 PANS, Micro: Churches, Halifax, St Mark's Anglican Church, Marriage Register, 1920–9
39 PANS, MG 36, HRC, R.1854, Vacated Balances, Rent Ledger, 1919–25
40 PANS, MG 36, HRC, R.1411, 30 Stairs Place
41 *Evening Mail*, 13 Nov. 1928; Canada, *Census*, 1931, vol. 5, 1343. This responsibility perhaps fell unevenly upon the older children, as in Jessie Muir's family. A contemporary Maritime fictional account in which the eldest son in a working-class family in Rington (Sydney) must support the family after the death of his father appears in Rev. P.J. Rankin's *On This Rock* (Ottawa 1930).
42 *Morning Chronicle*, 10 Jun. 1920; *Citizen*, 14 May 1920
43 *Evening Mail*, 14 May, 5 Nov. 1925; 4 Aug. 1927
44 PANS, MG 36, HRC, R.842, 13 Kane Place
45 PANS, Micro: Churches, Halifax, United Memorial United Church, Session Minutes, 3 Jan. 1923, 29 Dec. 1927, 11 Jan. 1926. The spending of funds on non-assistance items was not the result of any lack of need. At this point, several prominent members of the congregation were in serious difficulty.
46 Diane Duke, 'An Analysis of the Pension System for the Victims of the Halifax Explosion, 1917,' essay prepared for Legal History Course, Dalhousie Law School 1988, 11. These female-headed households with children in full-time school attendance received additional payments for children who suffered injury or the loss of a parent. NAC, RG 19, Department of Finance, vol. 4885, file 5743-04-03, 'Notes and Explanations of Items on Financial Statement,' 7. Access to pension records of the HRC is

restricted under federal legislation and it is impossible to determine which Richmond Heights residents were receiving support.

47 Nova Scotia, *JHA*, 1921, App. 34, 'Report of the Commission on Mothers' Allowances,' 1

48 Ibid., 12

49 Ibid., 13–14. Nova Scotia, *Statutes*, 1930, ch. 4, 'An Act to Provide for the Payment of Allowances towards the Maintenance of the Dependent Children of Certain Mothers.' The delay in the legislation was at least in part the result of poor provincial finances, with all social programs throughout the 1920s being deferred until the repeal of prohibition in Dec. 1929. E.R. Forbes, 'Prohibition and the Social Gospel in Nova Scotia,' in *Challenging the Regional Stereotype: Essays on the Twentieth-Century Maritimes* (Fredericton 1989)

50 There were 73 widows with one child under 16; 102 with two children; 61 with three children; 37 with four children; 17 with five children; 10 with six children; 2 with seven children, and 1 widow with eight children. Nova Scotia, *JHA*, 1921, App. 34, 'Report of the Commission on Mothers' Allowances,' 22

51 Ibid., 12. In the case of the Children's Aid Society, it had a policy of leaving at least one child with the mother, to ensure she did not escape her responsibility of motherhood.

52 Ibid., 22. The Workmen's Compensation Act allowed $30 per widow and an additional $7.50 per child to a maximum of $60 a month. Nova Scotia, *JHA*, 1921, App. 31, 'Report for 1920 of Workmen's Compensation Board,' 7

53 Nova Scotia, *Statutes*, 1930, s. 1, ch. 4

54 Duke, 'Analysis of the Pension System,' 27

55 Desmond Morton and Glenn Wright, *Winning the Second Battle: Canadian Veterans and the Return to Civilian Life, 1915–1930* (Toronto 1987), 53

56 PANS, MG 36, HRC, R.1358, 22 Sebastian Place

57 PANS, RG 39, 'D,' Supreme Court, Halifax Divorce Court, vol. 31, Case 389, 1924

58 *Evening Mail*, 12 Jan. 1928; Nova Scotia, *JHA*, 1920, App. 28, 'Report of the Superintendent of Neglected and Delinquent Children,' 7

59 PANS, MG 36, HRC, R.1854, Vacated Balances, Rent Ledger, 1919–25

60 *Evening Mail*, 27 May; 7, 9 Aug. 1929

61 DUA, MS 2, 240, Halifax Visiting Dispensary, Registry of Calls

62 DUA, MS 2, 240, Halifax Visiting Dispensary, Record of Patients, 1924–37

63 PANS, MG 36, HRC, R.1364, 28 Sebastian Place, 2[?] Apr. 1925

64 Nova Scotia, *JHA*, 1926, App. 28, 'Thirteenth Annual Report of the Superintendent of Neglected and Delinquent Children,' 30

65 PANS, MG 36, HRC, R.1855, Vacated Balances; PANS, MG 36, HRC,

R.1411, 20 Stairs Place; *Evening Mail*, 21 Jan. 1919, 18 Aug. 1923. After June 1922, desertion was an extraditable offence, but there was still tremendous difficulty in tracking down culprits; Canada, Department of External Affairs, *Treaties and Agreements affecting Canada in Force between His Majesty and the U.S.A, 1814–1925* (Ottawa 1927), 504; PANS, MG 36, HRC, R.1364, 28 Sebastian Place, Apr. 1925; PANS, MG 36, HRC, R.1854, Vacated Balances, Rent Ledger, 1919–25

66 PANS, MG 36, HRC, R.1854, Vacated Balances, Rent Ledger, 1919–25; John R. Gillis, *For Better, For Worse. British Marriages, 1600 to the Present* (Oxford 1985), 209–10. Two such examples appeared, in the *Morning Chronicle*, 5 Aug. 1920, and the *Evening Mail*, 9 Apr. 1926.

67 James Snell, 'Marital Cruelty: Women and the Nova Scotia Divorce Court, 1900–1939,' *Acadiensis* 18, no. 1 (Autumn 1988): 3–32, and his *In the Shadow of the Law: Divorce in Canada, 1900–1939* (Toronto 1991)

68 PANS, RG 39, 'D,' Supreme Court, Halifax Divorce Court, vol. 21, 35, Case 487, 1926; Case 159, 1919; and vol. 31, Case 389, 1924

69 See Judith Fingard, 'Soldiers, Wives, and Prostitutes in Victorian Halifax,' paper presented to Halifax Research Group, Dalhousie University 1988

70 PANS, MG 36, HRC, R.1854, Vacated Balances, Rent Ledger, 1919–25, 19 Mar. 1923

71 Ibid., 1 Dec. 1922, 19 Mar. 1923

72 PANS, MG 36, HRC, R.424 (2 files), 33 Columbus Place, 12 May no year

73 *Evening Mail*, 12 Aug. 1924, 2 Nov. 1920, 7 June 1924

74 *Evening Mail*, 25 Mar., 22 Sept. 1927. PANS, MG 36, HRC, R.1854, Vacated Balances, Rent Ledger, 1919–25; Canada, Department of Labour, Royal Commission on Industrial Relations, Minutes of Evidence (Microfilm), Reel 4, 4416; Mark Rosenfeld, '"It Was a Hard Life,": Class and Gender in the Work and Family Rhythms of a Railway Town, 1920–1950,' *Historical Papers* (Ottawa 1988), 251

75 *Evening Mail*, 7 Oct. 1924

76 PANS, MG 36, HRC, R.776, 26 Hennessey Place

77 *Evening Mail*, 29 Mar. 1926

78 PANS, MG 36, HRC, R.1879, Mortgage and Rental Records, Accounts Payable, 1920s–40s; *Evening Mail*, 20 May 1926

79 *Evening Mail*, 12 June 1924

80 *Evening Mail*, 15 Nov. 1923

81 *Evening Mail*, 12 June 1924, 15 Nov. 1923; Rosenfeld, 'It Was a Hard Life,' 252–4

82 PANS, MG 36, HRC, R.404, 13 Columbus Place, 18 Mar. 1924

83 *Evening Mail*, 24 Feb. 1928

84 Linda Gordon, *Heroes in Their Own Life: The Politics and History of Family Violence, Boston, 1880–1960* (New York 1988), 83

CHAPTER 6 Men

1 The 1920 lease was co-signed by his wife in the same signature, and the 1923 lease was marked with an x. *Mail-Star*, 17 June 1989; *Halifax City Directory*, 1920–9; *Monthly Bulletin*, July 1920, Feb. 1929; PANS, MG 36, HRC, R.1016, 30 Livingstone Place

2 *Evening Mail*, 24 Dec. 1931; *Mail-Star*, 14 Apr. 1936, 10 June 1939, 2 Sept. 1943, 31 Aug. 1948, 17 May 1951

3 Andrew Tolson, *The Limits of Masculinity* (London 1977), 12–13

4 Ibid., 47; *Monthly Bulletin*, Apr. 1923

5 William F. Coltrell, *The Railroader* (Stanford 1940), 24–5

6 *Halifax City Directory*, 1919–29

7 David Frank, 'The 1920s: Class and Region, Resistance and Accommodation,' in E.R. Forbes and D.A. Muise, eds, *The Atlantic Provinces in Confederation* (Toronto 1993), 264–6

8 George Meredith Rountree, *The Railway Worker: A Study of the Employment Problems of the Canadian Railways* (Montreal 1936), 155–6

9 David Montgomery, *Fall of the House of Labor: The Workplace, the State and American Labor Activism, 1865–1925* (Cambridge 1987), 459. See also, David Montgomery, 'Thinking about American Workers in the 1920s,' *International Labor and Working-Class History* 32 (Fall 1987), 4–24.

10 Sanford Jacoby, *Employing Bureaucracy: Managers, Unions and the Transition of Work in American Industry, 1900–1945* (New York 1985), 195–6; DUA, MS 4, 180, Maritime Telephone and Telegraph, H 301, Personnel Benefits Employees' Benefit Fund 1917, Pensions, Disability Benefits and Death Benefits. Maritime Telephone and Telegraph also introduced a Group Life Insurance Plan and an Employee Stock Savings Plan, and while 89 per cent of employees participated in the former only 107 of the eligible 400 joined the latter. DUA, MS 4, 180, Maritime Telephone and Telegraph, H 303, Employees Stock Savings Plan, 1927; H 313, Rulings of the trustees, 19 Oct. 1927, 70; *Monthly Bulletin*, Apr. 1927

11 *Evening Mail*, 16 May 1923

12 *Evening Mail*, 9 July 1921

13 *Evening Mail*, 27 July 1921, 29 Nov. 1923

14 *Evening Mail*, 18 May 1929

15 Frank Stricker, 'Affluence for Whom? – Another Look at Prosperity and the Working Classes in the 1920s,' *Labor History* 24, no. 1 (Winter 1983): 5–33

16 M.C. Urquhart and K.A.H. Buckley, *Historical Statistics of Canada* (Cambridge 1965), Series J, 139–46, Cost of Living Index, 304

17 Canada, Department of Labour, *Labour Gazette*, Mar. 1921, 634

18 Ibid., Mar. 1931, 485

19 Terry Copp, *The Anatomy of Poverty: The Condition of the Working Class in Montreal, 1897–1929* (Toronto 1974), 152, 159

20 Canada, *Census*, 1931, Vol. 5, T. 41, 704–5

21 PANS, MG 36, HRC, R.1360, 24 Sebastian Place

22 PANS, MG 36, HRC, R.1340, 4 Sebastian Place

23 PANS, MG 36, HRC, R.851, 22 Kane Place, 5 Apr. 1926

24 PANS, MG 36, R.776, 26 Hennessey Place

25 Elaine Tyler May, *Great Expectations: Marriage and Divorce in Post-Victorian America* (Chicago 1980), 146–50. See also Mirra Komarovsky, 'The Breakdown of the Husband's Status,' in Elizabeth Pleck and Joseph Pleck, eds, *The American Man* (Englewood Cliffs, N.J. 1980); Lizabeth Cohen, *Making a New Deal: Industrial Workers in Chicago, 1919–1939* (Cambridge 1990), 246–9. This argument was discussed in *Labor History's* symposium on the book, 32 (Fall 1991), by Patricia Cooper and Nancy Gabin.

26 PANS, MG 36, HRC, R.276.72, 34 Cabot Place, note from J.M. Hire. Men were not always aware of their household finances. A tenant of 33 Columbus Place was surprised to find himself behind in his rent, as he 'thought [it] was being paid by my wife monthly.' PANS, MG 36, HRC, R.424 (2 files), 33 Columbus Place, 27 July 1928

27 PANS, MG 36, HRC, R.1446, 12 Stanley Place, 3 Jan. 1929

28 PANS, MG 36, HRC, R.1450, 16 Stanley Place, R.1869, Rental Accounts by street with section on wooden houses, 1919–27; DUA, MS 2, 240, Halifax Visiting Dispensary, Record of Patients, 1924–37, no. 80; *Evening Mail*, 4 Aug. 1920, 5 May 1926

29 Michael Roper and John Tosh, 'Introduction,' *Manful Assertions: Masculinities in Britain since 1800* (London 1991), 18

30 Michael Kimmel, 'The Contemporary "Crisis" of Masculinity in Historical Perspective,' in Harry Brod, ed., *The Making of Masculinities: The New Men's Studies* (Boston 1981); Marilyn Lake, 'The Politics of Respectability: Identifying the Masculinist Context,' *Historical Studies* 22, no. 86 (Apr. 1986): 116–31; Joe L. Dubbert, 'Progressivism and the Masculine Crisis,' in Pleck and Pleck, eds, *American Man*

31 *Citizen*, 17 Nov. 1922

32 Peter Gabriel Filene, 'In Time of War,' in Pleck and Pleck, eds, *American Man*

33 John Clarke and Chas Critcher, *Devil Makes Work: Leisure in Capitalist Britain* (Urbana 1985), 71

34 PANS, Micro: Misc., 'S' Societies, Halifax Boy Scouts, Minutes of Meetings of Halifax District Boy Scouts, 1920–9, 1927; Micro: Churches, Halifax, United Memorial Session Minutes, 1925; *Morning Chronicle*, 30 Sept. 1920; *Halifax City Directory*, 1923; *Evening Mail*, 5 Apr. 1923; PANS, MG 20, Knights of Pythias, vol. 507

35 PANS, sound archives transcript, Mf 136, no. 16–17, Christina Simmons Collection, 19

36 E.R. Forbes, 'Prohibition and the Social Gospel in Nova Scotia,' in his *Challenging the Regional Stereotype: Essays on the Twentieth-Century Maritimes* (Fredericton 1989), 30–1. See PANS, MG 20, vol. 526, HRC Minutes, 7 Oct. 1926.

37 PANS, RG 42, City Court Book, 1915–35. For Carl, see Peter Brock, *The Man Who Built Churches: The Story of B.D. Stevens, A Parable for Our Time* (Lawrencetown Beach 1990), 49, and PANS, MG 36, R. 395, 4 Columbus Place

38 Judith Fingard, *The Dark Side of Life in Victorian Halifax* (Halifax 1989), 27; Roy Rosenzweig, *Eight Hours for What We Will: Workers and Leisure in an Industrial City, 1870–1920* (Cambridge 1983), 35–64. Fred Thompson describes the drinking habits of the man who was president of the Halifax Trades and Labor Council for most of the decade. DUA, MS 10, 2, Social Radicalism Collection: Fred W. Thompson. A.1, Correspondence: Fred W. Thompson to J. Bell, 9 Aug. 1976, 5

39 *Evening Mail*, 4 June 1929

40 Nova Scotia, *JHA*, 1930, App. 27, Plebiscite Returns, 20; Nova Scotia, *Statutes*, 1929, s. 36, ch. 2

41 *Evening Mail*, 11 Mar. 1927; *Citizen*, 4 July 1919, 29 Aug. 1919, 18 Mar. 1921, 5 June 1925, 14 Apr. 1922; PANS, MG 36, HRC, R.1077, 11 Merkel Place

42 *Citizen*, 4 July 1924

43 *Evening Mail*, 21 Aug. 1929

44 Canada, Department of Labour, *Tenth Annual Report on Labour Organization in Canada, 1920* (Ottawa 1921), 276. Only Montreal, Toronto, and Quebec City could boast more organized workers.

45 The organizations reorganized included the Blacksmiths (*Evening Mail*, 22 July 1929), Labourers (*Evening Mail*, 18 May, 18 Aug. 1928; *Citizen*, 20 Apr. 1928), Barbers (*Evening Mail*, 11 May, 15 Aug. 1928), Theatre and Stage Employees (*Citizen*, 9 Aug. 1929), Plasterers (*Evening Mail*, 8 Apr. 1927), Fish Handlers (*Citizen*, 29 June, 21 Dec. 1928; *Evening Mail*, 28 Jan. 1929), Shipyard Workers (*Citizen*, 2 Nov. 1928; *Evening Mail*, 31 Oct. 1928), Teamsters and Chauffeurs (*Citizen*, 1, 15 June 1928), Telegraph Operators (*Evening Mail*, 9 Sept. 1929), Bakers (*Evening Mail*, 6 Nov. 1929), and

Musicians (*Evening Mail*, 6 Aug. 1929); Department of Labour, *Twentieth Annual Report on Labour Organization in Canada, 1930* (Ottawa 1931), T. 6, 214.

46 Suzanne Morton, 'Labourism and Independent Labor Politics in Halifax during the 1920s' (MA thesis Dalhousie University 1986); John Manley, 'Communists and the Canadian Labour Movement during a Period of Retreat: The 1920s,' unpublished paper, Dalhousie University 1979; *Evening Mail*, 8 Sept. 1928

47 *Evening Mail*, 3, 6 Sept. 1927

48 *Evening Mail*, 13 Oct. 1928

49 *Evening Mail*, 29 July 1921, 10 Dec. 1927

50 *Evening Mail*, 22 Dec. 1921; 13 Nov. 1924; *Halifax District Trades and Labour Council Journal 1928*

51 Joseph F. Kett, *Rites of Passage: Adolescence in America, 1790 to the Present* (New York 1977), 258; John Gillis, *Youth and History: Tradition and Change in European Age Relations, 1700 – Present* (New York 1974), 134

52 *Evening Mail*, 25 Mar. 1925; 13 July 1922, 22 July 1926, and 9 Oct. 1928

53 *Evening Mail*, 1 Oct. 1924, 20 Apr. 1926, 25 Sept. 1928; PANS, MG 36, HRC, R.842, 13 Kane Place; R.861, 18 Kane Place, misfiled; R.983, 3 Livingstone Place; R.1358, 22 Sebastian Place

54 *Evening Mail*, 21 July 1921, 19 June 1924, 18 July 1929

55 *Evening Mail*, 9 Feb. 1923

56 PANS, MG 36, HRC, R.1358, 22 Sebastian Place, 27 Apr. 1927; R.511, 12 Duffus, 17 Oct. 1921; *Evening Mail*, 2 Feb. 1921; Neil Sutherland, *Children in English-Canadian Society: Framing the Twentieth Century Consensus* (Toronto 1976), 95–6

57 *Citizen*, 9 May 1919

58 Cohen, *Making a New Deal*, 179; *Evening Mail*, 28 Oct., 1 Dec. 1926, 8 Oct. 1927

59 *Evening Mail*, 14 Jan., 18 Apr. 1921; *Halifax Chronicle*, 5, 6 June 1928. The six teams represented the *Herald* and *Mail*, Shipyards, Navy, Moirs, CNR, and *Halifax Chronicle*. *Evening Mail*, 19 Feb. 1921, 9 July 1928; *Monthly Bulletin*, Aug. 1920

60 Expense was an important factor in the feasibility of sport. In 1922 the 'proposal to form outlaw hockey league falls through. The officials regret to report that owing to the large expense which would be entailed in securing the rink and fitting out the teams (the boys being unable to stand any expense owing to unemployment) the project had to be abandoned.' *Evening Mail*, 13 Jan. 1922; Colin Howell, 'Baseball, Class, and Community in the Maritime Provinces, 1870–1910,' *Histoire sociale / Social History* 22 (Nov. 1989): 266

61 A Stairs Street man played for the West End Federals and St Agnes team.
62 *Daily Echo*, 30 May 1925, reported 1,800 people; 1 June 1925, 1,500 fans. *Halifax Chronicle*, 25 May 1927, a crowd of 2,000
63 *Daily Echo*, 21, 28 Apr., 23 May, 1 June 1925; *Morning Chronicle*, 10 May 1926; 10 May 1927
64 *Mail-Star*, 6 Mar. 1957; 8 Mar. 1955
65 Philip Terrie, 'Urban Man Confronts the Wilderness: The Nineteenth-Century Sportsman in the Adirondacks,' *Journal of Sport History* 5, no. 3 (Winter 1978): 7–20; Thomas Altherr, 'The American Hunter-Naturalist and the Development of the Code of Sportmanship,' *Journal of Sport History* 5, no. 1 (Spring 1978): 7–22; Altherr, '"Mallards and Messerschmitts": American Hunting Magazines and the Image of American Hunting during World War II,' *Journal of Sport History* 14, no. 2 (Summer 1987): 151–63
66 Edward Anthony Rotundo, 'Manhood in America: The Northern Middle Class, 1770–1920' (PhD diss., Brandeis University 1982), 302, 307. An interesting account of hunting and masculinity appears in Ted Ownby, *Subduing Satan: Religion, Recreation and Manhood in the Rural South, 1865–1920* (Chapel Hill 1990).
67 Dennis Hardy and Colin Ward, *Arcadia for All: The Legacy of a Makeshift Urban Landscape* (Oxford 1984); Jeffrey Hantover, 'The Boy Scouts and the Validation of Masculinity,' in Pleck and Pleck, eds, *American Man*
68 *Citizen*, 29 Apr., 12 May 1927, 28 Apr. 1928, 3, 31 May 1929
69 *Citizen*, 20 Apr. 1923, 4 Oct. 1924, 24 Apr., 15 May 1925, 4 May 1928
70 Halifax Board of Trade, 'Halifax, Fishing All Summer in Lake, Stream and Sea' (Halifax 1909). See Edward Beck, *Sporting Guide to Nova Scotia* (Halifax 1909), and Dominion Atlantic Railway, *Hunting and Fishing in Nova Scotia* (Halifax 1919). In addition, Harry Piers's journals often described his fishing expeditions to nearby lakes in Spryfield, Harrietsfield, and Bedford. PANS, MG 1, vols 1046–51
71 *Citizen*, 17 May 1929; The *Evening Mail* reported that railway worker Edward Hilton caught a five-pound salmon on a fishing trip, 22 May 1924. See also 25 May 1922, 12 May 1926, and Robert Daw's fishing trip, *Daily Star*, 17 Apr. 1927.
72 Nova Scotia, *JHA*, 1921, 1922, 1923, 1924, 1925, 1926, App. 24, 'Report of Commissioner of Forests and Game'; 1927, 1928, 1929, App. 9, 'Department of Lands and Forests'; 1930, App. 12, 'Department of Lands and Forests'
73 Nova Scotia, *JHA*, 1928, App. 9, 'Department of Lands and Forests,' 58
74 *Daily Star*, 22 Jan. 1927
75 *Evening Mail*, 23 July 1925, 6 May 1921, 1 June 1922; R.W. Ross, 'Housing in Halifax,' *Social Welfare* (Oct. 1920); *Evening Mail*, 11 Sept. 1923, 12 and 19 Aug. 1926

76 *Evening Mail*, 7 July 1927; 6 Sept. 1928; Glady McTier, interview, Ottawa, July 1988. In Ross McKibbin, 'Work and Hobbies in Britain, 1880–1950' (Jay Winter, ed., *The Working Class in Modern British History* [Cambridge 1983]), the author mentions competition among British working-class gardeners (129); *Evening Mail*, 21 May 1921; PANS, MG 36, HRC, R.748, 2 Hennessey Place

77 McKibbin, 'Work and Hobbies,' 130. It is interesting to note that in the past seventy years a similar phenomenon has occurred in relation to female activities such as baking or sewing, which once would have composed a part of domestic production and now are considered hobbies.

CHAPTER 7 Young Women

1 Valerie Steele, *Fashion and Eroticism: Ideals of Feminine Beauty from the Victorian Era to the Jazz Age* (New York 1985), 237

2 Lisa Duggan, 'The Social Enforcement of Heterosexuality and Lesbian Resistance in the 1920s,' in Amy Swerdlow and Hanna Lessinger, eds, *Class, Race and Sex: The Dynamics of Control* (New York 1983)

3 Veronica Strong-Boag, 'The Girl of the New Day: Canadian Working Women in the 1920s,' *Labour / Le Travail* 4 (Fall 1979): 131–64; Graham Lowe, 'Women, Work and the Office: The Feminization of Clerical Occupations in Canada, 1901–31,' in Veronica Strong-Boag and Anita Clair Fellman, eds, *Rethinking Canada: The Promise of Women's History* (Toronto 1986), 107–22

4 This chart is based on 1931 categories. 'Clerical' before 1931 refers to office workers and clerks in finance, law, and government. 'Warehousing' refers to packers. Canada, *Census*, 1911, vol. 6, 326–35; 1921, vol. 4, 382–99; 1931, vol. 2, 31, vol. 5, 572–5, vol. 7, 267–77, and 739–45

5 In England the number of domestic servants also remained high and increased 1920–31 to 23 per cent of wage earning women. Pam Taylor, 'Daughter and Mothers – Maids and Mistresses: Domestic Service between the Wars,' in John Clarke, Chas Critcher, and Richard Johnson, eds, *Working-Class Culture: Studies in History and Theory* (New York 1979), 121

6 Canada, *Census*, 1931, vol. 5, 63

7 For this trend in a slightly earlier period see PANS, MG 20, Halifax Local Council of Women, vol. 539, 3, 1909–11, 'Application for Position' section in the Halifax Local Council of Women's Welcome Hostel Registry.

8 Discussions of women's work culture appear in Kathy Peiss, *Cheap Amusements: Working Women and Leisure in Turn of the Century New York* (Philadelphia 1986); Susan Porter Benson, *Counter Cultures: Saleswomen, Managers,*

and Customers in American Department Stores, 1890–1940 (Urbana, Ill. 1986); Joanne Meyerowitz, Women Adrift: Independent Wage Earners in Chicago, 1880–1930 (Chicago 1988); Barbara Melosh, 'The Physician's Hand': Work Culture and Conflict in American Nursing (Philadelphia 1982); and Leslie Woodcock Tentler, Wage-Earning Women: Industrial Work and Family Life in the United States, 1900–1930 (New York 1979).

9 PANS, MG 3, vol. 1872, Moirs Scrapbook
10 Evening Mail, 19 Nov. 1927
11 Margaret E. McCallum, 'Separate Spheres: The Organization of Work in a Confectionery Factory: Ganong Bros., St. Stephen, New Brunswick,' Labour / Le Travail 24 (Fall 1989): 69–90
12 Sharon Myers, '"I Can Manage My Own Business": Female Industrial Workers in Halifax at the Turn of the Twentieth Century' (MA thesis, Saint Mary's University 1989), 14–15; Tentler, Wage-Earning Women, 42; PANS, MG 36, HRC, C.32.3E, Children's Department; 'Moirs Double Shift Day and Night,' Evening Mail, 18 Jul. 1927; Nova Scotia, JHA, 1910, App. 26, 'Report of the Commission on the Hours of Labor'
13 Halifax City Directory, 1919–29
14 Evening Mail, 19 Nov. 1927
15 David Brody, 'The Rise and Decline of Welfare Capitalism,' in his Workers in Industrial America: Essays on the Twentieth Century Struggle (Oxford 1980), 48–81; Stuart Brandes, American Welfare Capitalism (Chicago 1970)
16 Citizen, 6 Aug. 1927; Joy Parr, The Gender of Breadwinners: Women, Men and Change in Two Industrial Towns, 1880–1950 (Toronto 1990), 48–9; DUA, MS 4, 180, Maritime Telephone and Telegraph, H 301, Maritime Telephone and Telegraph Personnel Benefits; Evening Mail, 26 Jan. 1927, 19 June 1926, 11 July 1927
17 Evening Mail, 5, 9 May 1927, 16 Feb. 1927
18 Florence J. Murray, At the Foot of Dragon Hill (New York 1975). Her brother, Charlie Murray, would later become a prominent member of the Communist party and a labour organizer. Nicholas Fillmore, Maritime Radical: The Life and Times of Roscoe Fillmore (Toronto 1992), 180; Gary Burrill, 'The Thorn inside the Body,' New Maritimes (July/Aug. 1991), 30
19 For a discussion of the restricted participation of daughters in housework in Swansea, Wales, during the 1960s, see Diana Leonard, Sex and Generation: A Study of Courtship and Weddings (London 1980), 58–60. The question of young women and the double day reminds us of the range of experience that was possible. Young women in other neighbourhoods in the city who might be more likely to board would probably be responsible for much more of their own maintenance. See Carolyn Strange and Cynthia Wright,

'Single Women, Double Day: The Management of "Ontario Business Women's" Leisure in the 1920s,' paper in progress, presented to the Canadian Historical Association, June 1989, 2.

20 Glady McTier was born in Halifax in 1911 and interviewed by the author in Ottawa, July 1988.

21 *Monthly Bulletin*, Aug. 1926

22 Isabel Mann, 'A Day in the Life of a VON,' Yarmouth 1922, pamphlet in Ontario Archives; Stella Shore, telephone interview, July 1989, Halifax, Nova Scotia

23 For an example from fiction see Charles Bruce, *The Channel Shore* (Toronto 1954).

24 *Evening Mail*, 5 Nov. 1927

25 Meyerowitz, *Women Adrift*, 6

26 Nova Scotia, *JHA*, 1920, App. 33, 'Report of Commission on Hours of Labor, Wages, Working Conditions of Women Employed in Industrial Occupations,' 15

27 Stella Shore, telephone interview, July 1989

28 *Citizen*, 4 July 1930

29 PANS, MG 36, HRC, R.1855, Vacated Balances, Rent Ledger, 1 Dec. 192[1]

30 DUA, MS 4, 180, Maritime Telephone and Telegraph, H 302, Maritime Telephone and Telegraph, Employee Benefits, 1920; *Monthly Bulletin*, June 1925; Meyerowitz, *Women Adrift*, 9, 15; Peiss, *Cheap Amusements*, 45; Tentler, *Wage-Earning Women*, 111–14

31 PANS, RG 35, vol. 102, City of Halifax, 16, H. 3, Halifax Policewoman's Report, 1931–3, 4 Apr. 1932. Thanks to Karen Dubinsky for this point.

32 Ibid., 6 Sept. 1931

33 Carolyn Strange, 'The Perils and Pleasures of the City: Single, Wage-Earning Women in Toronto, 1880–1930' (PhD diss., Rutgers, State University of New Jersey 1991), ch. 4, 'Good Times and the "Girl Problem,"' 218

34 *Evening Mail*, 29 Jan. 1920, 6 July 1921; *Citizen*, 27 Sept. 1929

35 *Eastern Federationist* (New Glasgow), 10 May 1919; *Citizen*, 7 May 1920

36 *Evening Mail*, 13 Oct. 1920

37 *Citizen*, 9, 16 Dec. 1927, 1 June 1928; *Evening Mail*, 8 Mar. 1929; Linda Kealey, 'Sophie,' *New Maritimes* (Nov. 1987): 12–13; Janice Newton, 'The Alchemy of Politicalization: Socialist Women and the Early Canadian Left,' in Franca Iacovetta and Mariana Valverde, eds, *Gender Conflicts: New Essays in Women's History* (Toronto 1992), 128–31

38 *Citizen*, 30 Nov. 1929, 14 Dec. 1928. Equal pay for equal work had been a constant platform of the local labour parties and the Provincial Federation of Labour. *Citizen*, 9 May 1919, 19 Sept. 1919, 26 Sept. 1919; Kealey, 'Sophie,' 13

39 *Evening Mail*, 3 Dec. 1928
40 *Citizen*, 25 May, 1 June 1928
41 *Citizen*, 1 Apr. 1927. Emphasis in original
42 Myers, '"I Can Manage My Own Business,"' 85
43 *Monthly Bulletin*, Oct. 1922, Oct. 1923, Apr. 1926; Myers, '"I Can Manage My Own Business,"' 82
44 *Evening Mail*, 27 June 1921, 10 Feb. 1921, 9 Apr. 1926, 15 Mar. 1928
45 Strong-Boag, *New Day Recalled*, 21
46 David Montgomery, *Fall of the House of Labor: The Workplace, the State and Labor Activism, 1865–1925* (Cambridge 1987), 458; Meyerowitz, *Women Adrift*, 30; Benson, *Counter Cultures*, ch. 4, 'Made, Not Born,' and Michele Martin, 'Subjugating the Voice: Telephone Companies' Regulation of Workers' and Consumers' Self-Expression,' paper presented to the Canadian Historical Association, June 1989
47 St Patrick's had a separate school for boys and girls and therefore the only available statistics. Nova Scotia, *JHA*, 1921–30, App. 5, 'Report of the Superintendent of Education'
48 Paul Axelrod, 'Moulding the Middle Class: Student Life at Dalhousie University in the 1930s,' *Acadiensis* 15, no. 1 (Autumn 1985): 91
49 PANS, MG 36, HRC, R.1855, Vacated Balances, Rent Ledger; R.398, 7 Columbus Place
50 *Evening Mail*, 12 Sept. 1928
51 L.D. McCann, 'Metropolitanism and Branch Businesses in the Maritimes, 1881–1931,' *Acadiensis* 13, no. 1 (Autumn 1983): 112–25
52 Nova Scotia, *JHA*, 1910, App. 26, 'Report of the Commission on the Hours of Labor,' 88–91; Benson, *Counter Cultures*, 231
53 Benson, *Counter Cultures*, 233
54 Ibid., 230
55 Elizabeth Ewen, 'Immigrant Women in the Land of Dollars,' (PhD diss., State University of New York at Stony Brook 1979), 94; Susan E. Kennedy, *If All We Did Was to Weep at Home: A History of White Working-Class Women in America* (Bloomington, Ind. 1979), 167; Benson, *Counter Cultures*, 235
56 Peiss, *Cheap Amusements*, 51–5
57 Ellen Gee, 'Fertility and Marriage Patterns in Canada 1851–1971' (PhD diss., University of British Columbia 1978), 168
58 Based on his British sources, Gillis found that the unskilled married younger than the skilled. John R. Gillis, *For Better, For Worse: British Marriages, 1600 to the Present* (Oxford 1985), 289
59 Sallie Westwood described textile-industry rituals of England in the 1970s, as did Joy Parr for Paris, Ontario, in the 1920s and 1930s. Sallie Westwood, *All Day Every Day: Factory and Family in the Making of Women's Lives*

(London 1984); Parr, *Gender of Breadwinners*, 30–2. In her study of courtship and wedding customs in Swansea, Wales, in the late 1960s, Diana Leonard found work-leaving rituals were most frequent and elaborate in situations with 'a lot of young women working together.' Leonard, *Sex and Generation*, 145–6

60 DUA, Maritime Telephone and Telegraph, *Monthly Bulletin*, June 1924
61 *Monthly Bulletin*, June 1920
62 *Evening Mail*, 18 June 1927
63 *Monthly Bulletin*, May 1920; For other examples of showers see, e.g. *Monthly Bulletin*, June 1924; *Evening Mail*, 28 May 1919, 3 June 1920, 28 June 1921, 5 Nov. 1924
64 *Evening Mail*, 8 Sept. 1919, 13 Sept. 1922, 16 June 1920, 28 Sept. 1926, 16 Nov. 1927
65 *Evening Mail*, 24 Oct. 1924; 28 Sept., 16 June 1926; 1 Sept. 1925; 16 June 1920; and 8 Aug. 1923
66 *Evening Mail*, 18 June 1919, 21 June 1922, 8 Aug. 1923, 25 July, 20 Sept. 1929. For further information on the growth of branch plants in Halifax see McCann, 'Metropolitanism and Branch Businesses.'
67 Jane Synge, 'Young Working-Class Women in Early Twentieth Century Hamilton: Their Work and Family Lives,' in A.H. Turrittin, ed., *Proceedings of the Workshop Conference on Blue-Collar Workers and Their Communities* (Toronto 1976), 139
68 *Monthly Bulletin*, June 1924
69 *Citizen*, 4 July 1930, emphasis mine

Conclusion

1 O.R. [Oscar Ryan], *The Worker*, 8 Jan. 1927
2 Betty DeBerg, 'American Fundamentalism and the Disruption of Traditional Gender Roles, 1880–1930' (PhD diss., Vanderbilt University 1988), 183
3 See Ellen Ross, *Love and Toil: Motherhood in Outcast London, 1870–1918* (London 1993)
4 *Maritime Merchant* (Halifax), 26 Dec. 1929

Index